EDUCATION
Perspectives and Issues

EDUCATION

Perspectives and Issues

Swapan Kumar Kolay
Mousumi Kolay

GYAN

ISBN : 978-81-212-1249-6
Price :

First Published, 2015

Published by

Gyan Publishing House
23, Main Ansari Road, Darya Ganj,
New Delhi- 110 002
Ph. : 2328 2060, 2326 1060
E-mail: books@gyanbooks.com

Laser Typesetting : Sanya Computers, Delhi
Printed at : G. Print Process, Delhi

Cataloging in Publication Data—DK
Courtesy: D.K. Agencies (P) Ltd. <docinfo@dkagencies.com>

Kolay, Swapan Kumar, 1966- **author.**
Education : perspectives and issues / Swapan Kumar Kolay, Mousumi Kolay.
pages cm
Includes bibliographical references (pages).
ISBN 9788121212496

1. Education—India—Bastar (District) 2. Education—India—Dhamtari. 3. Education and state—India—Bastar (District) 4. Education and state—India—Dhamtari. I. Kolay, Mousumi, author. II. Title.

DDC 370.954137 23

Contents

Foreword

I welcome the publication of *"Education: Perspectives and Issues"* written by Dr Swapan Kumar Kolay and Mrs Mousumi Kolay. The new knowledge arising from their study has the potential to transform Education system and management at the grass roots level. The book is mainly focussed on education perspectives at grass roots and present status.

Indian education system promoting ample opportunities to enhance the knowledge of its citizens, the authors brought out such tangible information for the use of the education field. The authors have tried to give a new dimension of research which has a practical academic utility. It appears that the academicians in India will give a new direction of research and open vistas in 21st century.

The present book makes unique contribution and gives an important thought to the policy-makers, administrators, students and researchers. It can be said with a note of appreciation to authors for their scholarly attempt to bring out this book with a systematic and meaningful effort for the empowerment of primary and secondary education.

Prof (Dr) A.K. Jalaluddin

Preface

The book on *"Education: Perspectives and Issues"* by Dr Swapan Kumar Kolay and Mrs. Mousumi Kolay provides an in-depth discussion of education concerns and challenges at grassroots. This book highlights the education policies and other social fabricators. The key features of this book are to give an overview of challenges facing by educationail organisations and governments in the field of Primary and Middle Education. The book highlights the role of community and administration in the empowerment process and carefully examines each of these concerns. It outlines a conceptual framework for participation and empowerment that is centered on the concept of dissemination of education at grassroot level. This book clearly elucidated the Social Change, Development, Education Interventions and Field Practice. This book is definitely useful for Students, Teachers, Policy Makers and Practitioners.

Dr Swapan Kumar Kolay

Mrs Mousumi Kolay

Acknowledgements

At the outset I express my deep sense of gratitude and heartfelt thanks to Personnel of Rajiv Gandhi Siksha Mission, Raipur for providing financial assistance in the form of Research Project at the initial stage of this work. It is my privilege to remember the elderly support given by Prof N.D.R Chandra Vice-Chancellor, Bastar University, Jagdalpur. I thank Dr Indu Anant, Registrar for her support. I am very thankful to Mr Rajat Kumar, Director and Smt Pratima Abasthi, Additional Director, Rajiv Gandhi Siksha Mission, Raipur for their cooperation.

I am thankful to Mr Karan C. Chandrakar, APC, Raipur, Mr Stanley Jones, APC and Dr Nitin Dandsena, APC, Jagdalpur for their help in the field. My heartfelt gratitude to H.P Sharam, APC, Damtari and K.K Joshi, the staffs in education department in Bastar District, for their support.

My heartfelt thanks to Teachers, Block Educational Officers, Students and their parents from Bastar and Damtari districts for their constant support during the collection of data. I owe much gratitude to them; without their co-operation and support I could not complete this report. I am grateful to several persons who helped me at various stages of the study and its subsequent culmination in the form of this report.

Dr Swapan Kumar Kolay

Mrs Mousumi Kolay

Acronyms

CBSE	Central Board of Secondary Education
CISCE	Council of Indian School Certificate Examination
DPEP	District Primary Education Programme
EFA	Education For All
ICDS	Integrated Child Development Scheme
ICT	Information and Communication Technology
IGNOU	Indira Gandhi National Open University
IIM	Indian Institute of Management
IIT	Indian Institute of Technology
KGBV	Kasturba Gandhi Balika Vidyalaya
MFL	Modern Foreign Languages
NAAC	National Assessment and Accreditation Council
NBA	National Board of Accreditation
NCERT	National Council of Educational Research and Training
NGO	Non-Governmental Organisation
NIT	National Institutes of Technology
NPE	National Policy on Education
NPEGEL	National Programme for Education of Girls at Elementary Level
PE	Physical Education
PEC	Parents Education Committee
PSHE	Personal, Social and Health Education
PTA	Parent Teacher Association
RTE	Right to Education

SC	Schedule Caste
SSA	Sarva Siksha Abhiyan
ST	Schedule Tribe
TCPCs	Training-Cum-Production Centres
TLM	Teaching Learning Materials
UGC	University Grants Commission
UK	United Kingdom
UNESCO	United Nations Educational, Scientific and Cultural Organisation

CHAPTER 1 Introduction

Education leads to individual freedom and enablement, which yields significant societal advance gains and makes an individual self-reliant. Education is a postern to the opportunities and paybacks of economic and social development. We cannot imagine any society without education, for human growth and development, it plays a significant role and it focusses on the expansion of capacity and enrollments to meet manpower needs. The world is marching towards intellectuality and knowledge; in this context the societies should gear-up their educational strategies to maximise their output. There is a high demand for higher levels of education and dramatically countries approach for education has been increased, overtime. The Education for All, evinced growth in primary and secondary quality education. Furthermore, globalisation and the increasing demand for a more sophisticated labour force combined with the growth of knowledge-based economies gives a sense of urgency to the heightened demand for education.

In today's world, education has a vital mission—one which combines the policy peculiarities of being, at the same time terminal and preparatory, compulsory and post-compulsory, uniform and diverse, general and vocational. Primary and secondary education is now being recognised as the cornerstone of educational systems in the 21st century. Quality Primary and Secondary education is indispensable in creating a bright future for individuals and nations alike. The education should give a sense of support for the people that they can achieve maximum benefits. Those who had best at stepping stone probably they can see the good results in their socio-economic conditions. The State interventions should be focussed on improving employability and productivity of school leavers through support to vocational secondary schools and increasing people's competitiveness by improving the quality of education to raise the overall productivity and trainability of the labour force. The countries with low Primary and Secondary enrollment, should be focused on meeting specific shortages of educated manpower in the public and private sectors by raising Primary and Secondary school completion rates and improving the social conditions of the poor and reducing inequality by expanding access to primary and secondary education. The governments, NGOs, and private agencies should collaborate with educational leaders and international organisations to promote the sharing of knowledge, research, policy analysis and best practices designed to strengthen access, quality and equity in primary and secondary education.

Education plays a vibrant role in the social, economic, and human capital development. The Policy Makers, Administrators and Practitioners should focus on the systemic challenges to address the gap in the education. They should emphasise that it is important for the country that if we nurture our children and young people with the right education, their future will emerge as strong and prosperous which is good for them and as well as the country. The educational system should be characterised by a strong stratification, a high standardisation, and occupational specificity. The Policy Makers should concentrate on the enrollment in primary and secondary schools and they should streamline the families from lower social backgrounds who are away from the quality education system.

A sequel to the proclamation of the National Policy on Education, the Government has made efforts to sensitise the educational system across the country in such a manner so that, every child, irrespective of sex, caste, religion, economic condition can avail the opportunity to get education. The various schemes that have been launched in the states and UTs in the country to ensure primary education to all children are (a) Operation Blackboard, (b) Jawahar Rojgar Yojana and Employment Assurance Scheme (relating to school building component), (c) Non-formal Education, (d) Teachers Education Training, setting up of DIET etc., (e) Basic Education Project Funded by International Agencies, (f) Area Intensive Programmes for educationally backward minorities and (g) schemes funded and implemented by State Government on their own, e.g., Education Guarantee Schemes etc.

After six decades of Independence, the goal of tribal education has not been achieved so far. Inspite of the remarkable expansion of the elementary education system in the last two decades, a very large number of tribal children and more among tribal girls who are deprived section of the society in India, continue to out of school. Out of all the children enrolled at primary stage, a very high percentage drops out. Nearly 160 million children of 6-14 age groups do not enrolled in school (based on sixth education survey data and available statistics on 5-14 age group children in India, NCERT (2002)) and among those who enrolled, nearly half of them drop out before completing the primary education. About 10 million children of school going age are not attending elementary schooling even today (Aggarwal, 2002: Vol. 2). Elementary education is a priority area in the Tribal sub-plans from the 5th Five Year Plan. Education of ST children is considered important, not only because of the constitutional obligation but also as a crucial input for total development of tribal communities. Another important development in the policy towards education of tribals is the National Policy on Education (NPE), 1986 which specified among other things are the following:

(i) Priority will be accorded to opening primary schools in tribal areas.

(ii) There is need to develop curricula and devise instructional material in tribal language at the initial stages with arrangements for switchover to regional languages.

(iii) ST youths will be encouraged to take up teaching in tribal areas.

(iv) Ashram schools/residential schools will be established on a large scale in tribal areas.

(v) Incentive schemes will be formulated for the STs, keeping in view their special needs and lifestyle. The main causes of the non-implementation of this basic objective of our national policy are well known, viz., (a) financial inadequacy (b) non-availability of a sufficient number of suitable teachers (c) lack of motivation and (d) poverty (Aggarwal, 2002).

Education has still to play a significant role in the overall development of the poor people and especially among the poor tribal population of India where there is high dropout and low participation rates which is again gender sensitive. The impact of tribal education policy after independence can neither be said to be much satisfactory nor can't it be taken to be very disappointing (Thakur, 1995). Studying the shortcomings of the tribal education policy is the need of the hour as tribal people are the most backward communities in India. Russel (1932) in his divergent theories of education noted that "education is to be considered rather in relation to the community than in relation to the individual". Education is not only imparting theoretical knowledge, but a process of enculturation and socialisation. Education must be associated with the cultural pattern and way of life of specific communities. "One of the avenues to speedy development is education" (Sachhidananda, 1992). Education leads to overall development of an individual and in turn it influences development of a whole society.

But it has been observed throughout these years that the extent of benefits of these schemes varies from one district to another and from one region to another within the State. It has also been observed that the number of tribal children of deriving benefits of these schemes is far less that of others. The efforts were made by the Government and the Missionaries to educate tribal people. But the pace of development was slow for them. Venkataiah (2001) noted that tribal education is not a different kind of education, but it is to suit the special needs and aspirations of the tribal groups who are in the different stages of development.

Moreover, the education is based on the family support and assistance. The parents should address the differences in structural and individual risk aversion, and under what conditions of social background individual risk aversion might affect their children' intentions for further education after finishing Primary and Secondary Education. That structural risk aversion is the major force in the educational decision process, since the motive of status maintenance is pivotal in educational decision-making. Individual risk aversion comes into effect particularly for students from comparably lower social classes, since these students normally tend to maintain their status earlier than higher class students and thus need to make decisions, where individual risk aversion comes into play. The family plays significant role in the education process. The parents must cooperate with their children to continue their education for their betterment.

Children's future social and economic situation therefore strongly depends on the "right" school track choice. With respect to the determinants of this choice, one comes across a vast literature on the transmission of socio-economic status suggesting for high social selectivity. This means that parental education, as a compound measure for parents' cognitive skills and for investments into their children, is still the most important factor for children's educational attainment (Heineck, 2009, Ermisch, 2001). The overall goal of school systems is, generally, to provide children with the values, knowledge, skills and behaviours to live well as children, as adults and as citizens.

The World is changing fast, and everyone needs to catch up. The Indian schooling system is enhancing the quality and standards. The primary and secondary schools with a fast and easy ways to enhance teaching and learning techniques for the betterment of the knowledge societies. Primary and Secondary education has been seen as the foundation of society, enabling economic wealth, social prosperity and political stability. Primary and secondary education is therefore increasingly being viewed as a fundamental right across the globe and essential for the exercise of all human rights. All individuals are entitled to education and develop. Primary and secondary education forms the foundation for all levels of learning and development. It empowers and equips individuals with analytical capabilities, instills confidence and fortifies them with determination to achieve goal-setting competencies. Therefore, the primary and secondary education plays a pivotal role in improving the socio-economic condition of the nation.

The evolution of the education system in India has been about balancing the competing claims between the constitutional compulsion towards providing eight years of compulsory education (as required by the Directive Principles of State Policy in the constitution), the manpower requirements of a growing economy and meeting the demand for overall expansion of the system. The first and most important lesson is that, no education system can be better than the quality of its teachers. Raising the status of teaching also requires a significant strengthening of teachers' authority in the classroom. The Governments and school authorities should seriously work on raising achievement and narrowing attainment gaps, focus sharply on the progress of every child and teach a rigorous and demanding curriculum in an inspiring way, opening up opportunity to many more children to access the primary and secondary education.

The evidence from around the world shows that the most important factor in determining the effectiveness of a school system is the quality of its teachers (Barber, 2007). The best education systems draw their teachers from the most academically able, and select them carefully to ensure that they are taking only those people who combine the right personal and intellectual qualities (Auguste, 2010). These systems train their teachers rigorously at the outset, focusing particularly on the practical teaching skills they will need. At each stage of their career, and especially as they move into leadership positions, teachers in the highest performing systems receive further focused training and development (Barber, 2007). In the highest performing Schools, teachers and teaching are held in the highest esteem. Rightly so, because all the evidence shows that good teachers make a profound difference. The countries like India needs change in the teacher training curriculum and empower them with new teaching and learning techniques which makes them self-reliant.

Eight out of 10 of the world's children live in developing countries (World Bank, 2003). For economists working on education, the study of developing countries offers both policy questions of fundamental importance and a rich set of experiences to examine. In view of the widespread consensus on the importance of education and the existence of several reviews on the impact of education on income and other outcomes, Government of India enacted The Right of Children to Free and Compulsory Education Act, 2009, in a nut shell, Right to Education Act. Extending access to education is part of a worldwide agenda. The Education for All (EFA) initiative from the United Nations is an essential element of the Millennium Development Goals, in part, because education is seen as being crucial to human development, and also because so many children do not have access to education UNESCO (2005).

Differences in access to and outcomes from, education depend not only on children's individual circumstances, but also crucially on the location in which they live and in many cases, where they live within that location. Many children are at risk of not attending school, or of receiving a sub-standard education. In some parts of the world, schooling is not available because of a shortage of school places, a lack of quality teachers, or because schools are too far from where children live. Throughout the world, there is an increased awareness of differences in access to and outcomes of education. This has to be understood in the power of education to reduce poverty, to improve the lives of individuals and groups, and to transform societies (Grubb and Lazerson, 2004).

The process of mainstream education reform, began in many countries in the mid-1980s, when concerns about economic competitiveness and the efficiency of school systems led to the introduction of marketplace principles in education (Ball, 2006). Such reforms were underpinned by the idea that competition and choice raise standards and accountability. However, it could be argued that competitive environments result in winners and losers and that in such a climate, some children may be seen as more attracted to schools than others. Children who are considered difficult to teach and those who find learning difficult are at increased risk for exclusion when schools operate in a competitive educational marketplace (McLaughlin and Rouse, 2000, Gillborn and Youdell, 2000).

1.1 Indian Education

Indian education system is different than other system. The education system which was evolved first in antique India, is known as the Vedic system of education. In other words, the antique system of education was based on the Vedas and therefore it was given the name of Vedic Educational System. The antique education system has been a source of motivation to all educational systems of the world. The elements, which our present system, lacks, and which were the predominant facets of our ancient system relate to admission policies (upnayan), monitorial system, low teacher pupil ratio, healthy teaching surroundings, free schooling and college education, sympathetic treatment, role of punishment in discipline, regulation governing student life. The main aim of any system of education should be advance of a wholesome personality. Moral strength and moral excellence were developed to the fullest extent.

Indian education was based on religious rituals and some caste people were eligible to study during ancient days.

Traditional education was meant for some sections only. With the arrival of British rule the Indian education scenario had been changed. Under British rule from the 1700 to 1947, India's education policies were changed dramatically. British rulers had given great opportunity to Indians to access the education. The education system geared to preserving the position of the more privileged classes. Because of the efforts of the British rulers, the under privileged communities were able to access the Higher education. Previously education was meant for Brahmins and during the colonial rule the fruits of education reached to the downtrodden. At present, still India adopts British structure of education.

The primary school starts from first standard and ends at fifth standard of the age group six-eleven and high school education starts from sixth standard ends at 10th standard the age of 11 to 14. In India primary education and High school education are compulsory. The great efforts are made by Indian government to increase the standards of the Indian education and allocated huge funds for primary and secondary education. In respect of Primary education, however, the Constitution has made an exception on the lines recommended by the Hartog Committee. The intimate relationship between the provision of a minimum of free and compulsory education for all children and the successful working of a democracy which the Constitution decided to create is obvious. The Constitution, therefore, makes the following provision as a directive principle of State policy under Part IV:

> "45. The State shall endeavour to provide within a period of ten years from the commencement of this Constitution, for free and compulsory education for all children until they complete the age of 14 years."

1.2 Importance of Primary Education in India

The Importance of Primary education has been neglected in India knowingly or unknowingly since our independence and the Government of India has is now realised and willing to improve primary education by making legislation and planning to cover all the sections of age group of 6-14 years of age and assuring for the deserved free education.

Education in India has a history stretching back to the ancient urban centres of learning at Taxila and Nalanda. The

Nalanda University was the oldest University-system of education in the world. Western education became ingrained into Indian society with the establishment of the British Raj. Education in India falls under the control of both the Union Government and the states, with some responsibilities lying with the Union and the states having autonomy for others. The various articles of the Indian Constitution provide for education as a fundamental right (*Source*: Wikipedia).

India has made a huge progress in terms of increasing primary education attendance rate and expanding literacy to approximately two thirds of the population. India's improved education system is often cited as one of the main contributors to the economic rise of India. Much of the progress in education has been credited to various private institutions. The private education market in India is estimated to be worth $ 40 billion in 2008 and will increase to $ 68 billion by 2012.

However, India continues to face challenges. Despite growing investment in education, 35 per cent of the population is illiterate and only 15 per cent of the students, reach high school.

1.3 Education System in India and its Stages, Today

The education system in India is very qualitative and meaningful unlike others. The education system has given lot of changes in the country and at the grassroots; such a populous country has turned the closed education to open education. Previously the education in India was restricted to some other communities and they ruled the education systems. During the colonial period the education seeds sprung-up. The following are the Indian education system patterns:

1.3.1 Pre-primary

It consists of children of three-five years of age studying in nursery, lower kindergarten and upper kindergarten. At this stage student is given knowledge about school life and is taught to read and write some basic words.

1.3.2 Primary

It includes the age group of children of 6-11 years studying in classes from first to fifth.

1.3.3 Middle

It consists of children studying in classes from sixth to eighth.

1.3.4 Secondary

It includes students studying in classes ninth and tenth.

1.3.5 Higher Secondary

Includes students studying in eleventh and twelfth classes.

1.3.6 Undergraduate

Here, a student goes through higher education, which is completed in college. This course may vary according to the subject pursued by the student. For medical student this stage is of four and a half years plus one year of compulsory internship, while a simple graduate degree can be attained in three years.

1.3.7 Postgraduate

After completing graduation a student may opt for post graduation to further add to his qualifications.

1.4 Education Governing Bodies

1.4.1 The Central Board of Secondary Education (CBSE)

This is the main governing body of education system in India. It has control over the central education system. It conducts exam. and looks after the functioning of schools accredited to central education system.

1.4.2 The Council of Indian School Certificate Examination (CISCE)

It is a board for Anglo Indian Studies in India. It conducts two examinations 'Indian Certificate of Secondary Education' and 'Indian School Certificate'. Indian Certificate of secondary education is a k-10 examination for those Indian students who have just completed class 10th and Indian school certificate is a k-12 public examination conducted for those studying in class 12th.

1.4.3 The State Government Boards

Apart from CBSE and CISCE each state in India has its own State Board of education, which looks after the educational issues.

1.4.4 The National Open School

It is also known as National Institute of Open Schooling. It was established by the Government of India in 1989. It is a ray of hope for those students who cannot attend formal schools.

1.4.5 The International School

It controls the schools, which are accredited to curriculum of international standard.

1.5 Elementary Education

According to the Constitution of India, elementary education is a fundamental right of children in the age group of 6-14 years. India has about 688,000 primary schools and 110,000 secondary schools. According to statistics two third of school going age children of India are enrolled in schools but the figures are deceptive as many don't attend schools regularly. At least half of all students from rural area drop out before completing school. The government has rolled out many plans to increase the percentage of elementary education. The plans such as—Sarva Siksha Abhiyan (SSA), District Primary Education Programme (DPEP), Operation Black-board and Mid Day Meal have been successful to great extent.

1.6 Sarva Siksha Abhiyan (SSA)

The main goal of this programme is that, all children of 6-11 years of age should complete primary education by the year 2007 and all children of 6-14 years of age should complete eight years of schooling by 2010. This plan covers the whole country with special emphasis on girls education and education of Schedule Caste (SC) and Schedule Tribe (ST) children and children with special needs. The SSA centers are mainly opened in those areas, which do not have any school or where schools are very far off. Special girl oriented programmes include:

- Girls education at elementary level.
- National Programme for Education of Girls at Elementary Level (NPEGEL)
- Kasturba Gandhi Balika Vidyalaya (KGBV)
- Mahila Samakhya Scheme

1.7 District Primary Education Programme (DPEP)

This programme was launched in 1994 with the objective

of universalisation of primary education. Its main features are Universal Access, Universal Retention and Universal Achievement. It aims that the primary education should be accessible to each and every child of school going age, once a child is enrolled in school he/she should be retained there. The final step is achieving the goals of education. The main components of this programme are:

- Construction of classrooms and new schools
- Opening of non-formal schooling centers
- Setting up early childhood education centers
- Appointment of teachers
- Providing education to disabled children.

The programme has been successful to the large extent as 1,60,000 schools and 84,000 alternative schools have been opened under this programme. And work is going on for the construction of new buildings of 52,758 schools. 4,20,203 disabled students have been successfully enrolled into the schools.

1.8 Operation Blackboard

It was started in 1987-88. The aim of this programme is to improve human and physical resource availability in primary schools of India. According to this programme every primary school should have at least two rooms, two teachers and essential teaching aids like black-board, chalk, duster etc.

1.9 National Bal Bhavan

The National Bal Bhavan was opened with the aim of developing overall personalities of children of all strata of society irrespective of their caste, creed, religion and gender. It supplements school education by helping children to learn in play way and natural environment.

Other important endeavours taken up by Indian government for the development of education in India includes:

- Navodaya Vidyalaya Samiti
- Kendriya Vidyalaya Sangathan
- Integrated Education for Disabled Children
- National Council of Educational Research and Training.

1.10 Secondary Education

The enrollment at secondary school throughout the country was close to 28 million in 1998-99. Efforts are being made to increase this figure through the implementation of proposed new educational strategies. Education system in India is making fast progress. The data of students' enrollment at primary and secondary level of school education testifies to it.

National Policy of Education (1992) laid down many objectives for the development of education system in India but it has not been successful in achieving all of them. It has specified that the examination system should discourage the memorising but it is what is going on. The education in India seems to encourage rote learning instead of experimentation and questioning. There is some disparity in assessment as all the State Boards have different standards of evaluation. The reservation on the basis of caste and religion is also a negative point in Indian education. Corruption is visible in the allocation of seats of institutions of higher studies and student politics is another sore point. These are some of the issues, which need to be worked upon.

1.11 Role of Government

When one examines the role of Government of India which the Constitution assigns to the central government in education and compares it with the role which other federal governments play in education, or even with the role which the Government of India itself played in the earlier years of our history, one can easily conclude that the following activities may be undoubtedly regarded as "federal functions in education":

1. Educational and cultural relations with other countries;
2. The clearing house functions of collecting and broadcasting ideas and information;
3. The coordinating function of harmonising the educational activities of the Centre and the States;
4. Education in the Union Territories;
5. Scientific research;
6. Technical education;
7. Propagation, development and enrichment of Hindi;

1.12 Journey of Indian Education

Time	*Elementary Education*	*Secondary Education*	*Higher Education*	*Across Segments*
1990-2011	District Primary Education Programme launched to universalise primary education (1994) Mid-Day Meal scheme (1995) Sarva Shiksha Abhiyaan launched (2001)	Formation of Navodaya Vidyalaya and National Open School (Eight Plan–1992–1997) Establishment of IITGuwahati in 1994	Establishment of IIMs at Kozhikode (1996) and Indore (1998) National Boardof Accreditation (NBA) and National Assessment and Accreditation Council (NAAC) established (1994) Work underway to set up 8 IITs, 7 IIMs, 20 IITs, 10 NITs and 5 Indian Institutes of Science Education and Research (2011)	NPE 1986 revised basedon review by Acharya Ramamurti Committee (1992) Constitution amended to make Free and Compulsory Education a fundamental right (2002) Right to Education Act (2009)
1974-1990	Launch of centrally assisted schemes suchas Operation Blackboard (1986), Nonformal education scheme (1986), Shiksha Karmi Project (1987) and Mahila Samakya (1989)	Vocationalisation of Secondary Education scheme launched (1987–88) Computer Literacy and Studies in Schools (CLASS) initiated (1984–85)	Enactment of the All India Council for Technical Education Act, 1987 Establishment of Indira Gandhi National Open University (IGNOU) in 1985 and IIM Lucknow in 1984	Launch of integrated child development scheme (ICDS) For children up to six years of age (1975) Education made a concurrent subject (1976) Second National Policyon Education adopted (1986)
1951-1974	Expansion of basic and elementary education (First Plan 1951–56) Primary education made free and compulsory (Fourth Plan 1969–74)	Diversification of the secondary education system (Second Plan 1956–61) Establishment of IIT Guwahati in 1994	Enactment of The University Grants Commission Act, 1956 Setting up of IITs (Kharagpur 1951; Mumbai 1958; Kanpur and Chennai 1959) and IIMs (Ahmadabad and Kolkata 1961; Bangalore 1963) Enactment of Apprentices Act, 1961 and Institute of Technology Act, 1961	First National Policy on Education adopted (1968)

8. Preservation and promotion of national culture inclusive of patronage to national art;
9. Patronage to the study of ancient Indian culture in general and the study of Sanskrit in particular;
10. Education of the handicapped;
11. Promotion and coordination of educational research;
12. Special responsibility for the cultural interests of the minorities;
13. Responsibility for the weaker sections of the people, i.e., the Scheduled Castes and Scheduled Tribes;
14. Responsibility for strengthening national unity through suitable programmes and particularly through those of emotional integration;
15. Grant of scholarships in an attempt to scout for talent, especially at the University stage;
16. Advanced professional and vocational training;
17. Maintenance of Central Institutions or agencies for education;
18. Provision of free and compulsory education up to the age of 14 years.

1.13 UK School Curriculum

The quality of a school depends on a variety of factors including infrastructure, presence and motivation of teachers, minimum teaching standards and a minimum achievement level of pupils. Since the primary aim of an educational institution is to ensure that all the learners acquire the desired skills and knowledge (Aggarwal, 2000), the quality of a school can be estimated by the extent to which students have acquired knowledge, skills, values and attitudes, which refer to the actual learning outcomes.

Throughout the post-war period there have been many attempts to reform the UK education system, often with an explicit intention to try and make it more productive. The list of education policy reforms that have been attempted over the last 50 years is quite extensive, and recently the UK (and in particular England and Wales) has introduced many innovative market-oriented reforms to its educational system, in an attempt to raise standards. The most striking recent reform is that parents have increasingly been given much more choice in terms of the school attended by their children, and schools have been forced to be more accountable. Other notable reforms include a nationally prescribed curriculum, vigorous attempts to raise participation in post-compulsory schooling and the introduction of tuition fees for higher education.

To tackle the problem of poor literacy and numeracy, as well as address general concerns about poor standards, the UK introduced two other significant national policies. Firstly, in the late 1980s a standardised national curriculum was introduced for pupils aged between seven and sixteen. The purpose of the national curriculum was to raise standards by ensuring that all students study a prescribed set of subjects up to a minimum level until the age of 16. The second policy reform, in 1998, was the introduction of the National Literacy and Numeracy Strategies. These strategies involved all primary schools allocating part of the daily curriculum to literacy and numeracy hours, with the specific aim of developing pupils' basic skills. The content of these daily literacy and numeracy lessons, and indeed how they should be taught, was tightly prescribed by central government.

1.13.1 Primary Curriculum Subjects

The National Curriculum for England at Key Stages, one and two. It includes, programmes of study and attainment target level descriptions for all Key Stage one and two subjects.

1. Religious Education

   Details of the non-statutory guidance for religious education in English schools.

2. Information and Communication Technology

   The most recent programmes of study for ICT at KS one and two have now been disapplied and are no longer statutory. Schools are free to develop their own curricula for ICT that best meet the needs of their pupils, or to continue to follow the existing programmes.

3. History

   The statutory programme of study for Key Stages one and two history.

4. Geography

   The statutory programme of study for Key Stages one and two geography.

5. Citizenship

   The non-statutory programme of study for Key Stages one and two citizenship. Personal, social and health education (PSHE)

   The non-statutory programme of study for Key Stages one and two PSHE.

6. Science

   The statutory programme of study for Key Stages one and two science.

7. Physical education (PE)

   The statutory programme of study for Key Stages one and two PE.

8. Music

   The statutory programme of study for Key Stages one and two music.

9. Modern foreign languages (MFL)

   The non-statutory programme of study for Key Stages one and two modern foreign languages

10. Mathematics

    The statutory programme of study for Key Stages one and two mathematics.

11. English

    The statutory programme of study for Key Stages one and two English.

12. Design and Technology

    The statutory programme of study for Key Stages one and two design and technology.

13. Art and Design

    The statutory programme of study for Key Stages one and two art and design.

1.13.2 Secondary Curriculum Subjects

The National Curriculum for England at Key Stages three and four. It includes programmes of study and attainment target level descriptions for all Key Stage three and four subjects.

1. Religious Education

   Details of the non-statutory guidance for religious education in English schools.

2. Mathematics

   The statutory programme of study for Key Stages three and four mathematics.

3. ICT

   The most recent programmes of study for ICT at Key Stages three and four have now been disapplied and are no longer statutory. Schools are free to develop their own curricula for ICT that best meet the needs of their pupils, or to continue to follow the existing programmes.

4. English

   The statutory programmes of study for Key Stages three and four English.

5. Citizenship

   The statutory programme of study for Key Stages three and four citizenship.

6. Art and Design

   The statutory National Curriculum for England for Key Stage three art and design.

7. Design and Technology

   The statutory National Curriculum for England for Key Stage three design and technology.

8. Geography

   The statutory National Curriculum for England for Key Stage three geography.

9. History

   The statutory National Curriculum for England for Key Stage three history.

10. Modern Foreign Languages (MFL)

    The statutory National Curriculum for England for Key Stage three modern foreign languages.

11. Music

    The statutory National Curriculum for England for Key Stage three music.

12. Physical Education (PE)

    The statutory programme of study for Key Stages three and four PE.

13. Personal, social, health and economic education (PSHEE)

    The non-statutory programme of study for Key Stages three and four PSHEE.

14. Science

    The statutory programme of study for Key Stages three and four science.

1.14 School Curriculum of Ireland

During the 20th century, the economic demand of labour with secondary education skills rose due to the rise of big businesses, advances in science and technology, and large-scale retailing that led to the increase of returns on education.

As per the Education Act, 1998 the American government is adopting following curriculum.

1.14.1 Curriculum

1. The Minister may, from time to time, following such consultation with patrons of schools, national associations of parents, recognised school management organisations and recognised trade unions and staff associations representing teachers, as the Minister considers appropriate, prescribe the curriculum for recognised schools, namely—

   (a) The subjects to be offered in recognised schools,

   (b) The syllabus of each subject,

   (c) The amount of instruction time to be allotted to each subject and

(d) The guidance and counselling provision to be offered in schools.

2. Without prejudice to the generality of subsection (1), the Minister—

   (a) Shall have regard to the desirability of assisting schools to exercise their powers as provided for under subsection (4),

   (b) Shall have regard to the characteristic spirit of a school or class of school in exercising his or her functions under this section,

   (c) May give directions to schools, where he or she considers it appropriate, to ensure that the subjects and syllabuses pursued in those schools are appropriate and relevant to the educational and vocational needs of the students in those schools,

   (d) Shall ensure that the amount of instruction time to be allotted to subjects on the curriculum as determined by the Minister in each school day shall be such as to allow for such reasonable instruction time, as the board with the consent of the patron determines, for subjects relating to or arising from the characteristic spirit of the school, and

   (e) Shall not require any student to attend instruction in any subject which is contrary to the conscience of the parent of the student or in the case of a student who has reached the age of 18 years, the student.

3. The Minister may—

   (a) Consult with the National Council for Curriculum and Assessment and such other persons or bodies of persons as the Minister considers appropriate on any matter relating to the curriculum for recognised schools, and

   (b) Establish, as the Minister considers appropriate, such bodies of persons to conduct research and to advise him or her on matters relating to his or her duties under this section.

4. A school may, subject to the requirement that the curriculum as determined by the Minister is taught in

that school, provide courses of instruction in such other subjects as the board considers appropriate.

1.14.2 Content of Curriculum

The revised primary school curriculum was introduced into national schools in 1999. It consists of six curriculum areas that are further divided into 11 subjects. These are:

- Language: English
- Mathematics
- Social, Environmental and Scientific
- Education: History, Geography, Science
- Arts Education: Music, Visual Arts, Drama
- Physical Education
- Social Personal and Health Education.

There are guidelines on the time to be allocated to each of the curriculum areas.

1.14.3 Aims of Curriculum

The aims of the curriculum are to ensure that all children are provided with learning opportunities that recognise and celebrate their uniqueness, develop their full potential and prepare them to meet the challenges of the 21st century. The focus is on the child as learner, and the use of a variety of teaching methodologies is an essential feature of the curriculum. The curriculum aims to foster the development of key skills in communication, problem-solving, critical thinking, inquiry, investigation and analysis, and social and personal awareness and interaction. In particular, it places key emphasis on the acquisition of literacy and numeracy skills. The curriculum emphasises the need for greater attention to be paid to students with special educational needs and emphasises the importance of achieving functional literacy and numeracy. It also draws attention to the needs of gifted children.

1.15 Importance of Inclusive Education

Inclusive education is a process of increasing the participation of all students in schools, including those with disabilities. Inclusive education means that all students attend and are welcomed by their neighbourhood schools in age-appropriate, regular classes and are supported to learn, contribute and participate in all aspects of the life of the school. It is about restructuring the cultures, policies and practices in schools so that they respond to the diversity of students in their locality. Inclusive education is different from special education, which takes a variety of forms including special schools, small units, and the integration of individual children with specialised support. Inclusion can be seen as an attempt to move ideas of education for all beyond 'mainstreaming' where children may be integrated that is in the same physical location but not necessarily share an educational experience with their peers. Inclusion implies children away from school due to different reasons, have 'access to the curriculum' in the best way to meet their needs.

According to UNESCO, inclusive education is seen as "a process of addressing and responding to the diversity of needs of all learners through increasing participation in learning, cultures and communities, and reducing exclusion from education and from within education." The goal is that the whole education system will facilitate learning environments where teachers and learners embrace and welcome the challenge and benefits of diversity. Within an inclusive education approach, learning environments are fostered where individual needs are met and every student has an opportunity to succeed.

In third world countries like India, inclusive education plays vital role in the primary and secondary education. In India, there are many disparities are prevailed here due to different regions and religions, in this context inclusive education is necessary to reach out the unreached. The Education for All (EFA) initiative from the United Nations is an essential element of the Millennium Development Goals, in part because education is seen as being crucial to human development, and also because so many children do not have access to education UNESCO (2005). Across the world, there are many reasons why children do not attend school, including high levels of mobility, social conflict, child labour and exploitation, poverty, gender and disability. Many children are at risk of not attending school, or of receiving a sub-standard education. In some parts of the world, schooling is not available because of a shortage of school places, lack of quality teachers, or because schools are too far from where children live. Sometimes families choose not to send their children to school because of fears about safety and security, the poor quality of schooling or because of the economic costs. Such costs might include school fees, having to buy uniforms, books and materials, and so-called 'opportunity costs' that arise when young people are not economically active because they are in school.

An inclusive education plan will represent a key element of downtrodden children and young people's plan and will replace plans such as the learning and behaviour support Plan. It will link directly to the school improvement and social inclusion elements of the plan, the accessibility strategy, school organisation plan and admissions arrangements and to the work plans of the downtrodden children's. "An educationally inclusive school is one in which the teaching and learning, achievements, attitudes and well-being of every young person matters. Effective schools are educationally inclusive schools. This shows, not only in their performance, but also in their ethos and their willingness to offer new opportunities to pupils who may have experienced previous difficulties. This does not mean treating all pupils the same way. Rather it involves taking account of pupils' varied life experiences and needs." (*Evaluating Educational Inclusion. Guidance for Inspectors and School,* OFSTED, 2000). OFSTED (2000) describes educational inclusion as, "more than a concern about any one group of pupils such as those pupils who have been or are likely to be excluded from school. Its scope is broad. It is about equal opportunities for all pupils, whatever their age, gender, ethnicity, attainment and background. It pays particular attention to the provision made for and the achievement of different groups of pupils within a school".

Mainstream inclusive educational reform initiatives designed to raise standards can be both a facilitator and a barrier to the education of children with learning needs. In many cases these two strands of policy development, inclusion on the one hand and higher standards on the other, do not necessarily make comfortable partners. On the one hand it can be argued that higher standards are good for all children because schools are held accountable for the progress of all learners. On the other hand, it has been argued that the difficulties children experience in learning are a consequence of unresponsive education systems. As a result children are often seen as having 'additional support needs' when there is a discrepancy between what a system of schooling ordinarily provides and what the child needs to support their learning. Thus, the professional focus tends to be on what is 'additional to or different from' the provision which is generally available, rather than on what can be done to make schooling more accessible for all (Florian, 2007).

In addition, there are persistent beliefs that when children find learning difficult, it is because there is something wrong with them. The 'classic' special education view assumes that it is not possible to include children with learning difficulties in mainstream settings because their needs are different. The assumption that underpins this view is that it is desirable to group children according to the nature of their abilities, disabilities or difficulties. There are those who claim that because children are different, there will be a diversity of instructional needs. In turn, this requires teaching groups to be formed according to these perceived individual characteristics. According to Kaufman *et al.* (2005), successful teaching of children who are different, requires that they be grouped homogeneously so that special pedagogical approaches can be deployed by teachers who have been trained to use them. It could be argued that when special education is conceptualised in this manner, it is a barrier to the development of inclusion because it absolves the rest of the education system from taking responsibility for all children's learning.

1.15.1 Inclusive Education: Defining Principles

An inclusive education system is one which:

(i) Places children, not institutions, at the centre and focuses on their needs and well-being.

(ii) Inclusive education has the highest expectations of all children and their potential to achieve success, whatever their circumstances.

(iii) The inclusiveness recognises that parents/careers have the right to be fully involved at all times and that they must be engaged as active partners in making decisions about their children's education and well-being.

(iv) It ensures that the views of children and young people are sought and given due weight according to their age, maturity and capability.

(v) Inclusive education recognises every child's entitlement to gain full access to a broad and balanced curriculum, alongside their peers in a mainstream setting in their local communities wherever possible, enabling full and active participation in the life of the school and the highest possible levels of achievement.

(vi) Inclusive curriculum ensures this entitlement by maintaining a flexible, responsive continuum of provision to match a rage of need. Such a rage includes appropriately adapted, differentiated and targeted curriculum delivery, reflecting language and cultural diversity as appropriate, and services which can help to enhance the capacity of schools and early years settings to meet a diverse range of needs.

(vii) Provides opportunities for children attending special schools to learn alongside mainstream peers and vice versa, and interchange of staff between the two sectors.

(viii) Emphasises that those responsible for meeting children's educational needs—primarily the Governors and staff of our schools—must take responsibility for providing high quality education for all children, with the School Authority and other agencies providing appropriate support.

(ix) Works in direct partnership with health, social care and the voluntary sector in meeting the needs of children and delivering improved outcomes for them, through services, schools and other settings, jointly planning and implementing strategy in ways which make best use of resources.

(x) Relates to all aspects of educational provision, as proposed in the Extended schools guidance, and involves youth services, libraries and other sources of support, advice and information.

(xi) Has the full support of elected Members of the County Council.

1.15.2 The Benefits of Inclusive Education

Inclusive education provides benefits for all students and school personnel and serves as an example for an inclusive society. In a review of exploration on inclusion for both elementary and secondary schools, students' academic performance was found equal to or better in inclusive settings for general education students, even those considered to be high achievers. In a study of inclusive programming at the elementary level, in which a co-teaching model was implemented, both students with disabilities and low achieving general education students experienced improvements in social skills and all students experienced increase in self-esteem related to their abilities and accomplishments. Students with disabilities experience increased self-esteem by the mere fact they are attending classes in an inclusive education setting rather than in a special education setting. Students who have transitioned to middle schools after participating in inclusive settings and curriculum from specific feeder elementary schools are scoring higher. In addition, student gains in self-esteem, desirable behaviour, attendance, grades, and test scores have been noted for students with and without disabilities in inclusive classrooms. Finally, a greater number of students are better prepared to transition from elementary to secondary levels after participating in inclusive elementary programmes.

Three concerns typically identified when considering outcomes for students without disabilities are whether or not inclusion will result in reduced academic outcomes, less teacher time and attention, or learned "undesirable" behaviours from student with disabilities. Studies using quasi-experimental designs to compare outcomes of students with and without disabilities in inclusive classrooms found that none of the concerns were realised. Students without disabilities experience growth in social cognition and gain a greater understanding and acceptance of students with disabilities and of diversity in general when they experience inclusive programming. Students without disabilities also experience increased self-esteem and overall improvement in their own self-concept. Parents of students without disabilities confirmed the findings of overall improved outcomes as a result of the inclusion of students with severe disabilities within the regular education classroom.

1.15.3 Recommended Practices in Inclusive Schools

1. Embrace diversity,
2. Provide access to knowledge, skills, and information to all students,
3. Tailor learning to meet individual needs,

4. Encourage co-teaching and collaboration among general and special Educators,
5. Collaborate with families and community members,
6. Think outside the box in terms of school structure and finance,
7. Maintain high expectations of all students,
8. Engage in continuous improvement and
9. Promote and support inclusive communities.

The University of Minnesota and the Council for Exceptional Children identified key characteristics related to achieving positive learning outcomes for students with disabilities. They include a clear and common vision, active leadership, high expectations of all students, stakeholder involvement in school leadership, innovative practices, and professional development activities among staff, and the development of an inclusive and collaborative community of learning. The use of a collaborative or co-teaching model, in which two to three adults share the responsibility of meeting the diverse needs of all students, results in better academic and social outcomes for those students. Adequate and appropriate resources, support for both students and teachers, teacher training and planning time, and a commitment to a vision of success for all students is vital to the success of inclusive programming.

According to the *National Study of Inclusive Education,* students in cooperatively taught inclusive classes were on-task more often, had more opportunities for one-on-one instruction, and were engaged in more individual work. The use of cooperative learning strategies results in, for students with and without disabilities, increased social skills, greater communication skills, the development of problem-solving skills, and enhanced learning. The use of technology, including audiotaped books, closed captioning, and computer networks and software, is seen as a diversity accommodation tool and enhances the learning opportunities for all students. Students who were trained in collaborative learning on computers in small groups had higher achievement, better self-esteem, and more positive attitudes towards learning than students working individually. These results were particularly notable for students with low abilities.

Three skills that teachers need in order to work successfully in an inclusive school are the ability to collaborate and team with other professionals, develop and implement strategies to accommodate diverse learners, and the ability to develop solutions that will enhance the learning experiences of all children. Regular educators require specialised training in order to work effectively with students with disabilities and special educators are concerned they need more content area training, especially when working in middle school classrooms.

1.16 Importance of Creativity in Education

Creativity is an elusive and contested concept. There have been many attempts to define it. Creativity has been described as 'a state of mind in which all our intelligences are working together' (Lucas, 2001) and as 'the ability to solve problems and fashion products and to raise new questions' (Gardner, 1993). Few experts agree on a precise definition, but when we say the word 'creativity', everyone senses a similar feeling. When we are creative, we are aware of a special excitement. Creativity can be understood as having the power or quality to express yourself in your own way. Children are naturally creative. They see the world through fresh, new eyes and then use what they see in original ways. One of the most rewarding aspects of working with children is the chance to watch them create. Every child is born with creative potential, but this potential may be stifled if care is not taken to nurture and stimulate creativity. Young children are naturally curious. They wonder about people and the world. Even before they enter primary school, they already have a variety of learning skills acquired through questioning, inquiring, searching, manipulating, experimenting, and playing. Children need opportunities for a closer look; they need time for the creative encounter. Creative learning is a natural human process that occurs when people become curious and excited. Children prefer to learn in creative ways rather than just memorising information provided by teachers or parents. They also learn better and sometimes faster.

The term "creativity," as it relates to the classroom, goes beyond art class and school projects. At its best, creativity in the classroom is about how a teacher captivates students and inspires them to learn. Teachers who are practised in the art of developing creativity are generally focused on creating a classroom culture that thrives on creativity. They build a repertoire of strategies designed to spark new ideas and bring out a spirit of creativity in students, and they adapt and create ideas for their own curriculum needs. What is needed is teaching that is innovative. Children need to experience the unpredictable and the uncertain. They need lessons that produce surprise. As Fisher argued, creative learners need creative teachers who provide both order and adventure, and who are willing to do the unexpected and take risks (Fisher, 2002).

Creativity is the act of turning new and imaginative ideas into reality. According to Linda Naiman, founder of Creativity at Work, "Creativity involves two processes: thinking, then producing. Innovation is the production or implementation of an idea. If you have ideas, but don't act on them, you are imaginative but not creative." Naiman promotes the use of arts-based learning to develop creativity, innovation, and collaborative leadership in organisations. A creative curriculum offers children plenty of opportunities for creative behaviour. Such a curriculum will call for original work, independent learning, self-initiated projects, and experimentation. Using curriculum materials that provide progressive warm-up experiences, procedures that permit one thing to lead to another, and activities that recognise and reward creative thinking makes it easier for teachers to provide opportunities for creative learning.

Children have a seemingly endless supply of creative energy. It shows up in their quirky impromptu rhymes and songs, in their imaginative play, and in their innate ability to make something out of anything. However, research on creativity points to a so-called "fourth grade slump" across various cultures (Torrance, 1967). It appears that when children begin school, their level of creativity is evident and often flourishing but, by the time they reach the fourth grade, they have become more conforming, less likely to take risks, and less playful or spontaneous than in earlier years. Today's children must be given the chance to develop their creativity to the fullest extent possible; not only for the benefit of their own future but also for the communities we all inhabit.

CHAPTER 2 The Right to Children to Free and Compulsory Education Act, 2009

The following act of Parliament received the assent of the President on the 26th August, 2009 and is hereby published for general information:

An act to provide for free and compulsory education to all children of the age of six to fourteen years. Be it enacted by Parliament in the sixtieth Year of the Republic of India as follows:

2.1 Preliminary

2.1.1 Extent and Commencement

(1) This act may be called the Right to Children to free and Compulsory Education Act, 2009.

(2) It shall extend to the whole of India except the State of Jammu and Kashmir.

(3) It shall come into force on such date as the Central Government may, by notification in the official Gazette, appoint.

2.1.2 Definition

In this Act, unless the context otherwise requires :

(a) "appropriate Government" means:

(i) in relation to the school established, owned or controlled by the Central Government, or the administrator of the Union territory, having no legislature, the Central Government.

(ii) in relation to a school, other than the school referred to in sub- clause (i), established within the territory of-

(A) a State, the State Government;

(B) a Union territory having legislature, the Government of that Union territory;

(b) "capitation free" means any kind of donation or contribution or payment other than the free notified by the school;

(c) "child" means a male or female child of the age of six to fourteen years;

(d) "child belonging to the disadvantage group" means a child belonging to the Schedule Caste, the Schedule Tribe, the socially and educationally backward class or such other group having disadvantage owing to social, cultural, economical, geographical, linguistic, gender or such other factor, as may be specified by the appropriate Government, by notification;

(e) "child belonging to weaker section" means a child belonging to such parent or guardian whose annual income is lower than the minimum limit specified by the appropriate Government, by notification;

(f) "elementary education" means the education from first class to eight class;

(g) "guardian" in relation to a child, means a person having the care and custody of that child and includes a natural guardian or guardian appointed or declared by a court or a statute;

(h) "local authority" means a Municipal Corporation or Municipal Council or Zila Parishad or Nagar Panchayat or Panchayat, by whatever name called, and includes such other authority or body having administrative council over the school or empowered by or under any law for the time being in force to function as a local authority in any city, town or village;

(i) "National Commission for Protection of Child Rights" means the National Commission for Protection of Child Right constituted under section 3 of the Commissions for Protection of Child Right Act, 2005;

(j) "notification" means a notification published in the Official Gazette;

(k) "parent" means either the natural or step or adaptive father or mother of a child;

(l) "prescribed" means prescribed by rules made under this Act.

(m) "Scheduled" means the Schedule annexed to this Act.

(n) "school" means any recognised school imparting elementary education and includes-

(i) a school established, owned or controlled by the appropriate Government or a local authority;

(ii) an aided school receiving aid or grants to meet whole or part of its expenses from the appropriate Government or the local authority;

(iii) a school belonging to specified category, and

(iv) an unaided school not receiving any kind of aid or grants to meet its expenses from the appropriate Government pr the local authority;

(o) "screening procedure" means the method of selection for admission of a child, in preference over another, other than a random method.

(p) "specified category", in relation to a school, means a school known as Kendriya Vidyalaya, Navodaya Vidyalaya, Sainik School or any other school having a distinct character which may be specified, by notification, by the appropriate Government;

(q) "State Commission for Protection of Child Rights" means the State Commission for Protection of Child Rights constituted under section 3 of the Commissions for Protection of Child Rights Act, 2005.

2.2 Right to Free and Compulsory Education

2.2.1 Right to Child to Free and Compulsory Education

(1) Every child of the age of six to fourteen years shall have a right to free and compulsory education in a neighbourhood school till completion of elementary education.

(2) For the purpose of the sub-section (1), no child shall be liable to pay any kind of fee or charges or expenses which

may prevent him or her from pursuing and completing the elementary education:

Provided that child is suffering from disability, as defined in clause (i) of section 2 of the Persons with Disabilities (Equal opportunities, Protection and Full Participation) Act, 1996, shall have the right to pursue free and compulsory elementary education in the accordance with the provisions of Chapter V of the said Act.

2.2.2 Special Provisions for Children not Admitted to or have not Completed, Elementary Education

Where the child above six years of the age has not been admitted in any school or through admitted, could not complete his or her elementary education, then he or she shall be admitted in a class appropriate to his or her age:

Provided that where a child is directly admitted in a class appropriate to his or her age, then, he or she shall, in order to be at par with others, have a right to received special training, in such manner, and within such time-limits, as may be prescribed:

Provided further that a child so admitted to elementary education shall be entitled to free education till completion of elementary education even after fourteen years.

2.2.3 Right to Transfer to other School

(1) Where in a school, there is no provision for completion of elementary education, a child shall have a right to seek transfer to any other school, excluding the school specified in sub-clauses (iii) and (iv) of clause (n) of section 2, for completing his or her elementary education.

(2) Where a child is required to move from one school to another, either within a State or outside, for any reason whatsoever, such child shall have a right to seek transfer to any other school, excluding the school specified in sub-clauses (iii) and (iv) of clause (n) of section 2, for completing his or her elementary education.

(3) For seeking admission in such other school, the Head-teacher or in-charge of the school where such child was last admitted, shall immediately issue the transfer certificate:

Provided the delay in producing transfer certificate shall not be a found for either delaying or denying admission such other school.

Provide further that the Head-teacher or in-charge of the school delaying issuance of transfer certificate shall be liable for disciplinary action under the service rules applicable to him or her.

2.3 Duties of Appropriate Government, Local Authority and Parents

2.3.1 Duty of Appropriate Government and Local Authority to Establish School

For carrying the provisions of this Act the appropriate Government and the local authority shall establish, within such area or limits of neighbourhood, as may be prescribed a school, where it is not so established, within a period of three years from the commencement of this Act.

2.3.2 Sharing of Financial and other Responsibilities

(1) The Central Government and State Government shall have enactment responsibility for providing funds for carrying out the provisions of this Act.

(2) The Central Government shall prepare the estimates of capital and recurring expenditure for the implementation of the provisions of the Act.

(3) The Central Government shall provide to the State Government as grants-in-aid of revenues, such percentage of expenditure referred it in sub-section (2) as it may determine, from time to time, in consultation with the State Governments.

(4) The central Government may make a request to the President to make reference to the Finance Commission under sub-clause (d) of clause (3) of article 280 to examine the need for additional resources to be provided to any State Government so that the said State Government may provide its share of funds for carrying out the provisions of the Act.

(5) Notwithstanding anything contained in sub-section (4), the State Government shall, taking into consideration the sums provided by the Central Government to a State

Government under sub-section (3), and its other resources, ne responsible to provide funds for implementation of the provisions of the Act.

(6) The Central Government shall-

(a) develop a framework of national curriculum with the help of academic authority specified under section 29;

(b) develop and enforce standards for training of teachers;

(c) provide technical support and resources to the State Government for promoting innovations, researches, planning and capacity building.

2.3.3 Duties of Appropriate Government

The appropriate Government shall—

(a) Provide free and compulsory elementary education to every child:

Provided that where a child is admitted by his or her parents or guardian, as the case may be, in a school other than a school established, owned, controlled or substantially financed by funds provided directly or indirectly by the appropriate Government or a local authority, such child or his or her parents or guardian, as the case may be, shall not be entitled to make a claim for reimbursement of expenditure incurred on elementary education of the child in such other school.

Explanation—The term "compulsory education" means obligation of the appropriate Government to—

(i) provide free elementary education to every child of the age of six to fourteen years; and

(ii) ensure compulsory admission, attendance and completion of elementary education by every child of the age of six of fourteen years;

(b) ensure availability of a neighborhood school as specified in section 6;

(c) ensure the child belonging to weaker section and the child belonging to disadvantaged group are not discriminated against and prevented from perusing and completing elementary education on any grounds;

(d) provide infrastructure including school building, teaching staff and learning equipment;

(e) provide special training facility specified in section;

(f) ensure and monitor admission, attendance and completion of elementary education by every child;

(g) ensure good quality elementary education conforming to the standards and norms specified in the schedule;

(h) ensure timely prescribing of curriculum and courses of study for elementary education; and

(i) provide training facility for teachers.

2.3.4 Duties of Local Authority

Every local authority shall—

(a) provide free and compulsory elementary education to every child:

provide that where a child is admitted by his or her parents or guardian, as the case may be, in a school other than a school established, owned, controlled or substantially financed by funds provided directly or indirectly by the appropriate Government or a local authority, such child or his or her parents or guardian, as the case may be, shall not be entitled to make a claim for reimbursement of expenditure incurred on elementary education of the child in such other school;

(b) ensure availability of a neighborhood school has specified in section 6;

(c) ensure that the child belonging to disadvantaged group are not discriminated against and prevented from pursuing and completing elementary education on any grounds;

(d) maintain record of children up to the age of fourteen years residing within its jurisdiction, in such manner as may be prescribed;

(e) ensure and monitor admission, attendance and completion of elementary education by every child residing within its jurisdiction;

(f) provide infrastructure including school building, teaching Staff and learning material;

(g) provide special training facility specified in section;

(h) ensure good quality education conforming to the standards and norms specified in the Schedule;

(i) ensure timely prescribing of curriculum and course of the study for elementary education

(j) providing training facility for teacher

(k) ensure admission of children of migrant families;

(l) monitor functioning of schools within its jurisdiction and

(m) decide the academic calendar.

2.3.5 Duties of Parents and Guardian

It shall be the duty of every parent or guardian to admit or cause to be admitted his or her child or ward, as the case may be, to an elementary education in the neighbourhood school.

2.3.6 Appropriate Government to Provide for Pre-school Education

Within a view to prepare children above the age of three years for elementary education and to provide early childhood care and education for all children until they complete the age of six years, the appropriate Government may make necessary management for providing free pre-school education for such children.

2.4 Responsibilities of Schools and Teacher

2.4.1 Extent of Schools Responsibility for Free and Compulsory Education

(1) For the purpose of this Act, a school—

(a) Specified sub-clause (i) of clause (n) of section2 shall provide free and compulsory elementary education to all children admitted therein;

(b) Specified sub-clause (ii) of clause (n) of section 2 shall provide free and compulsory elementary education to such proportion of children admitted therein as its annual recurring aid or grants so received bears to its annual recurring expenses, subject to a maximum of twenty five per cent;

(c) Specified in sub-clauses (iii) and (iv) of clause (n) of section 2 shall admit in class I, to the extent of at least twenty five per cent of the strength of that class children belonging to weaker section and disadvantaged group in the neighbourhood and provide free and compulsory elementary education till its completion:

Provide further that where a school specified in clause (n) of section 2 imparts pre-school education, the provisions of clauses (a) to (c) shall apply for admission to such pre-school education.

(2) The school specified in sub-clause (iv) of clause (n) of section 2 providing free and compulsory elementary education as specified in clause (c) of sub-section (i) shall be reimbursed expenditure so incurred by it to the extent of per-child-expenditure incurred by the State, or the actual amount charged from the child, whichever is less, in such manner as may be prescribed:

Provided that such reimbursement shall not excess pre-child-expenditure incurred by a school specified in sub-clause (i) of clause (n) of section 2;

Provided further that where such school is already under obligation to provide free education to a specified number of children on account of it having received any land, building, equipment or other facilities, either free of cost or at a concessional rate, such school shall not be entitled for reimbursement to the extent of such obligation.

(3) Every school shall provide such information as may be required by the appropriate Government or the local authority, as the case may be.

2.4.2 No Capitation Fee and Screening Procedure for Admission

(1) No school or person shall, while admitting a child, collect any capitation fee and subject the child or his or her parents or guardian to any screening procedure.

(2) Any school or person, if in contravention of the provisions of sub-section (1),—

(a) receives capitation fee, shall be punishable with fine which may extend to ten times to the capitation fee charged;

(b) subject a child to screening procedure, shall be punishable with fine which may extend to twenty five thousand rupees for the first contravention and fifty thousands rupees for each subsequent contraventions.

2.4.3 Proof of Age for Admission

(1) For the purposes of admission to elementary education the age of a child shall be determined on the basis of the birth certificate issued in accordance with the provisions of the Births, Deaths and Marriages registration Act, 1886 or on the basis of such other document as may be prescribed.

(2) No child shall be denied admission in a school for lack of age proof.

2.4.4 No Denial of Admission

A child shall be admitted in a school of the commencement of the academic year or within such extended period as maybe prescribed:

Provided that no child shall be denied admission if such admission is sought subsequent to the extended period;

Provided further that any child admitted after the extended period shall complete his studies in such manner as may be prescribed by the appropriate Government.

2.4.5 Prohibition of Holding Back and Expulsion

No child admitted in a school shall be held back in any class or expelled from school till the completion of elementary education.

2.4.6 Prohibition of Physical Punishment and Mental Harassment to Child

(1) No child shall be subjected to physical punishment or mental harassment

(2) Whoever, contravenes the provision of sub-section (1) shall be liable to disciplinary action under the service rule applicable to such person.

2.4.7 No School to be Established without Obtaining Certificate of Recognition

(1) No school, other than a school established, owned or controlled by the appropriate Government or the local authority, shall, after the commencement of this Act, be established or function, without obtaining a certificate of recognition from such authority, by making an application in such form and manner, as may be prescribed.

(2) The authority prescribed under sub-section (1) shall issue the certificate of recognition in such form, within such period, in such manner, and subject to such conditions, as may be prescribed:

Provided that no such recognition shall be granted to a school unless it fulfils norms and standards specified under section 19.

(3) On the contravention of the conditions of recognition, the prescribed authority shall, by an order in writing, withdraw recognition:

Provided that such order shall contain a direction as to which of the neighborhood school, the children studying in the derecognised school, shall be admitted:

Provided further that no recognisition shall be so withdrawn without giving an opportunity of being heard to such school, in such manner, as may be prescribed.

(4) With effect from the date of withdrawal of the recognisition under sub-section (3), no such school shall continue to function.

(5) Any person who establishes or runs a schools without obtaining certificate of recognition, or continue to run a school after withdrawl of recognisition, shall be liable to fine which may extend to one lakh rupees and in case of continuing contraventions, to a fine of ten thousand rupees for each day during which such contravention continues.

2.4.8 Norms and Standards for School

(1) No school shall be established, or recognised, under section 18, unless it fulfills the norms and standards specified in the Schedule.

(2) Where a school established before the commencement of this Act does not fulfill such norms and standards specified in the Schedule, it shall take steps to fulfill such norms and standards at its own expenses, within a period of three years from the date of such commencement.

(3) Where a school fails to fulfill the norms and standards within the period specified under sub section (2), the authority prescribed under section (1) of section 18 shall withdraw recognisition granted to such school in the manner specified under sub section (3) thereof.

(4) With effect from the date of withdrawal of recognisition under sub section (3), no school shall continue to function.

(5) Any person who continues to run a school after the recognisition is withdrawn, shall be liable to find which may extend to one lakh rupees and in case of continuing contravention continues.

2.4.9 Power to Amend Schedule

The Central Government may, by notification, amend the Schedule by adding to, or omitting there from, any norms and standards.

2.4.10 School Management Committee

(1) A school, other than a school specified in sub clause (iv) of clause (n) of section 2, shall continue a School Management Committee consisting of the elected representatives of the local authority, parents or guardians of children admitted in such school and teachers:

Provided that at least three fourth of members of such Committee shall be parents or guardians;

Provided further that proportionate representation shall be given to the parents or guardians of children belonging to disadvantaged group and weaker section:

Provided also the 50 per cent of Members of such Committee shall be women.

(2) The School Management Committee shall perform the following functions, namely:-

(a) monitor the working of the school;

(b) prepare and recommend the school development plan;

(c) monitor the utilisation of the grants received from the appropriate Government or local authority or any other source; and

(d) perform such other functions as may be prescribed.

2.4.11 School Development Plan

(1) Every School Management Committee, constituted under sub section (1) of School section 21, shall prepare School Development Plan, in such manner as may be prescribed.

(2) The School development Plan so prepare under sub section (1) shall be the basis for the plans and grants to be made by the appropriate Government or local authority, as the case may be.

2.4.12 Qualifications for Appointment and Terms and Conditions of Service of Teachers

(1) Any person possessing such minimum qualifications, as laid down by and academic authority, authorised by the Central Government, by notification, shall be eligible for appointment as a teacher.

(2) Where the state does not have adequate institutions offering courses or training in teacher education, or teachers possessing minimum qualifications as laid down under sub section (1) are not available in sufficient numbers, the Central Government may, if it deems necessary, by notifications, relax the minimum qualifications required for appointment as a teacher, for such period, not exceeding five years, as may be specified in that notification:

Provided that a teacher who, at the commencement of this Act, does not possess minimum qualifications as laid down under sub section (1), shall acquire such minimum qualification within a period of five years.

(3) The salary and allowances payable to, and the terms and conditions of service of, teachers shall be such as may be prescribed.

2.4.13 Duties of Teachers and Redressal of Grievances

(1) A teacher appointed under sub section (1) of section 23 shall perform the following duties, namely:-

(a) maintain regularity and punctuality in attending school;

(b) conduct and complete the curriculum in accordance with the provisions of sub section (2) of section 29;

(c) complete entire curriculum within the specified time

(d) assess the learning ability of each child and accordingly supplement additional instructions, if any, as required;

(e) hold regular meeting with parents and guardians and apprise them about the regularity in attendance, ability to learn, progress made in learning and any other relevant information about the child; and

(f) perform such other duties as may be prescribed.

(2) A teacher committing default in performance of duties specified in sub section (1), shall be liable to disciplinary action under the service rules applicable to him or her:

Provided that before taking such disciplinary action, reasonable opportunity of being heard shall be afforded to such teacher.

(3) The grievances, if any, of the teacher shall be redressed in such manner as may be prescribed.

2.4.14 Pupil- Teacher-Ratio

(1) Within six months from the date of commencement of this Act, the appropriate Government and the local authority shall ensure that the Pupil-Teacher-Ratio, as specified in the Schedule, is maintained in each school.

(2) For the purpose of maintaining the Pupil-Teacher-Ratio under sub section (1), no teacher posted in a school shall be made to serve in any other school or office or deployed for any non-educational purpose, other than those specified in section 27.

2.4.15 Filling up of Vacancies of Teachers

The appointing authority, in relation to school established, owned, controlled or substantially financed by funds provided by directly or indirectly by the appropriate Government or by a local authority, shall ensure that vacancy of teacher in a school under its control shall not exceed ten per cent of the total sanctioned strength.

2.4.16 Prohibition of Deployment of Teachers for Non-educational Purposes

No teacher shall be deployed for any non-educational purposes other than the decennial population census, disaster relief duties or duties relating to elections to the local authority or the State Legislatures or Parliament, as the case may be.

2.4.17 Prohibition of Private Tuition by Teacher

No teacher shall engage himself or herself in private tuition or private teaching activity.

2.5 Curriculum and Completion of Elementary Education

2.5.1 Curriculum and Evaluation Procedure

(1) The curriculum and the evaluation procedure for elementary education shall be laid down by an academic authority to be specified by the appropriate Government, by notification.

(2) The authority, while laying down the curriculum and the evaluation procedure under sub section (1), shall take into consideration the following, namely:

(a) conformity with the values enshrined in the Constitution;

(b) all round development of the child;

(c) building up child's knowledge, potentiality and talent;

(d) development of physical and mental abilities to the fullest extent;

(e) learning through activities, discovery and exploration in a child friendly and child-centered manner;

(f) medium of instructions shall, as far as practicable, be in child's mother tongue;

(g) Making the child free of fear, trauma and anxiety and helping the child to express views freely;

(h) Comprehensive and continuous evaluation of child's understanding of knowledge and his or her ability to apply the same.

2.5.2 Examination and Completion Certificate

(1) No child shall be required to pass any Board examination till completion of elementary education.

(2) Every child completing his elementary education shall be awarded a certificate, in such form and in such manner, as may be prescribed.

2.6 Protection of Right of Children

2.6.1 Monitoring of Child Right to Education

(1) The National Commission for Protection of Child Rights constituted order section 3, or, as the case may be, the State Commission for Protection of Child Rights constituted under section 17, of the Commissions for Protection of Child Rights Act, 2005, shall, in addition to the function assigned to them under that Act, also perform the following functions, namely:-

(a) examine and review the safeguards for rights provided by or under this Act and recommended measures for their effective implementation;

(b) inquire into complaints relating to child's right to free and compulsory education and

(c) take necessary steps as provided under sections 15 and 24 of the said Commissions for protections of Child Rights Act.

(2) The Commissions shall, while inquiring into any matters relating to child's right to free and compulsory education under clause (c) of sub section (1), have the same powers as assigned to them respectively under section 14 and 24 of the said Commissions for Protections of Child Rights Act.

(3) Where the State Commission for Protection of Child Rights has not been constituted in a State, the appropriate Government may, for the purpose of performing the functions specified in clauses (a) to (c) of sub section (1), constitute such authority, in such

manner and subject to such terms and conditions, as may be prescribed.

2.6.2 Redressal of Grievances

(1) Notwithstanding anything contained in section 31, any person having any grievance relating to the right of a child under this Act may make a written complaint to the local authority having jurisdiction.

(2) After receiving the complaint under sub section (1), the local authority shall decide the matter within a period of three months after affording a reasonable opportunity of being heard to the parties concerned.

(3) Any person aggrieved by the decision of the local authority may prefer an appeal to the State Commission for Protection of Child Rights or the authority prescribed under sub section (3) of section 31, as the case may be.

(4) The appeal performed under sub section (3) shall be decided by State Commission for Protection of Child Rights or the authority prescribed under sub section (3) of section 3, as the case may be, provided under clause (c) of sub section (1) of section 31.

2.6.3 Construction of National Advisory Council

(1) The Central Government shall continue, by notification a National Advisory Council, consisting of such number of Members, not exceeding fifteen, as the Central Government may deem necessary, to be appointed from amongst persons having knowledge and practical experience in the fields of elementary education and child development.

(2) The functions of National Advisory Council shall be to advice the Central Government on implementation of the provisions of the Act in an effective manner.

(3) The allowances and other terms and conditions of the appointment of Members of the National Advisory Council shall be such as may be prescribed.

2.6.4 Construction of State Advisory Council

(1) The Government shall continue, by notification, a State Advisory Council consisting of such number of Members,

not exceeding fifteen, as the State Government may deem necessary, to be appointed from amongst persons having knowledge and practical experience in the field of elementary education and child development.

(2) The function of the State Advisory Council shall be to advice the State Government on implementation of the provisions of the Act in an effective manner.

(3) The allowances and other terms and conditions of appointment of Members of the State Advisory Council shall be such as may be prescribed.

2.7 Miscellaneous

2.7.1 Power to Issue Directions

(1) The Central Government may issue such guidelines to the appropriate Government or, as the case may be, the local authority, as it deems tit for the purposes of implementation of the provisions of this Act.

(2) The appropriate Government may issue guidelines and give such directions, as it deems fit, to the local authority or the School Management Committee regarding implementation of the provisions of this Act.

(3) The local authority may issue guideline and give such directions, as it deems/fit, to the School Management Committee regarding implementation of the provisions of this Act.

2.7.2 Previous Sanction for Prosecution

No prosecution for offences punishable under sub section (2) of section 13, sub section (5) of section 18 and subsection (5) of section 19 shall be instituted except with the previous sanction of an officer's authorised on this behalf, by the appropriate Government, by notification.

2.7.3 Protection of Action Taken in Good Faith

No suit or other legal proceeding shall lie against the Central Government, the State Commission for Protection of Child Rights, the local authority, the School Management Committee or any person, in respect of anything which is in good faith done or intended to be done, in pursuance of this Act, or any rules or order made there under.

2.7.4 Power of Appropriate Government to Make Rules

(1) The appropriate Government may, by notification, make rules, for carrying out the provisions of this Act.

(2) In particular, and without prejudice to the generally of the foregoing powers, such rules may provide for all or any of the following matters, namely:-

(a) the manner of giving special training and the time-limit thereof, under first proviso to section ;

(b) the area or limits for establishment of a neighborhood school, under section 6;

(c) the manner of maintenance of records of children up to the age of fourteen years, under clause (d) of section 9;

(d) the manner and extent of reimbursement of expenditure, under sub-section (2) of section 12;

(e) any other document for determining the age of child under sub- section (1) of section 14;

(f) the extended period for admission and the manner of completing study if admitted after the extended period, under section 15;

(g) the authority, the form and manner of making application for certificate of recognisition, under sub-section (1) of section 18;

(h) the form, the period, the manner and the conditions for issuing certificate of recognisition, under sub-—section (2) of section 18;

(i) the manner of giving opportunity of hearing under section proviso to sub-section (3) of section 18;

(j) the other functions to be performed by School Management Committee under clause (d) of sub-section (2) of section 21;

(k) the manner of preparing School Development Plan under sub-section (j) of section 22;

(l) the salary and allocation payable to, and the terms and conditions of service of teacher, under sub-section (3) of section 23;

The duties to be performed by the teacher under clause (f) of sub-section (1) of section 24;

(m) the manner of redressing grievances of teachers under sub-section (3) of section 24;

(n) the form and manner of awarding certificate for completion of elementary education under sub-section (2) of section 30;

(o) the authority, the manner of its constitutions and the terms and conditions therefore, under sub-section (3) of section 31;

(p) the allowances and other terms and conditions of appointment of Members of the National Advisory Council under sub-section (3) of section 33;

(q) the allowances and other terms and conditions of appointment of Members of the State Advisory Council under sub section (3) of section 34.

(3) Every made under this Act and every notification issued under section 20 and 23 by the Central Government shall be laid, as soon as may be after it is made, before each House of Parliament, while it is in session, for a total period of thirty days which may be comprised in one session or in two or more successive sessions, and if, before the expiry of the session immediately following the session or the successive session aforesaid, both Houses agree in making any modification on the rule or notification or both Houses agree that the rule or notification should not be made, the rule or notification shall thereafter have effect only in such modified form or be of no effect, as the case may be; so, however, that any such notification or annulment shall be without prejudice to the validity of anything previously done under that rule or notification.

(4) Every rule or notification made by the State Government under this Act shall be laid, as soon as may be after it is made, before the State Legislatures.

2.8 Norms and Standards for School

Sl. No.	*Item*	*Norms and Standards*	
1.	Number of teachers:		
	(a) For first class to fifth class	Admitted children	Number of teachers
		Up to Sixty	Two
		Between sixty one to ninety	Three
		Between Ninety one to one hundred and twenty	Four
		Between one hundred and twenty one to two hundred	Five
		Above one hundred and fifty children	Five plus one Head teacher
		Above two hundred children	Pupil- Teacher- Ratio (excluding Head teacher) shall not exceed forty
	(b) For sixth class to eight class	(1) At least one teacher per class so that there shall be at least one e teacher each for— (i) Science and Mathematics (ii) Social Studies; (iii) Languages. (2) At least one teacher for every thirty five children (3) Where admission of children is above one hundred- (i) a full time head teacher (ii) part time instructors for— (A) Art Education (B) Work Education	

(Contd...)

(Contd...)

Sl. No.	*Item*	*Norms and Standards*
2.	Building	All weather building consisting of— (i) at least one class room for every teacher and an office- cum-Head teachers room; (ii) barrier- free access; (iii) separate toilets for boys and girls; (iv) safe and adequate drinking water facility to all children; (v) a kitchen where mid-day meal is cocking in the school; (vi) playground; (vii) arrangements for securing the school building by boundary wall or fencing.
3.	Minimum number of working days/ instructional hours in an academic year	(i) two hundred working days for first class to fifth class; (ii) two hundred and twenty working days for sixth class to eight class; (iii) eight hundred instructional hours per academic year for first class to fifth class; (iv) one thousand instructional hours per academic year for sixth class to eight class.
4.	Minimum number of working hours per week for the teacher	Forty-five teaching hours including preparation hours.
5.	Teaching learning equipment	Shall be provided to each class as required.
6.	Library	There shall be a library in each school providing newspaper, magazines and books on all subjects, including storybooks.
7.	Play material, games and sports equipment	Shall be provided on each class as required.

CHAPTER 3 Methodology and Study Setting

The objective of the study was to obtain grassroot data on how schools function, including the level of school resources and potential indicators of practices related to quality and equality issues in education after enactment of Right to Education Act-2009. The participating schools wanted to use the data collected to explore questions about school inputs, policies and processes related to Right to Education Act. The study was organised by the education department and also interested in learning the extent to which resources and good practices were equitably distributed among schools in the education systems. The Right of Children to Free and Compulsory Education Act, which was passed by the Indian parliament on fourth August, 2009, describes the modalities of the provision of free and compulsory education for children between six and fourteen in India under Article 21A of the Indian Constitution. India became one of 135 countries to make education a fundamental right of every child when the act came into force on First April 2010.

3.1 Importance of Research

For the purpose of the study of the 45 Hour Schedule the researchers adopted different research techniques. The Schools are adopting lot of activities under the Right to Education activities, these activities needs to be evaluated. Research can be defined as s systemic and objective process of gathering, recording, and analysing data to guide decision making. Research is mainly used to reduce the uncertainty of decisions. Moreover, the planned research is very typical to get the data from the respondents due to their incompetency. Research encompasses various facets of in any organisation including marketing, finance, human resources and manufacturing. Three types of research studies are mainly employed-market research, operations research and motivational research.

Research studies can be classified into two categories—basic research and applied research. Basic research refers to a focused, systematic study or investigation undertaken to discover new knowledge or interpretation and establish facts or principals in a particular field. Applied research refers to investigation undertaken to discover the applications and uses of theories, knowledge and principals in actual work or in solving problems. The key objective of any research is to provide accurate, relevant and timely information to the Policy makers, Administrators, implementers and management, so that they can make effective decision.

The educational factors and forces are playing a predominant role in implementing RTE in the Chhattisgarh. Since the proximity of educational services is scanty the RTE implementation is not on par with the other states. The terrain and the local conditions are main determinants for the implementation of any projects. Education helps each and every one for the betterment of the vulnerable and marginalised sections of society. Every human being ought to be gifted to lead a self-determined life so far as possible. Each person should be able to survive in peace and security. Each person ought to be able to say what he or she means. She/he should find out what she is competent of doing. We ought to be permitted to join whomsoever we wish to; and so on. And therefore also: We should be allowed to be healthy–not victims of illnesses and circumstances, which can all too easily be decoded as the result of avoidable bad luck and unjust burdens, to address this education must be a tool.

The Indian society is combating many social problems like poverty, illiteracy and internal security. Moreover, the primary and secondary education is also on decline with other third world countries. Many researches revealed that the education services are very scanty among the tribes in India comparatively other groups. Tribes lives in different environment and which promotes poor socialisation status due to their innocence and ignorance. Their educational levels and awareness levels are less to understand the importance of the education. These are the reasons which can influence their socio-economic and health status. Based on these circumstances the study was carried-out to find the status of implementation of RTE at government schools and 45 Hours Schedule.

In any research, decision making goes through four key interrelated stages: problem/opportunity identification, problem opportunity selection, problem opportunity solution, and implement the course of action. For the purpose of the study problem was identified with the help of multiple stakeholders like School Teachers, Students and parents of the students.

This research helps the Policy makers/Administrators/ management/organisation/institution in each of these stages by providing useful and timely information regarding the RTE and 45 Hours Schedule. We should decide upon the option of conducting research after considering various factors like awareness levels, proximity of the education services and intention to get and deliver the education services. These include time constrains, availability of resources, availability of data, nature of information that we can expect and the cost involved. Basically the collection of data involved many steps and it is linked with the perception of the respondents towards the problem.

3.2 Steps in the Research Process

There are many steps involved in collection of data regarding the steps in the research process, namely identification and definition of the problem or opportunity, planning and research design, selecting a research method, selecting a sampling procedure, data collection, evaluating the data and finally preparing and presenting the research. After completion of research process the researchers have been identified the schools for data collection.

3.2.1 Identifying and Design the Problem/Opportunity

The initial step in the research process is the identification of the problem or opportunity. Today it is a highly volatile environment governed by various macro environmental factors, systems and structures disorders constantly assess their relative position and identify the various problem areas or opportunities need to work upon in order to sustain themselves completely. To need to analyse the changing dynamics and to evolve the strategy to adapt to the changes taking place in the external environment. Whether these are potential problems areas or opportunities, it is very important to identify them accurately and at the earliest. Problem identification processes the problem definition stage. Although it has identified the problem in broader perspective, it needs to define the problem specifically in terms of what is to be researched.

It is important to define the problem in a precise manner. A well defined problem gives the researcher a proper direction for carrying out investigation. It also helps the utilising the resources provided for the research effectively. A researcher can focus his efforts on collecting relevant information, if the problem is defined properly. Some research problem such as conducting a survey on set of population can be clearly defined.

3.2.2 Exploratory Research

Exploratory research aims at understanding the topic being researched. Through exploratory research, one arrives at a set of questions that are to be answered in order to solve the problem. Exploratory research is undertaken in the initial stage of the research process. It is an informal process that helps in defining the identified problem. This process involves evaluating the existing studies on related topics, discussing topics. Discussing problem with experts, analysing the situation and so on. At the end of the process the researcher should be clear about what type of information needs to be gathered and how the research process should proceed.

Secondary data analysis and pilot studies are the most popular tools used in previously for some other research purpose. It can be obtained from magazines, journals, online articles and so on. Data from these secondary sources needs to be analysed so that the researchers have the knowledge to define the problem. Pilot study involves collecting data from the actual respondents in order to gain insight to the topic and help the researcher in conducting a large study. Here data is collected informally in order to find out the views of the respondents. Once the research problem is identified and clearly defined, a formal statement containing the research objectives must be developed.

3.2.3 Preparing the Statement Research Objectives

Once the problem is clearly defined, it becomes absolutely essential to determine the objectives of the research. The objectives of the research should be started in a formal research statement. The statement of objectives should be as precise as possible. Objectives as a guidelines for various steps in the research process and therefore we may develop by analysing the purpose of the research thoroughly. The objective of the research must be brief and specific; also, it is preferable to limit the number of objectives. The research objectives comprise the research questions and the hypothesis if the objective of the research is to study. Once the objectives and the research questions are identified, a researcher has to develop a hypothesis statement that reflects these research objectives.

3.2.4 Developing the Hypothesis

The Researchers had developed a Hypothesis which is based on the RTE and educational activities carried out by the schools. A hypothesis is a statement based on some presumption about the exercise of a relationship between two or more variable that can be tested through empirical data. For instance the exploratory research for the above problem may have resulted in the hypothesis. When a researcher is developing a hypothesis, must try to assume an answer for a particular research question and then test it for its validity.

A hypothesis normally makes the research question clearer to the researcher. The formulation of a hypothesis allows the researcher to make a presumption or 'guess' and can thus ensure that all the relevant aspects of the research are included in the research design.

If a research study is to be conducted the hypothesis adds factors of geographic location and life style of the research problem. For any research question, several hypotheses can be developed, but there are limits to the number of hypothesis that can be developed, but there are limit to the number of hypothesis that can be validated. Researcher should avoid including any hypothesis that has already been validated by other similar studies. However, a hypothesis cannot be developed for every research question. Moreover, a vague hypothesis may be of no use at all. Once the hypothesis is developed, the next stage in the research process, the research design phase, begins.

Before proceeding to the next stage it is essential to consider two points. The first one is to assess the value of information that is being sought. In this stage it is important to conduct the cost benefit analysis, where in the cost incurred on the obtaining the needed information is compared with the benefits accruing. If the costs are more than the benefits then it is better to halt the research, while the subsequent phase of the research process can be carried on if the benefit is greater than the cost. The second point is to ensure that the required information does not already exist as it would make the research effort futile.

3.2.5 Planning the Research Design

Once the problem or opportunity identification and definition stage is complete, the process of research design begins. Planning the research design is a crucial step in the research design process. A research design is the actual framework of a research that provides specific details regarding the process to be followed in conducting the research. The research is design based on the objectives formulated during the initial phase of the research. The research design includes all the details regarding the research such as where the information should be obtain from, the time and budget allotted for conducting the research, the appropriate measurement techniques and the sampling process. Factors like the research objective, the importance of the decision, cost involved in conducting the research and the availability of the data sources determine the selection of an appropriate research design.

This study conducted exploratory and descriptive research on the creation of a specific information regarding RTE, 45 Hours Schedule, importance education, parents perception and amenities in the schools to gain an understanding of how such standards are developed.

To address the objectives of this study, the researcher developed a multi-method research strategy that supported the exploratory and descriptive nature of the research. This chapter discusses the overall study design and the study's multiple data collection and data analysis activities used to collect sufficient data to answer the study's research questions. The chapter also highlights methodological issues and limitations encountered by the researcher.

3.3 Need for the Study

Across the world, there are many reasons why children do not attend school, including high levels of mobility, social conflict, child labour and exploitation, poverty, gender and disability. Many children are at risk of not attending school, or of receiving a sub-standard primary and secondary education. In some parts of the world, schooling is not available because of a shortage of school places, a lack of quality teachers, or because schools are too far from where children live. Sometimes families choose not to send their children to school because of fears about safety and security, the poor quality of schooling or because of the economic costs. Such costs might include school fees, having to buy uniforms, books and materials, and so-called 'opportunity costs' that arise when young people are not economically active because they are in school. Differences in access to and outcomes from, education depend not only on children's individual circumstances, but also crucially on the location in which they live and in many cases, where they live within that location.

India had been enacted Right to Education Act in 2009, to alleviate the inaccessibility of education to all. After the inception of years the research was conducted to find out the present status after implementation of Right to Education Act. The purpose of this study is to set out a vision for the development of a more inclusive education system in line with national and Local Authority corporate priorities. These include raising achievement, developing the capacity of schools and early year's settings to meet a more diverse range of needs and ensuring greater social inclusion. Its primary focus is on the development of the most effective possible means of enabling children to access the mainstream curriculum, in schools serving their local communities.

The researcher adopted mixed methods approach; the researcher investigated the issues relating to Child Development, 45 hours schedule of RTE in the schools, issues and problems related to implementation and other allied information. Moreover, the study concentrates on the empowerment of the teachers. How far, the teachers are utilising the time and educational resources for their betterment and as well as the students knowledge enhancement.

3.4 Aims and Objectives of the Study

For the purpose of study the following broad objectives are prepared:

- To study the status of implementation of 45 hours schedule of RTE in the schools.
- To study the awareness regarding the provisions of RTE act amongst HMs and Teachers.

- To assess the time being devoted on various aspects of academic activities as per scheduled time allocations under RTE.
- To study the issues/problems in implementation of teachers working period and lastly.
- To provide appropriate solutions/strategies of the 45 hours schedule for sorting out the issues.
- To make suggestions, if any, for policy and practice.

3.5 Study Setting

3.5.1 Bastar District Socio-economic and Demographic Profile

Bastar, the tribal district, before splitting into three districts, was one of the largest district in India, with an area of 39114 Sq Km, which was even greater than the Kerala state and some other countries like Belgium, Israel etc. In the year 1999, the district Bastar has been divided into three districts namely Bastar, Kanker and Dantewada. All these three districts come under Bastar Division with the divisional head quarter at Jagdalpur, which is the district head quarter of Bastar district. The beauty of Bastar district lies in its natural forest area and various types of tribals. The total forest area is 7112 sq km which is more than 75 per cent of the total area of the district. Of the total population more than 70 per cent are tribals like Gonds, Abhuj Maria, Darda Maria, Bison Horn Maria, Muria Doria, Dhruva, Bhatra, Halba etc.

3.5.1.1 Population 2011

In 2011, Bastar had population of 1,411,644 of which male and female were 697,359 and 714,285 respectively. In 2001 census, Bastar had a population of 1,198,067 of which males were 595,779 and remaining 602,288 were females. Bastar District population constituted 5.53 per cent of total Maharashtra population. In 2001 census, this figure for Bastar District was at 5.75 per cent of Maharashtra population.

3.5.1.2 Industrial Profile of Bastar District

Bastar District is a district of the state of Chhattisgarh in central India. Jagdalpur is the district headquarters of this district. Bastar was one of the 16 Madhya Pradesh districts that formed the new state of Chhattisgarh and in 1999; the district was divided into the present-day districts of Bastar, Dantewada, and Kanker.

3.5.1.3 Topography

Bastar district has all the characteristics of Bastar Plateau. The district is currently a part of the Red Corridor. Rice is grown predominantly during *kharif* season as rain fed crop having 2.39 lakh hectare area but the productivity of this crop is very low 08.53 qt/ha in Bastar region of Chhattisgarh. Exceptionally fortunate in its water resources, the region has good rainfall and rapid run off due to the undulating terrain. There is potential for rainwater harvesting. Lime stone and marble stone are the minerals found in present Bastar district.

3.5.1.4 Forest

Forests play an important role in the lives of the people of the district, providing food security and livelihood through the collection of minor forest produce, and employment (as casual labour) in the Forest Department. The forests provide for people's consumption needs—fuel and firewood, medicines, food and drink, implements and housing materials.

3.5.1.5 Administrative Set Up

The district is divided into 12 tehsils, 12 panchayat samitis, 296 *patwari* circles and 580 Gram Panchayats.

3.5.1.6 District Population Growth Rate

There was change of 17.83 per cent in the population compared to population as per 2001. In the previous census of India 2001, Bastar District recorded increase of 18.18 per cent to its population compared to 1991.

3.5.1.7 District Density 2011

The initial provisional data released by census India 2011, shows that density of Bastar district for 2011 is 140 people per sq. km. In 2001, Bastar district density was at 119 people per sq. km. Bastar district administers 10,083 square kilometers of areas.

3.5.1.8 Literacy Rate 2011

Average literacy rate of Bastar in 2011 were 54.94 compared to 44.27 of 2001. If things are looked out at gender wise, male and female literacy were 65.70 and 44.49 respectively. For 2001 census, same figures stood at 56.75 and 31.93 in Bastar district. Total literate in Bastar district were 658,587 of which male and female were 387,907 and 270,680 respectively. In 2001, Bastar District had 437,362 in its district.

3.5.1.9 Sex Ratio 2011

With regards to Sex Ratio in Bastar, it stood at 1024 per 1000 male compared to 2001 census figure of 1011. The average national sex ratio in India is 940 as per latest reports of Census 2011 Directorate. In 2011 census, child sex ratio is 991 girls per 1000 boys compared to figure of 1009 girls per 1000 boys of 2001 census data.

3.5.1.10 Child Population 2011

In census enumeration, data regarding child under 0-6 age were also collected for all districts including Bastar. There were total 212,819 children under age of 0-6 against 210,110 of 2001 census. Of total 212,819 male and female were 106,904 and 105,915 respectively. Child Sex Ratio as per census 2011 was 991 compared to 1009 of census 2001. In 2011, Children under 0-6 formed 15.08 per cent of Bastar District compared to 17.54 per cent of 2001. There was net change of -2.46 per cent in this compared to previous census of India.

3.5.2 Dhamtari District Socio, economic and Demographic Profile

Dhamtari district is situated in the fertile plains of Chhattisgarh Region. Dhamtari district is officially formed on 6th July, 1998 dividing the Raipur district currently the capital of Chhattisgarh along with Mahasamund. As a result the boundaries of the Raipur district is converted into the districts e.g., Raipur, Mahasamund and Dhamtari. Dhamtari, Kurud and Nagari are included in Dhamtari district as Tehsils and Dhamtari, Kurud, Nagari and Magarlod are included as blocks.

3.5.2.1 Location and Geographical Area

This District is situated between 20D42' N Latitude and 81D33' E Longitude. The District is surrounded by District Raipur in North and District Kanker as well as Bastar in South, part of Orissa state in East and District Durg and Kanker in West. Mahanadi is the principal river of this district and Mahanadi is so far named as Kankannadi, Chitrotpala, Neelotpala, Mandvahini and Jairath etc.

Table 3.1: Bastar at a Glance

Variable	*2011*	*2001*
Actual Population	1,411,644	1,198,067
Male	697,359	595,779
Female	714,285	602,288
Population Growth	17.83%	18.18%
Area sq. km	10,083	10,083
Density/km^2	140	119
Proportion to Chhattisgarh Population	5.53%	5.75%
Sex Ratio (Per 1000)	1024	1011
Child Sex Ratio (0-6 Age)	991	1009
Average Literacy	54.94%	44.27%
Male Literacy	65.70%	56.75%
Female Literacy	44.49%	31.93%
Total Child Population (0-6 Age)	212,819	210,110
Male Population (0-6 Age)	106,904	104,572
Female Population (0-6 Age)	105,915	105,538
Literates	658,587	437,362
Male Literates	387,907	278,762
Female Literates	270,680	158,600
Child Proportion (0-6 Age)	15.08%	17.54%
Boys Proportion (0-6 Age)	15.33%	17.55%
Girls Proportion (0-6 Age)	14.83%	17.52%

Source: Census of India, Ministry of Home Affairs, New Delhi, 2001 and 2011.

3.5.2.2 Topography

It is 305 Meter above the mean sea level. In the east, Satpura range is located. It is popularly known as Sihawa Pahad. In west lies district of Kanker. In North lies Raipur, the heart and capital city of Chhattisgarh. Southwards lays the boundary of Orrisa state. Ravishankar Sagar dam that irrigates almost 57000 Hectare of land. Asia's first ever Siphon dam was built in the year 1914 at Madamsilli. Besides Madamsilli, Sondhur dam, Dudhawa dam are the major projects.

3.5.2.3 Administrative Set Up

There are four tehsils, four Panchayat Samitis and 124 *patwari* circles in the district.

3.5.2.4 Population-2011

In 2011, Dhamtari had population of 799,199 of which male and female were 397,250 and 401,949 respectively. In 2001 census, Dhamtari had a population of 706,591 of which males were 352,524 and remaining 354,067 were females. Dhamtari district population constituted 3.13 per cent of total Maharashtra population. In 2001 census, this figure for Dhamtari district was at 3.39 per cent of Maharashtra population.

3.5.2.5 Population Growth Rate

There was change of 13.11 per cent in the population compared to population as per 2001. In the previous census of India 2001, Dhamtari district recorded increase of 20.23 per cent to its population compared to 1991.

3.5.2.6 Density-2011

The initial provisional data released by census India 2011, shows that density of Dhamtari district for 2011 is 236 people per sq. km. In 2001, Dhamtari district density was at 209 people per sq. km. Dhamtari district administers 3,383 sq. kms. of areas.

3.5.2.7 Literacy Rate-2011

Average literacy rate of Dhamtari in 2011 were 78.95 compared to 74.89 of 2001. If things are looked out at gender wise, male and female literacy were 88.84 and 69.24 respectively. For 2001 census, same figures stood at 86.51 and 63.39 in Dhamtari District. Total literate in Dhamtari district were 551,569 of which male and female were 307,536 and 244,033 respectively. In 2001, Dhamtari district had 441,921 in its district.

3.5.2.8 Sex Ratio-2011

With regards to Sex Ratio in Dhamtari, it stood at 1012 per 1000 male compared to 2001 census figure of 1004. The average national sex ratio in India is 940 as per latest reports of Census 2011 Directorate. In 2011 census, child sex ratio is 969 girls per 1000 boys compared to figure of 976 girls per 1000 boys of 2001 census data.

3.5.2.9 Child Population-2011

In census enumeration, data regarding child under 0-6 age were also collected for all districts including Dhamtari. There were total 100,575 children under age of 0-6 against 116,514 of 2001 census. Of total 100,575 male and female were 51,073 and 49,502 respectively. Child Sex Ratio as per census 2011 was 969 compared to 976 of census 2001. In 2011, Children under 0-6 formed 12.58 per cent of Dhamtari district compared to 16.49 per cent of 2001. There was net change of -3.91 per cent in this compared to previous census of India.

Table 3.2: Dhamtari at a Glance

Description	*2011*	*2001*
Actual Population	799,199	706,591
Male	397,250	352,524
Female	401,949	354,067
Population Growth	13.11%	20.23%
Area sq. km	3,383	3,383
Density/km^2	236	209
Proportion to Chhattisgarh Population	3.13%	3.39%
Sex Ratio (Per 1000)	1012	1004
Child Sex Ratio (0-6 Age)	969	976
Average Literacy	78.95%	74.89%
Male Literacy	88.84%	86.51%
Female Literacy	69.24%	63.39%
Total Child Population (0-6 Age)	100,575	116,514
Male Population (0-6 Age)	51,073	58,960
Female Population (0-6 Age)	49,502	57,554
Literates	551,569	441,921
Male Literates	307,536	253,963
Female Literates	244,033	187,958
Child Proportion (0-6 Age)	12.58%	16.49 %
Boys Proportion (0-6 Age)	12.86%	16.73 %
Girls Proportion (0-6 Age)	12.32%	16.26%

Source: District. Statistical Hand Book, Dhamtari District.

3.6 Sampling Frame

There are many primary and middle schools in both settings. The government has been established primary and Middle schools to cater the educational needs of the children. For the purpose of the study the researchers have been taken the following blocks, in Bastar there are 345 primary and 137 middle schools, in Damtari 188 primary and 78 middle schools. These schools are completely run by the Government and following the Right to Education Act rules and regulations.

Table 3.3: Schools in Bastar and Dhamtari

District	*Block*	*Total Primary*	*Total Middle*
Bastar	Bastar	345	137
Dhamtari	Kurud	188	78
Total		**533**	**215**

For the purpose of study two Districts were selected in Chhattisgarh i.e., Bastar and Dhamtari, from these two districts two Blocks were selected. From each block 100 primary teachers and 100 secondary teachers were selected using snowball technique and interviewed. As such the total sample comprises two hundred.

Table 3.4: Sampling Frame

S. No.	*Name of the Location*	*Type of School*	*Sample Size*	
			Teachers	*Parents/Students*
1.	Bastar	Primary	50	50
	Bastar	Secondary	50	50
2.	Dhamtari	Primary	50	50
	Dhamtari	Secondary	50	50
Total Sample Size			**200**	**200**

3.7 Research Tools

Research results are based on the research tools. The tools persuade the research process and make the study easy and tell how to carry out. The following tools are generally and widely accepted by the researchers.

3.7.1 Schedule

A structured interview schedule was prepared for the respondents. Through this tool the respondents were elucidated their feelings about the RTE, 45 Schedule implementation, parents perception and school working description. The different interview schedule was prepared for primary and secondary schools.

3.7.2 Focussed Group Discussions

The investigator conducted four focused group discussions. The village president, secretary of village, the school teacher, two self help group members, students and parents were made to sit in an angular shape and the investigator assumed the role of a moderator. Certain issues such as RTE, 45 hour Schedule implementation, parents perception and school working description were discussed and the opinions of the members were elicited. All the members actively participated and contributed their knowledge.

3.7.3 Observation

The investigator had an opportunity to spend with the respondents and the parents of the students. The responses that were given by the respondents were observed and their body language, school environment and the surroundings were observed to interlink the information to that of actuality.

3.8 Data Collection

After preparing a suitable sample, the researcher collected the data from the units in this sample. As there are several research techniques, there are a number of data collection methods as well. For instance, in survey method the data is collected by asking the respondents to fill out a questionnaire administered to them, while in the observation technique the respondents are just observed without their direct participation in the research. Whatever, the method used to collect the data, it is very important that the data is collected without any error. Errors my creep in during the data collection process in several forms. Potential data collection errors may arise if the interviewee does not understand the question of if the interviewer records the answers inaccurately.

Data collection is done in two stages—pre-testing, and main study. Pre-testing involves collecting data from a small sub-sample to test whether the data collection plan for the main study is appropriate. This helped the researcher to minimise any potential errors that may crop up during the main study. The present result may also be used to decide on a way of tabulating the collected data. If the results of a pre-test are not appropriate for decision making, then the researcher may consider altering the research design. Once the data is collected to be satisfaction of the researcher, the research process enters the next stage, which is evaluation of the data.

3.9 Evaluating the Data

Once the data has been collected the next important phase in the research process is evaluating the data. The most important aspect of the data evaluation is to convert the data collected into a format which will facilitate in effecting decision making. The reason for analysing the data is to obtain research results and to prepare the research report. Several mathematical and statistical models are used to evaluate the data. Evaluation of data normally starts with editing and coding of the data. Editing is undertaken to verify the data and check for any potential errors or for any inconsistencies and so on. Another task of editing is to remove any error that may have cropped up during the interview such as recording the answer under the wrong columns of a questionnaire and so on. Coding is a process of assigning different symbols to different sets of responses. The coding process is done so that the data can be fed in and interpreted easily using computers. These days, technological advances have made it possible for data to be collected and directly fed into computers, removing the possibility of human errors. For instance, an interviewer may question respondents through telephone and records the answer directly into a computer, where the data is processed almost immediately, thus eliminating the scope for error which may arise if conventional methods of data collection are used.

3.10 Analysis

The interpretation of the data that has been collected by using different analytical techniques according to the requirements of the management is called analysis. Several statistical tools are used for data analysis, in order to make the analysis suitable for effective decision making. The statistical analysis of the data may range from simple frequency distribution tables to complex multivariate analysis.

3.11 Preparing and Presenting the Research Book

After the evaluation of the data, the last and the major phase that comes into picture is the preparation of a research book. The research book has been presented in oral as well written format. The research book contains a brief description of the objectives of the research, a summary of the research design adopted, a summary of the major findings and concludes with the limitations and recommendations. The purpose of conducting any research is to obtain information that can aid in efficient decision making. Therefore, it is very important to carefully analyse the information obtained and present it according to requirements. At this stage the research have been developed most efficiently and it has been portray the research findings most efficiently. Most often researchers fill the research reports with all the technical details. This has been avoided to the maximum possible extent in the actual research results and has to be presented lucidly in a concise format. The amount of information provided in the research book has been based on the requirement of the author. A research book also act as a historical document, in the sense that the researcher may refer to this document in the future if a research on the same lies is being conducted sometimes in the future.

3.12 Limitations of the Study

The illiteracy is one of the main limitations for the quality of the study. The tribes cannot reveal the information easily due to some ethnical backgrounds. Moreover, the respondents cannot accept the outsiders to ask something about their personal issues. The participatory observation method is not possible due to remote area, due to this reason the data collected and came back.

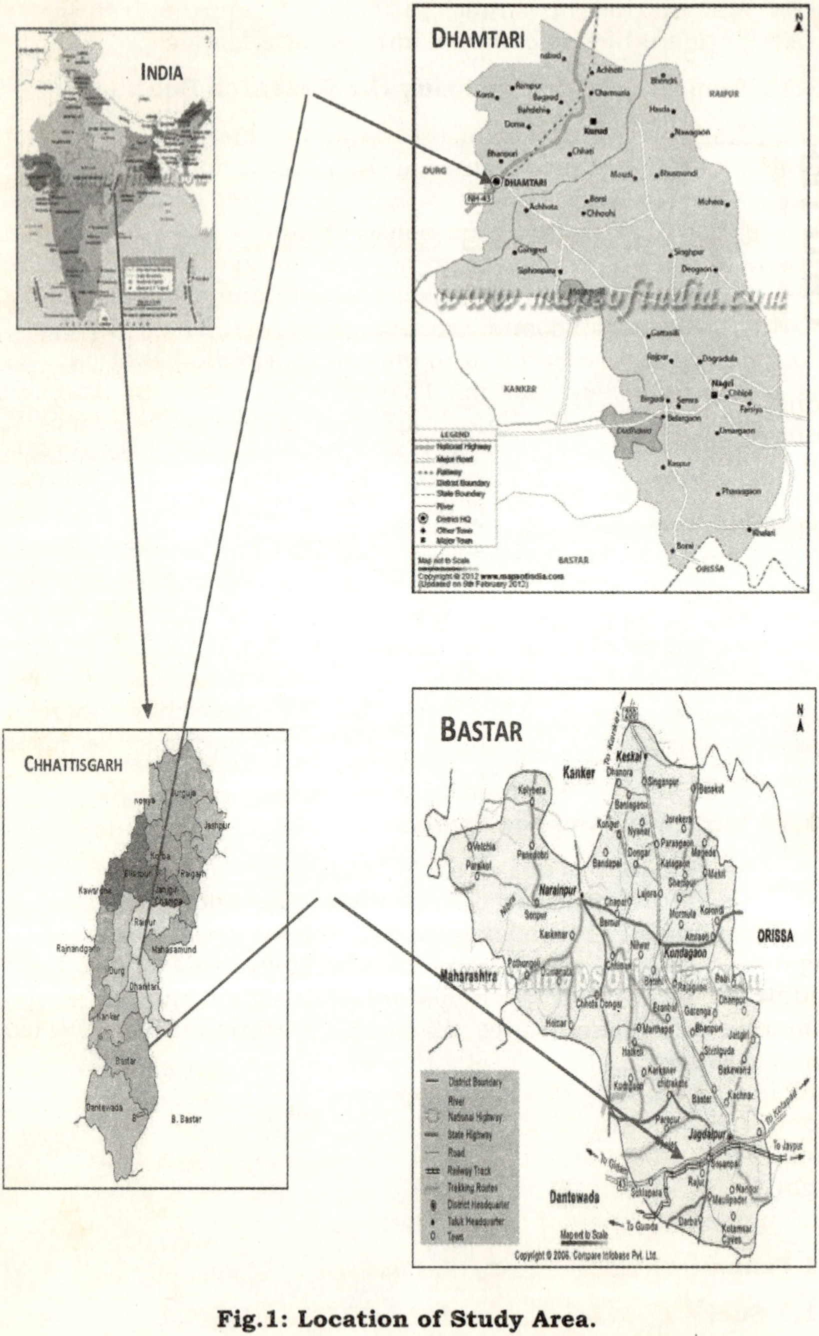

Fig.1: Location of Study Area.

CHAPTER 4 Results and Discussion

In educational premises, teachers often suffer from role conflict, not just when they try to take on roles society does not consider suitable, but also when they try to overcome their own biases and prejudices regarding what certain types of teachers can do or not do. If we compare the educational development of tribal school students with the non tribal school students the academic performance of tribal students is comparatively poor. Both central as well as State Governments have been appointing so many commissions and committees from time to time and implementing so many plans and programmes for the educational development of the tribal people. It has been proved that the role of teacher is very important for improving and providing quality secondary education in tribal area. But the teacher has to play different roles which may create obstacles on the way of work motivation. In order to find out the difference in role conflict and work motivation among tribal secondary school teachers, the present study is justified.

This chapter gives the overall picture of the results from the data collected in primary schools of Bastar and Dhamtari, Middle schools of Bastar and Dhamtari district, about 45 hour schedule implementation. The study has crystalised lot of results, which can be helpful for policy makers, administrators and implementers. For every project, success lays on the monitoring and evaluation. The education administrators have been taken a bold step to assess the 45 hour schedule under Right to Education. Further, the results discusses about the total implementation of the project.

4.1 Primary Schools in Bastar District

4.1.1 Social Characteristics of the Respondents

The data reveals that majority of the teachers (40.5 per

cent) were in the age group of 32-41. 14.5 per cent of the teachers were in the age group of 42-46 and the rest of the teachers are in different age groups. The parents/student data reveal that majority of the (43.0 per cent) were in the age group of 32-41. 13.0 per cent were in the age group of 22-26 while 7.0 per cent were in the age group of 27-31 and rest were in different age groups.

Table 4.1: Social Characteristics

Age Variable	Respondents	
	Teacher (n=50)	Parent/Student (n=50)
	per cent	per cent
22-26	10.0	13.0
27-31	12.0	7.0
32-36	18.5	25.5
37-41	22.0	17.5
42-46	14.5	14.0
47-51	12.0	11.0
> 51	11.0	12.0

As regards the educational qualifications, more than fifty per cent (55.6 per cent) of the teachers have were completed higher middle and 18.5 per cent of the teachers were in metric. A significant number of the teachers were able to complete B.A. and rest of the teachers completed B.Sc, Higher, Middle with D.Ed and M.A. On the other hand the educational qualification of the Parents/students indicate that majority of the parents/ teachers (36.5 per cent) were matriculated, (12.0 per cent) were B.A., (15.0 per cent) B.Sc, (21.5 per cent) higher secondary with D.Ed and rest (12.5 per cent) were higher Secondary and (2.5 per cent) were M.A. only.

Table 4.2: Educational Qualification

Variable	Respondents	
	Teacher (n=50)	Parent/Student (n=50)
	per cent	per cent
Metric	18.5	36.5
B.A.	14.8	12.0
B.Sc.	3.7	15.0
HS and D.Ed.	3.7	21.5
HS	55.6	12.5
M.A.	3.7	2.5

The data reveals that a majority of the teachers (40.7 per cent) belongs to Schedule Tribe and one fourths of the teachers (25.9 per cent) were in General Category. Other Backward Classes (18.5 per cent) and Schedule Caste (14.8 per cent) were in that order. The social class of parents/student depicted that (52.5 per cent) are Schedule Caste while (15.0 per cent) were OBC and (7.0 per cent) were general caste.

Table 4.3: Social Class

	Respondents (n=50)	
Variable	*Teacher (n=50)*	*Parent/Student (n=50)*
	per cent	*per cent*
SC	14.8	25.5
ST	40.7	52.5
OBC	18.5	15.0
General	25.9	7.0

4.1.2 Distance

The above table reveals that more than half of the teachers (52.0 per cent) were staying in the village and rest of the respondents (48.0 per cent) were staying outside the village where the school is located. As regards the distance from School, two fifths of the teachers (41.0 per cent) are staying less than five kilometers away and 37.0 per cent of the teachers staying between 6-10 kms. 11-15 kms. (14.5 per cent), 16-20 kms. (3.5 per cent) and > 20 kms. are in that order. Maximum students (81.73 per cent) are studying in same village and only (18.27 per cent) students studying in other village.

Table 4.4: Residence

	Respondents	
Distance	*Teacher (n=50)*	*Parent/Student (n=50)*
	per cent	*per cent*
Staying in		
Same Village	52.0	81.73
Other Village	48.0	18.27
Other village, Distance from School		
> 5	41.0	63.0
6-10	37.0	21.0
11-15	14.5	12.0
16-20	3.5	2.0
> 20	4.0	2.0

The data accentuated that (34.0 per cent) of teachers stated that their school is less than 10 kms. away from Block Resource Centre and 26.0 per cent schools 10-20 kms. away. 18.5 per cent of the teachers' schools were situated between 31-40 and 11.0 per cent schools were between 21-30 kms. An overwhelming fact was that 7.0 per cent of the schools were situated more than 51 kms. away from BRC. The data is almost similar from students/parents. The data indicate that the distance from BRC is less than 10 kms. (33.0 per cent), (25.0 per cent) school 10-20 kms. away, (18.0 per cent) school away in between 21-30 kms., (15.0 per cent) school 31-40 kms. away, (5.77 per cent) school were situated in between 41-50 kms. and rest (3.23 per cent) school were away more than 51 kms.

Table 4.5: Distance from BRC

Distance from BRC	*Respondents*	
	Teacher (n=50)	*Parent/Student (n=50)*
	per cent	*per cent*
< 10 km.	34.0	33.0
10-20	26.0	25.0
21-30	11.0	18.0
31-40	18.5	15.0
41-50	3.5	5.77
> 51	7.0	3.23

4.1.3 Facilities in the School

As per teachers opinion that a majority of the schools (81.5 per cent) does not have electricity facility and the rest of the schools (18.5 per cent) have the electricity facility. As regards the class rooms (49.0 per cent) of the schools have two rooms and 44.0 per cent schools have three rooms. (74.0 per cent) of the schools have toilet facility and rest of the schools (26.0 per cent) has no toilet facility. The study reveals that (71.0 per cent) of the schools have drinking water facility and rest of the schools (29.0 per cent) has not that facility. There are (40.0 per cent) of the schools were connected with the road and a majority of the schools (60.0 per cent) have not connected with the road. Buildings for primary schools in tribal and SC areas cannot design that the Anganwadis/Balwadis could also function, along with the primary schools, in the same buildings. When data gathered from parents/students, it is observed that (50.5 per cent) responding accepted that there were no electricity facility in the school and rest (19.5 per cent) parents/student accepted that there was electricity connection in the school. In primary level, the whole classes were going in single class room (68.75 per cent), (15.25 per cent) in two class room and rest, (1.0 per cent) were in four class room. Majority of the respondent (85.7) reveals that, they have toilet and drinking water facility in their school. (46.5 per cent) respondent stated that schools are connected with road and rest (54.5 per cent) schools are not connected.

Table 4.6: Facilities

Facilities	*Respondents*	
	Teacher (n=50)	*Parent/Student (n=50)*
	per cent	*per cent*
Electricity		
Yes	18.5	19.5
No	81.5	80.5
No of Class Rooms		
1.	4.0	68.75
2.	49.0	15.25
3.	44.0	15.0
4.	3.0	1.0
Toilet Facility		
Yes	74.0	85.74
No	26.0	14.26
Drinking Water Facility		
Yes	71.0	85.74
No	29.0	14.26
Road Connected		
Yes	40.0	46.5
No	60.0	54.5

4.1.4 Staffing

As per opinion of teachers that (37.0 per cent) of the schools have two teachers and (30.0 per cent) schools have three teachers. 18.0 per cent schools have one teacher, as such. As regards, the temporary teachers a majority of the schools (92.6 per cent) have no temporary teachers and (5.0 per cent) of the schools have two temporary teachers. Parents/students reveals that (64.0 per cent) primary school has only one permanent teacher, (18.0 per cent) school going through two permanent teacher and rest schools have three (11.0 per cent), four (3.5 per cent) and five (2.5 per cent) permanent teacher.

Table 4.7: Teachers Availability

Facilities	*Respondents* Teacher (n=50)	*Respondents* Parent/Student (n=50)
	per cent	*per cent*
Permanent Teachers		
0.	4.0	2.0
1.	18.0	64.0
2.	37.0	18.0
3.	30.0	11.0
4.	7.5	3.5
5.	3.5	2.5
Temporary Teachers		
0.	92.0	76.0
2.	5.0	14.0
3.	3.0	10.0

4.1.5 Prayer Timing

The data portrayed from the teachers that (78.0 per cent) of the teachers stated that schools were allocated 20 minutes for prayer and (12.0 per cent) of the schools are taking 30 minutes to complete the prayer. (75.0 per cent) parents/students opined that prayer timing is 30 minutes but teachers depicted it is taking only 20 minutes. The data depicted that (15.0 per cent) schools are taking less than 20 minutes time for prayer and (10.0) have taking 20 minutes for prayer.

Table 4.8: Prayer Timing

Player Timing	*Respondents* Teacher (n=50)	*Respondents* Parent/Student (n=50)
	per cent	*per cent*
Less than 20 Minutes	10.0	15.0
20 Minutes	78.0	10.0
30 Minutes	12.0	75.0

4.1.6 Teaching Hours

The data accentuated that (63.0 per cent) of the teachers stated that teachers are teaching four hours and (21.5 per cent) are teaching above four hours. As per parents/students that (12.5 per cent) of the teacher taking class up to four hours and (42.0 per cent) was teaching four hours and rest (45.5 per cent) teaching above four hrs.

Table 4.9: Teaching Hours

Teaching Hours	*Respondents*	
	Teacher (n=50)	*Parent/Student (n=50)*
	per cent	*per cent*
Less Than four Hours	15.5	12.5
4 Hours	63.0	42.0
Above four hours	21.5	45.5

4.1.7 Timing for Midday Meal

The study revealed that (74.0 per cent) of the school teachers state that teachers were allocated 40 minutes and (14.5 per cent) of the schools allocated more than 40 minutes for midday meal. On the other hand as per the parents/students that midday meal taken more than 40 minutes (75.0 per cent) and rest were taken 40 minutes (15.0 per cent).

Table 4.10: Mid-day Meal

Timing	*Respondents*	
	Teacher (n=50)	*Parent/Student (n=50)*
	per cent	*per cent*
< 40 Minutes	11.5	10.0
40 Minutes	74.0	15.0
> 40 Minutes	14.5	75.0

4.1.8 Timing for Preparation of Action Plans

The data reveals that (63.0 per cent) of the teachers, whereas according to parents/students (72.5 per cent) stated that teachers had taken one hour per day for preparation of action plan and (24.5 per cent) of the teachers have taken more than one hour. In this cases similar trend also observed among parents/students opinion.

Table 4.11: Preparation of Action Plans

Timing	Respondents	
	Teacher (n=50)	Parent/Student (n=50)
	per cent	per cent
< 1 hour per Day	12.5	2.0
1 hour per Day	63.0	72.5
> 1 hour per Day	24.5	25.5

4.1.9 Student Portfolio

The study revealed that (66.5 per cent) of the teachers (according to parents/students i.e., (50.5 per cent)) stated that teachers had allocated 30 minutes time for student portfolio and (18.5 per cent) of the teachers allocated more than 30 minutes for the same activity. According to parents/students; data reveals that majority of the teachers (50.5 per cent) take 30 minutes time to make student portfolio and (14.0 per cent) teachers take less than 30 minutes time and rest (35.5 per cent) take more than 30 minutes time for preparation.

Table 4.12: Student Portfolio

Timing	Respondents	
	Teacher (n=50)	Parent/Student (n=50)
	per cent	per cent
< 30 Minutes	15.0	14.0
30 Minutes	66.5	50.5
> 30 Minutes	18.5	35.5

4.1.10 Time Allocated for Discussion with Parents

The data accentuated that (48.0 per cent) of the teachers opine that teachers spared less than one hour for discussion with parents and (41.0 per cent) of the respondents spared one hour. Whereas 69.0 per cent parents/students opine that teachers take at least one hour for discussion with parents.

Table 4.13: Discussion with Parent

Timing	*Respondents*	
	Teacher (n=50)	*Parent/Student (n=50)*
	per cent	*per cent*
< 1 Hour	48.0	21.0
1 Hour	41.0	69.0
> 1 Hour	11.0	10.0

4.1.11 Time Spared for Staff Meeting

The data revealed that (74.0 per cent) of the teachers stated that teachers have been given 30 minutes time for staff meeting and (22.0 per cent) of the teachers allocated less than 30 minutes for the same. In this context, an instructional unit is a set of integrated lessons that is designed to accomplish learning objectives related to a curricular theme, an area of knowledge, or a general skill or process. Consistent with relevant federal, state, and local curriculum and/or academic standards, the teacher's instructional units provide for appropriate coverage of the key themes, concepts, skills, and standards related to the subject areas and are designed to expose students to a variety of intellectual, social, and cultural perspectives. The sequence of the teacher's units (as presented through timelines, curriculum maps, planning and pacing guides, and so forth) follows a logical progression, with an appropriate amount of time allocated to each instructional unit. The parent/student data reveals that (68.0 per cent) teachers take more than 30 minutes, (22.0 per cent) take 30 minutes and (10.0 per cent) teacher takes less than 30 minutes time for staff meeting.

Table 4.14: Staff Meeting

Timing	*Respondents*	
	Teacher (n=50)	*Parent/Student (n=50)*
	per cent	*per cent*
< 30 Minutes	22.0	10.0
30 Minutes	74.0	22.0
> 30 Minutes	4.0	68.0

4.1.12 Special Needs to Help the Children

The data explained that (70.5 per cent) of the teachers stated that they had given 40 minutes time to address the special needs of the children and (19.0 per cent) of the teachers opined that they had allocated less than 40 minutes time for the same activity. As per opinion of parents/students indicate that (38.5 per cent) teacher expand 40 minutes to help the children for their special need in study (26.0 per cent), teachers take less than 40 minutes and (35.5 per cent), take more than 40 minutes time.

Table 4.15: Special Need to Help the Children

Timing	Respondents	
	Teacher (n=50)	*Parent/Student (n=50)*
	per cent	*per cent*
< 40 Minutes	19.0	26.0
40 Minutes	70.5	38.5
> 40 Minutes	10.5	35.5

4.1.13 Tools/Format Fixed for Evaluation

The data reveals that (70.0 per cent) of the teachers stated that they allocated 30 minutes for tools or formats evaluation and (22.0 per cent) of the teachers opined that less than 30 minutes spared for the same. Majority of the parent/student opined that (54.5 per cent) take more than 30 minutes time for tools/format fixed for evaluation, (35.5 per cent) take 30 minutes and rest were take less than 30 minutes.

Table 4.16: Tools/Format Fixed for Evaluation

Timing	Respondents	
	Teacher (n=50)	*Parent/Student (n=50)*
	per cent	*per cent*
< 30 Minutes	22.0	10.0
30 Minutes	70.0	35.5
> 30 Minutes	8.0	54.5

4.1.14 Teachers and Students Attendance during Prayer

The study revealed that, (90.0 per cent) of the teachers stated that they presented during the prayer along with students and rest of the teachers neglected. Parent/student accepted that (92.0 per cent) present at the time of prayer and rest (8.0 per cent) were absent at that time.

Table 4.17: Tools/Format Fixed for Evaluation

Variable	*Respondents*	
	Teacher (n=50)	*Parent/Student (n=50)*
	per cent	*per cent*
Yes	90.0	92.0
No	10.0	8.0

4.1.15 Prayer Procedure

The data accentuated that (47.0 per cent) of the teachers opined that they were observed National song, National Anthem and Prayer and National Anthem alone (14.5 per cent), Group Song, National Song, National Anthem and prayer (14.0 per cent) were observed in the prayer. The data reveals that majority of the (parents/students) stated (68.0 per cent) that they do national song Anthem and prayer, (25.0 per cent) accentuated that they do group song, national song, anthem and prayer and rest were do only national song (2.0 per cent) or anthem (3.0 per cent) and both national song and anthem (2.0 per cent).

Table 4.18: Prayer Procedure

Variable	*Respondents*	
	Teacher (n=50)	*Parent/Student (n=50)*
	per cent	*per cent*
National Song	11.5	2.0
National Anthem	14.5	3.0
National Anthem and National Song	13.0	2.0
National Song, National Anthem and Prayer	47.0	68.0
Group Song, National Song, National Anthem and Prayer	14.0	25.0

4.1.16 Teaching Model

The data reveals that (45.0 per cent) of the teachers stated that they used lecture method, (32.5 per cent) of the teachers used *Mahapurus* thought and 22.5 used both variables used as teaching model. Parents/students data indicate that (65.0 per cent) teacher gave lecture only while (25.0 per cent) teachers gave lecture and *Mahapurus* thought also.

Table 4.19: Teaching Model

Variable	*Respondents*	
	Teacher (n=50)	*Parent/Student (n=50)*
	per cent	*per cent*
Lecture	45.0	65.0
Mahapurus Thought	32.5	10.0
Lecture and Mahapurus Thought	22.5	25.0

4.1.17 Attendance after Assembly

The data accentuated that a majority of the teachers (92.0 per cent) stated that they had taken attendance after assembly and rest of the teachers were negated. According to parents/ students, the data reveals that (98.0 per cent) teachers took attendance after assembly and rest (2.0 per cent) of the teachers say they did not.

Table 4.20: Attendance Taking After Assembly

Variable	*Respondents*	
	Teacher (n=50)	*Parent/Student (n=50)*
	per cent	*per cent*
Yes	92.0	98.0
No	8.0	2.0

4.1.18 Teaching: Cognitive Teaching

The study revealed that a majority of the teachers (75.5 per cent) teachers stated that they used cognitive teaching for class I-II and rest of the teachers negated. (85.0 per cent) of the teachers stated they taught Class III-V through cognitive mode. Majority of the parents/students stated that teachers used cognitive teaching for class I-II (65.0 per cent) (III-V) (60.5 per cent) and rest negated.

Table 4.21: Cognitive Teaching (Class I-V)

Variable	*Respondents*	
	Teacher (n=50)	*Parent/Student (n=50)*
	per cent	*per cent*
Cognitive teaching (Class I- II)		
Yes	75.5	65.0
No	24.5	35.0
Cognitive teaching (Class III- V)		
Yes	85.0	60.5
No	15.0	39.5

4.1.19 Whole Class Approach

The data reveals that a majority of the teachers (81.5 per cent) opined they adopted whole class approach and rest of the teachers negated. Parents/students indicate that more than (90.0 per cent) teacher adopted whole class approach.

Table 4.22: Whole Class Approach

Variable	*Respondents*	
	Teacher (n=50)	*Parent/Student (n=50)*
	per cent	*per cent*
Yes	81.5	91.0
No	18.5	9.0

4.1.20 Group Based Activity

The data revealed that (89.5 per cent) of the teachers stated that they adopted group based activity and rest of the sample despised. (72.5 per cent) parents/students opined that teachers adopted group based activities and rest of the teachers negated.

Table 4.23: Group Based Activity

Variable	*Respondents*	
	Teacher (n=50)	*Parent/Student (n=50)*
	per cent	*per cent*
Yes	89.5	72.5
No	10.5	27.5

4.1.21 Mode of Continuous Evaluation

As per opinion of teachers the data revealed that (41.0 per cent) of the teachers adopted oral, (25.5 per cent) used written and 33.5 per cent used both for continuous evaluation. The study of parent/student opinion revealed that (46.0 per cent) teacher addressing oral and written evaluation while (32.0 per cent) taking written examination only.

Table 4.24: Mode of Continuous Evaluation

Variable	*Respondents*	
	Teacher (n=50)	*Parent/Student (n=50)*
	per cent	*per cent*
Oral	41.0	22.0
Written	25.5	32.0
Oral and Written	33.5	46.0

4.1.22 Co-Cognitive Teaching

Majority of the teachers opined that (70.5 per cent) adopted Co-cognitive technique for teaching of class I-V and rest of the teachers were negated. Parents/students stated that (82.0 per cent) teachers doing co-cognitive teaching in primary school.

Table 4.25: Co-Cognitive Teaching (Class I- V)

Variable	*Respondents*	
	Teacher (n=50)	*Parent/Student (n=50)*
	per cent	*per cent*
Yes	70.5	82.0
No	29.5	18.0

4.1.23 Art

The data reveals that (37.0 per cent) of the teachers stated that they gave chance for drawing and (21.0 per cent) of the teachers adopted drawing, music and dance. (17.5 per cent) of the teachers organised drawing, music, dance, art and craft, literary and cultural activities and (14.5 per cent) of the teachers organised drawing and dance. Majority of the parents and teacher stated that (65.0 per cent) school has organised drawing, music, dance, art and craft literary and cultural activities, (17.0 per cent) school gave chance for drawing and dance, (3.0 per cent) adopted drawing only and rest have organised other kind of art activities.

Table 4.26: Art

Variable	*Respondents*	
	Teacher (n=50)	*Parent/Student (n=50)*
	per cent	*per cent*
Drawing	37.0	3.0
Drawing and Dance	14.5	17.0
Drawing, Music and Dance	21.0	5.0
Drawing, Music, Dance, Art and Craft, Literary and cultural Activities	17.5	65.0
Others	10.0	10.0

4.1.24 Work Experience

The data accentuated that a majority of the teachers (56.5 per cent) stated that they have given project and (29.0 per cent) opined that they have displayed creative work and (14.5 per cent) of the teachers opined that they adopted both for work experience. Majority of the parents/students stated that (49.5 per cent) teacher display creative work, (16.0 per cent) given project work and display creative work both and (34.0 per cent) gave only project work.

Table 4.27: Work Experience

Work	*Respondents*	
	Teacher (n=50)	*Parent/Student (n=50)*
	per cent	*per cent*
Project Work	56.5	34.5
Display Creative Work	29.0	49.5
Project Work and Display Creative Work	14.5	16.0

4.1.25 Physical Education and Health

The data revealed that (33.5 per cent) of the teachers stated that they gave physical education through sports and games,

(18.5 per cent) of the teachers adopted yoga and (15.5 per cent) of the teachers used yoga, sports and games, nutritional food, knowledge about diseases and cleanliness about the surrounding for physical education and health. Majority of the parents/ students (42.0 per cent) addressing sports and games as a physical education, (30.0 per cent) used sports games and cleanliness, (11.5 per cent) used yoga, (7.0 per cent) used yoga sports and games and rest 37.5 per cent used yoga sports, games, nutritional food, knowledge about the surroundings.

Table 4.28: Physical Education and Health

Variable	*Respondents*	
	Teacher (n=50)	*Parent/Student (n=50)*
	per cent	*per cent*
Yoga	18.5	11.5
Sports and Games	33.5	42.0
Yoga, Sports and Games	7.0	7.0
Sports and Games and Cleanliness	9.0	30.0
Yoga, Sports and Games, Nutritional Food, Knowledge about Diseases	6.0	9.5
Yoga, Sports and Games and Knowledge about Diseases	10.5	18.0
Yoga, Sports and Games, Nutritional Food, Knowledge about Diseases and cleanliness about the Surrounding	15.5	12.0

4.1. 26 Social/Personal Attitudes and Values

Majority of the teachers (35.5 per cent) opined that they adopted attitude, life skill and awareness towards environment and (29.0 per cent) of the respondents used attitude, life skill, awareness towards environment and value system for improvement of social/personal attitudes and values. (48.5 per cent) parents/students stated that teacher addressing knowledge about attitude, life skill, awareness towards environments, (10.0

per cent) parents/students accepted only attitude, (11.0 per cent) learning life skill, and rest (30.0 per cent) accepted attitude, life skill, awareness towards environment and value system.

Table 4.29: Social/Personal Attitudes and Values

Variable	*Respondents*	
	Teacher (n=50)	*Parent/Student (n=50)*
	per cent	*per cent*
Attitude	21.5	10.0
Life Skill	14.0	11.0
Attitude + Life Skill+ Awareness towards Environment	35.5	48.5
Attitude + Life Skill+ Awareness towards Environment + Value System	29.0	30.5

4.1.27 Mid-day Meal Distribution

The data accentuated that 37.0 per cent of the teachers stated that they could complete mid-day meal distribution between 31-40 minutes. 30.5 per cent of the teachers had taken 10-21 minutes, 14.5 per cent of the teachers had taken 41-50 minutes for the same. Majority of the Parents/Students (35.0 per cent) opined that distributed mid day meal in between 41-50 minutes, (10.0 per cent) had taken 21-30 minutes and (25.0 per cent) had taken more than 50 minutes respectively.

Table 4.30: Mid-day Meal Distribution

Time	*Respondents*	
	Teacher (n=50)	*Parent/Student (n=50)*
minutes	*per cent*	*per cent*
10-20	30.5	20.0
21-30	7.0	10.0
31-40	37.0	25.0
41- 50	14.5	35.0
> 50	11.0	10.0

Surveys had found out that village children went to school only for mid-day meals and no one was interested in actual education. The automatic promotion of children up to class V also de-motivated pupils from studying. This foundational weakness also had an impact on secondary and higher education outcomes. Health and nutritional problems faced by people in remote areas was also brought up, particularly the inability of Primary Health Centers to provide medicines to the ailing.

4.1.28 Preparation of Action Plan for Teaching and Evaluation

The data reveals that a majority of the teachers opined that (90.5 per cent) prepared action plan for teaching and evaluation and rest of the teachers (9.5 per cent) were neglected. The teacher's evaluation process includes the major formal and informal assessments to be used (i.e., observations, exams, research papers, performance, projects, portfolios) and the evaluation criteria for each. The teacher's evaluation methods are appropriate for the learning goals and the content. The evaluation criteria match state, local, and/or individually determined expectations for student progress and achievement. The teacher's record-keeping system provides a confidential and well-organised system for storing, retrieving, and analysing all necessary student data. The parent/student data quite similar as teachers opinion.

Table 4.31: Preparation of Action Plan

	Respondents	
Preparation	*Teacher (n=50)*	*Parent/Student (n=50)*
	per cent	*per cent*
Yes	90.5	90.0
No	9.5	10.0

4.1.29 Preparation of Activities for Class Room Teaching

The study revealed that 97.0 per cent of the teachers stated that they prepared activities for class room teaching. The teacher's rules and procedures for managing student behaviour, whether developed independently by the teacher or collaboratively with the students, are clearly stated, appropriate for the students, and consistent with school and district policies.

The rules are stated in positive terms, when possible, and focus on behaviours rather than on students. The teacher's procedures for managing essential non-instructional routines (e.g., transitioning between activities and/or subjects, taking roll, collecting student work, preparing learning centers or labs, retrieving instructional materials or resources) promote efficiency and minimise the loss of instructional time. Majority of parents/ students stated that (92.0 per cent) teacher prepare activities plan for school/children.

Table 4.32: Preparation of Activities

Preparation of Activities	*Respondents*	
	Teacher (n=50)	*Parent/Student (n=50)*
	per cent	*per cent*
Yes	97.0	92.0
No	3.0	8.0

4.1.30 Preparation of Teaching and Learning Material

The data revealed that a majority of the teachers (85.5 per cent) stated that they prepared Teaching and Learning material and rest of the respondents (14.5 per cent) was neglected. The content of the teacher's instructional plans is drawn from multiple sources that are accurate and current and is applicable to the students' grade-level academic standards, instructional needs, ability and developmental levels, and interests. The sources of the content expose students to a variety of intellectual, social, and cultural perspectives as appropriate. The teacher selects a variety of instructional strategies and materials in order to present content in formats that accommodate learning differences and that translate into real-life contexts for the students. Instructional technology is included as appropriate. The instructional strategies are logically sequenced and include sufficient opportunities for initial learning, application and practice, and review. The strategies lead the students to increasingly higher levels of thinking and problem solving. They promote active student engagement during both independent and collaborative learning tasks, and they provide opportunities for the teacher and students to vary their roles in the instructional process (i.e., instructor, facilitator, coach, audience). 86.4 per cent parents/students reveal that teachers prepare TLM for teaching students while 13.6 per cent were neglected.

Table 4.33: Preparation of TLM

Preparation of TLM	*Respondents*	
	Teacher (n=50)	*Parent/Student (n=50)*
	per cent	*per cent*
Yes	85.5	86.4
No	14.5	13.6

4.1.31 Application of Techniques

The data accentuated that 85.0 per cent of the teachers opined that they applied techniques for teaching and rest of the respondents were negated. The teacher's objectives define what the students should know (i.e., the factual, conceptual, procedural, and/or meta-cognitive knowledge) and be able to do (e.g., the cognitive processes—remembering, understanding, applying, analysing, evaluating, and/or creating) upon completing the unit. The teacher's objectives are student-oriented, explicit, and assessable statements of intended learning outcomes. There is a clear connection between the unit objectives and grade-level academic standards (or, for preschool children or students with severe disabilities, between the unit objectives and appropriate developmental and/or functional expectations). The unit objectives are consistent with the long-range goals, assessment results from previous instructional units, state and local curriculum guidelines, individualised education programmes (IEPs), and the needs and interests of the students. The unit objectives are logically linked to previous and future learning objectives. On the other hand (82.0 per cent) parents/students opined that the teacher applied technique for teaching and rest of them negated.

Table 4.34: Application of Techniques

Application of Techniques	*Respondents*	
	Teacher (n=50)	*Parent/Student (n=50)*
	per cent	*per cent*
Yes	85.0	82.0
No	15.0	18.0

4.1.32 Plan for Group Work of the Children

The study revealed that three fourths of the teachers (76.0 per cent) stated they planned for group work and (24.0 per cent) of the teachers were negated. The teacher develops lesson and unit plans on the basis of accurate conclusions that he or she has drawn from analyses of the particular students' prior performance (i.e., their behaviour, progress, and achievement Majority of the parents/teachers stated that (80.0 per cent), that teachers creating plan for group work and rest (20.0 per cent) not participated in it.

Table 4.35: Plan for Group Work

Plan for Group Work	*Respondents*	
	Teacher (n=50)	*Parent/Student (n=50)*
	per cent	*per cent*
Yes	76.0	80.0
No	24.0	20.0

4.1.33 Action Plan for Teaching and Learning

The data portrayed that (92.0 per cent) of the teachers were planned for action plan for teaching and learning. (70.0 per cent) parents/students revealed that teacher planned for teaching and learning.

Table 4.36: Action Plan for Teaching and Learning

Teaching and Learning	*Respondents*	
	Teacher (n=50)	*Parent/Student (n=50)*
	per cent	*per cent*
Yes	92.0	70.0
No	8.0	30.0

4.1.33.1 Teacher-Pupil Ratio

A major element of the approach to strengthening education will be to improve current learning levels by lowering the teacher pupil ratio. Government has already committed to fill-up all the existing teacher vacancies and sanctioning the additional posts necessary to achieve teacher-pupil ratio of 1:40. The teacher pupil ratios for primary, upper primary and high schools are shown in Table 4.37.

Table 4.37: Teacher People Ratio

Year	*Primary*	*Upper Primary*	*High School*
2000-01	45	38	34
2001-02	41	39	34
2002-03	37	33	29
2003-04	35	31	31
2004-05	29	25	30
2005-06	28	25	30
2006-07	29	24	29
2007-08	28	23	28
2008-09	27	22	29
2009-10	28	23	28

Source: School Education Department.

4.1.33.2 Dropout Rates

Dropout rate is defined as a percentage of the number of children to total enrolment dropping out of the educational system in a particular year. The ratio does not take into account repeaters and children who enter the system after class-I. It is expected that every child who enters class-1 completes class-VII without discontinuing the school in between. With this view, efforts are being made to tackle the problem of dropouts with the support of School Management Committees. The Dropout Rate during 2011-12 in Primary Stage (Classes I-V) is 15.60, in Upper Primary Stage (Classes I-VII) is 20.79 and in Secondary Schools is 45.71. Details of Dropout rates are shown in Table 4.38.

4.1.33.3 Reasons for Dropouts

The preceding analysis shows the existence of high dropout rates at schools in Bastar. In order to understand the causes for dropouts and non-enrollment of children and also to identify the socio-economic barriers at the primary and secondary education a sample survey of 60 respondents, i.e., teachers, parents and students was undertaken to elicit their opinion on the causes for dropouts in study area. Since local teachers possess greater knowledge about the children, their parents and also about the local problems, we had selected them purposefully. The sample area also selected purposively

Table 4.38 : Dropout Rates

Year	*I – V*			*I – VII*			*I - X*		
	Boys	*Girls*	*Total*	*Boys*	*Girls*	*Total*	*Boys*	*Girls*	*Total*
1971-72	69.34	72.53	70.65	77.80	86.91	81.59	87.62	94.37	90.56
1981-82	72.53	62.87	60.31	64.40	73.19	67.98	78.28	85.91	81.35
1991-92	58.48	57.04	54.28	61.17	69.17	64.65	72.76	79.31	75.54
2001-02	35.36	33.64	34.54	51.98	55.77	53.78	71.62	73.28	72.37
2003-04	42.42	42.80	42.61	52.71	55.92	54.27	65.28	68.53	66.70
2004-05	31.77	32.14	31.95	51.96	54.46	53.17	62.30	65.24	63.69
2005-06	24.61	24.85	24.73	50.26	52.37	51.30	62.24	65.20	63.67
2006-07	26.76	27.04	27.04	42.14	44.32	43.22	62.99	65.33	64.13
2007-08	19.10	18.48	18.79	33.26	35.23	34.24	62.30	64.00	63.13
2008-09	16.14	15.15	15.65	34.39	35.41	34.89	60.12	61.38	60.73
2009-10	16.34	15.24	15.80	26.38	26.50	26.44	52.73	54.2	53.36
2010-11	18.10	16.73	17.43	22.56	22.11	22.34	45.83	46.59	46.21
2011-12	15.93	15.27	15.60	21.51	20.06	20.79	45.43	45.99	45.71

Source: School Education Department.

representing different situations. This district represents urban and tribal conditions and presents a situation with low dropout rates. The sample is drawn from aided, unaided, Government and Private school teachers giving weightage to the experience and/or service of the teachers concerned, place of work etc., dropout students and parents the opinions of these 60 respondents are tabulated and their views are presented below:

- Educational background of the parents
- Poor economic conditions of the family
- Excessive involvement of children in domestic work
- Negligence of parents
- Caste factor
- Frequent shifting of the families, for seasonal work, from one place to other place for seeking livelihood, may also influence the dropout rate.
- Due to ill health, like incidence of malaria fever, some of the student's dropout from the schools.
- According to the teachers some of the students discontinued their studies due to lack of hostel facilities.
- Child marriages are also affecting the dropout rate.

4.1.34 Learned/Followed Teaching Learning Material

The data revealed that a majority of the teachers (89.0 per cent) opined that they were learned and followed teaching and learning material and rest of the teacher were neglected. Majority of the parents/students (91.0 per cent) stated that teacher followed teaching learning material and rest (9.0 per cent) of the respondents were neglected.

Table 4.39: Learned/Followed Teaching Learning Material

Followed Teaching Learning Material	*Respondents*	
	Teacher (n=50)	*Parent/Student (n=50)*
	per cent	*per cent*
Yes	89.0	91.0
No	11.0	9.0

4.1.35 Plan for the Uses of Library

The study revealed that (67.0 per cent) of the teachers opined that they planned useful books for the library and (25.0 per cent) of the teachers used books and book coroner for the use of library. (72.0 per cent) parents/students opined that teachers used books, (10.0 per cent) used books corner and (18.0 per cent) used books and books corner only.

Table 4.40: Plan for the Uses of Library

Plan for use of Library	*Respondents*	
	Teacher (n=50)	*Parent/Student (n=50)*
	per cent	*per cent*
Books	67.0	72.0
Book Corner	8.0	10.0
Books and Book Corner	25.0	18.0

4.1.36 New Information and New Technique for the Class Room

The data accentuated that (92.0 per cent) of the teachers stated that they developed new information and new techniques for the class room. (90 per cent) students/parents opined that teachers gather new information and technique from the teachers and rest (10.0 per cent) negated.

Table 4.41: New Information and New Technique

New Information and New Technique	*Respondents*	
	Teacher (n=50)	*Parent/Student (n=50)*
	per cent	*per cent*
Yes	92.0	90.0
No	7.0	10.0

4.1.37 Preparation of Portfolio for Individual Children

The study revealed that (86.0 per cent) of the teachers' opined that they prepared portfolio for individual children and rest of the teachers (14.0 per cent) negated. The teacher routinely obtains student baseline data, analyses the data to determine student learning needs, and uses this information to develop appropriate instructional plans. At appropriate intervals throughout instruction, the teacher analyses student performance on informal assessments (i.e., individual and group performance tasks, quizzes, assignments) and formal assessments (i.e., tests, projects, portfolios, research papers, performances) to determine the extent to which both individual students and groups of students are progressing towards accomplishing the learning objectives. (84.0 per cent) parents/ students stated that teachers make portfolio for individual children and (16.0 per cent) parents/students not agreed with this. On the basis of these analyses, the teacher determines the impact of instruction on student learning and makes appropriate decisions about the need to modify his or her instructional plans.

Table 4.42: Portfolio for Individual Children

Portfolio for Individual Children	*Respondents*	
	Teacher (n=50)	*Parent/Student (n=50)*
	per cent	*per cent*
Yes	86.0	84.0
No	14.0	16.0

4.1.38 General Information of Children

The data revealed that (52.0 per cent) of the teachers stated that they take name only. One fifths of the teachers (22.0 per cent) have taken name, weight, height, blood group, other physical and family background. (55.0 per cent) parents/ students reveal that teachers take their name only as a information of children, (12.0 per cent) take family background also, (25.0 per cent) take name weight and height, (3.0 per cent) take family background, name, height and weight and rest 5.0 per cent take name, weight, height, blood group, other physical and family background also.

Table 4.43: Information of Children

Information of child	*Respondents*	
	Teacher (n=50)	*Parent/Student (n=50)*
	per cent	*per cent*
Name	52.0	55.0
Family Background	8.0	12.0
Name, Weight and Height	10.5	25.0

Family Background, Name, other and Height Weight and Height	7.5	3.0
Name, Weight, Height, Blood Group, Other Physical and Family Background	22.0	5.0

4.1.39 Areas of Interest of Children

The data revealed that (92.0 per cent) of the teachers stated that they have find out the areas of interests of the children. Whereas (91.0 per cent) parents/students opined that teachers have find out the areas of interests of the children.

Table 4.44: Area of Interest of Children

Area of Interest of Child	*Respondents*	
	Teacher (n=50)	*Parent/Student (n=50)*
	per cent	*per cent*
Yes	92.0	91.0
No	8.0	9.0

4.1.40 Measuring of Learning Improvement

The data accentuated that (78.0 per cent) of the teachers stated that they measured the learning status and improvement and rest of the teachers (22.0 per cent) negated. The teacher makes decisions about student performance, progress, and achievement on the basis of explicit expectations that clearly align with the learning objectives and achievement goals, the assessments, and the students' level of ability. The teacher may present his or her evaluation criteria in the form of scoring rubrics, vignettes, grading standards, answer keys, rating scales, and the like. Assessments are appropriately weighted on the basis of the relative importance of each in determining overall progress and achievement. The teacher maintains accurate, current, well-organised, and confidential records of assessment results. The teacher uses available information technology to store and assist with the analysis of student data. On the other hand (63.0 per cent) parents/students revealed that teachers measured learning improvement of children and rest (37.0 per cent) negated.

Table 4.45: Measuring of Learning Improvement

Measurement	Respondents	
	Teacher (n=50)	Parent/Student (n=50)
	per cent	per cent
Yes	78.0	63.0
No	22.0	37.0

4.1.41 Collection of Information Regarding Special Work

The data portrayed that a majority of the teachers (82.0 per cent) opined that they had collected information regarding special work. (72.0 per cent) parents/students stated that teachers collected information about children.

Table 4.46: Collection of Information

Collection of Information	Respondents	
	Teacher (n=50)	Parent/Student (n=50)
	per cent	per cent
Yes	82.0	72.0
No	18.0	28.0

4.1.42 Assessing the Past and Present Status

The study reveals that (89.0 per cent) of the teachers stated that they are assessing the past and present status of the students. Less than three forth of parents/students (72.0 per cent) reveal that teachers collect information about the assessment of past and present status of students.

Table 4.47: Assessing the Past and Present Status

Collection of Information	Respondents	
	Teacher (n=50)	Parent/Student (n=50)
	per cent	per cent
Yes	89.0	72.0
No	11.0	28.0

4.1.43 Discussion with Parents to Solve the Problems

The data reveals that a majority of the teachers (79.0 per cent) stated that they discussed with the students parents to solve the problems and rest of the teachers negated. Family involvement is the strongest predictor of child educational outcomes. This dimension associated significantly with children's motivation to learn, attention, task persistence, receptive vocabulary skills, and low conduct problems. Family involvement in education has been identified as a beneficial factor in young children's learning (National Research Council, NRC, 2001; U.S. Department of Education, 2000). It is, therefore, a key component of national educational policies and early childhood programmes. Much of the research on parent involvement, as it relates to children's outcomes, has emphasised the relationship between specific parent involvement behaviours and children's achievement. Parental involvement at school (i.e., with school activities, direct communication with teachers and administrators) is associated with greater achievement in mathematics and reading. Higher levels of parent involvement in their children's educational experiences at home (i.e., supervision and monitoring, daily conversations about school) have been associated with children's higher achievement scores in reading and writing, as well as higher report card grades. Other research has shown that parental beliefs and expectations about their children's learning are strongly related to children's beliefs about their own competencies, as well as their achievement. Parents who evidenced high levels of school contact (volunteering in the classroom, participating in educational workshops, attending Policy Council meetings) had children who demonstrated greater social competency than children of parents with lower levels of school contact. It was hypothesised that home-based involvement would be most strongly associated with positive classroom learning outcomes and that direct school-based involvement would predict lower levels of conduct problems. Home-Based Involvement activities, such as reading to a child at home, providing a place for educational activities, and asking a child about school, evidenced the strongest relationships to later preschool classroom competencies. These activities were related to children's approaches to learning, especially motivation and attention/persistence, and were found to relate positively to receptive vocabulary.

The attitude of the parents signifies that the supporting nature of family in their children's education. The parental attitude can be negative or positive. The negative attitude of the parents regarding education and schooling can prevent their children from getting education. With less parental support in school work, low level of motivation and poor self-esteem of children can result positive attitude of the parents can be beneficial to their children in many cases and can be reflected in improvement in class performance, creating interest among children to learn, and higher achievement scores in reading and writing.

The growing awareness regarding education makes many families value their children's education and act favourably towards schooling and education of their children. They become a part of the decision making process of school, and decide their children's future regarding higher education. Therefore, it is imperative to assess the degree of favourableness of attitude in tribal communities so as to estimate the success of awareness programmes and endeavours with regard to "Sarva Sikhsha Abhiyan" or universal elementary education.

The reason behind the not so favourable attitude towards schooling among the respondents might be due to their low socio-economic status and parent's labour market position. The respondents were mostly poor with average income per month ranging from Rs 3000-to 4000 and their main livelihood was based on agriculture and non-agricultural labour. They had little knowledge about facilities of the urban and developed environment. Their existing environment might have created a narrow mentality towards schooling where they fail to perceive a direct relationship between their children's education and a better future. The second aspect is the father's labour market position. The data indicate (25.0 per cent) parents/students opined that teachers discuss with parents and (75.0 per cent) parents/students neacted.

Table 4.48: Discussion with Parents

Discussion with parents	*Respondents*	
	Teacher (n=50)	*Parent/Student (n=50)*
	per cent	*per cent*
Yes	79.0	25.0
No	21.0	75.0

4.1.44 Contact with the Parents and Parent Teacher Association

As per opinion of teachers that (71.0 per cent) of the teachers contacted with the parents in the parent teacher association and (29.0 per cent) of the teachers did not contact. As there is no education in the family background for generations, and the tribal child living in the fringes of non-tribal society finds himself cognitively unequal to the non-tribal child, the inferiority complex is built into his mind right from the beginning of formal schooling. This is one of the factors responsible for the lower educational achievement of the children. As the adults are not convinced of the benefits of formal education, it is not possible to escape the large scale wastage and stagnation. In the absence of trained ST candidates, outsiders are appointed as teachers and administrators, who without access to their language, lack first-hand communication.

In view of all, these tribal education can never be uniform. It must seek solutions to group specific problems in different states. There is a misplaced apprehension in some quarters that in finding separate solutions for integration of different groups, the seeds of disunity may grow. It must, however, be understood that the distinction is between apathetic attitude leading to inaction on the part of the planners which gets response of dissatisfaction verging on hatred towards the system and its mangers and a conscious strategy based on empathy leading to a national unity based on self fulfillment of small groups. A conscious strategy of unity in diversity cannot lead to disunity. It's clear from the data as per opinion of parents/ students that only (28.0 per cent) teachers contact with parents and rest (72.0 per cent) avoid communication.

Table 4.49: Contact with the Parents

Contact with the Parents	*Respondents*	
	Teacher (n=50)	*Parent/ Student (n=50)*
	per cent	*per cent*
Yes	71.0	28.0
No	29.0	72.0

4.1.45 Discussion with Parents and PTAs

The data depicts that (43.5 per cent) of the teachers stated that they discussed with the parent during parents teacher association regarding quality of education, educational survey, school activity/programme, health awareness and (27.0 per cent) of the teachers stated they discussed about quality education and (18.0 per cent) of the teachers were discussed Social Activity and other programmes. Educationists have often spoken of the problem-solving education. The problems posed by the elitist teacher and the textbook are not the problem of life. If at all such problems have any relevance, then they are relevant to the lives of the privileged. As the formal education system expects the child to conform to the logic of the present which has kept him submerged in ignorance and poverty, he has little motivation for giving attention to it, not to speak of pursuing it with any seriousness. Education for tribal's and other such socio-economically under privileged can only be meaningful if it is problem-posing rather than problem solving. The present education system has not adopted any conscious strategy to remedy this deficiency. Even conversation and discussions using the spoken school language which would stimulate students to question and thus result in greater classroom interaction has not been made to teach tribal language as well as the dominant language either both are taught in parallel streams of the student is taught entirely through the mother tongue medium in the elementary stage to be confronted with the dominant language at the post primary stage. Unless a conscious strategy for transition from the home language to school language is built into the formal elementary education of the tribal children it is almost impossible to meet their educational needs. This transfer programme has to be effected not only in the spoken material, but also in the reading material. Unless special reading manuals are prepared keeping in view the difficulties of the tribal child he is bound to lag behind.

Table 4.50: Discussion

Discussion with parents	*Respondents*	
	Teacher (n=50)	*Parent/Student (n=50)*
	per cent	*per cent*
Quality of Education	27.0	17.0
Educational Survey	11.5	14.0
School Activity/ Programme	18.0	14.0
Quality of Education, Educational Survey, School Activity/Programme, Health Awareness	43.5	55.0

4.1.46 Discussion about Dropout and Un-enrolled Children

The data revealed that (92.5 per cent) of the teachers stated that they discussed about dropout and un-enrolled children. A large number of school going children are not even able to access schools. There are many reasons for this—

- Poor infrastructure—few schools especially in rural and remote tribal areas. Those that are there have poor classrooms, no compounds, no latrines and no drinking water facilities.
- Parents are not certain about the safety of the girl child travelling to school even if it is only ½ km away from home.
- Apparently simple issues like the need to cross a highway/stream on the way to school keeps kids away.

Even if the child does get enrolled in a school, there is no guarantee that (s) he will attend. There are number of factors that keep the child away.

- Teachers are held accountable for enrolment, seldom for attendance; they don't see the need to push.
- The child needs to work, at home or in the family enterprise (farming, trading etc.) or in another enterprise to bring in money to help feed the family.
- The pedagogy is so boring and the subjects so irrelevant that no self-respecting child will be lured to stay on.
- Teachers are often uninterested in teaching. Their knowledge is limited.

(84.0 per cent) parents/students stated that teachers discuss about dropouts and un-enrolled children and rest (16.0 per cent) did not discuss.

Table 4.51: Discussion about Dropout and Un-enrolled Children

Discussion	*Respondents*	
	Teacher (n=50)	*Parent/Student (n=50)*
	per cent	*per cent*
Yes	92.5	84.0
No	5.5	16.0

4.1.47 Discussion about the Regular Attendance

Discussion about the regular attendance is very vital to improve the standards and quality education. The study revealed that all the respondents stated that they were discussed about the regular attendance. School performance is marked by absenteeism, inadequately trained teachers with indifferent attitudes, non-availability of teaching materials, inadequate supervision, and little support. Many poor families, having lost faith in government schools, are forced to send their children to private schools even when they have access to 'free' public schools. Several cases of discrimination are reported—against girls, against children belonging to socially disadvantaged and minority communities, and against the poor. Corporal punishment is common and many children are afraid of going to school for fear of being beaten, if not publicly ridiculed or rebuked by teachers and other students.

4.1.48 Discussion Regarding School Plan and Unit Plan

The data accentuated that (59.5 per cent) of the teachers stated that they had discussed about the only school plan. (17.0 per cent) of the teachers opined that they discussed school plan and unit plan. (42.0 per cent) parents/students stated that teachers discuss on school plan, (16.0 per cent) discuss on unit plan, (12.0 per cent) discuss on TLM and its uses and 30.0 per cent) discuss on school plan and unit plan.

Table 4.52: Discussion Regarding School Plan and Unit Plan

Discussion	*Respondents*	
	Teacher (n=50)	*Parent/Student (n=50)*
	per cent	*per cent*
School Plan	59.5	42.0
Unit Plan	12.5	16.0
TLM and its uses	11.0	12.0
School plan and Unit Plan	17.0	30.0

4.1.49 Discussion about Particular Activity in the Classroom

The data reveals that a majority of the teachers (93.0 per cent) stated that they discussed about particular activity in the classroom. (59.0 per cent) Parents/students opined that teachers discuss about particular activity in the class and rest (41.0 per cent) were avoiding the discussion.

Table 4.53: Discussion about Particular Activity

Discussion	*Respondents*	
	Teacher (n=50)	*Parent/Student (n=50)*
	per cent	*per cent*
Yes	93.0	59.0
No	7.0	41.0

4.1.50 Discussion about Writing and Reading Material

The data portrayed that (91.0 per cent) of the teachers stated that they discussed about writing and reading material. In developing countries throughout the world the educational context is characterised not by monolingual settings, but rather multilingual situations. Often children are asked to enroll in a primary school where the Medium of Instruction (MI) is not her home language, but rather the language of the Government, or another dominant society Studies throughout the world demonstrate the importance of the MI in determining a child's educational attainment. According to Mehrotra (1988) "In a situation where the parents are illiterate, if the medium of instruction in school is a language that is not spoken at home the problems of learning in an environment characterised by poverty are compounded and the chances of drop-out increase correspondingly. In this context, the experience of the high-achievers has been unequivocal: the mother tongue was used as the medium of instruction at the primary level in all cases. ... There is much research which shows that students learn to read more quickly when taught in their mother tongue. Second, students who have learned to read in their mother tongue learn to read in a second language more quickly than do those who are first taught to read in the second language. Third, in terms of academic learning skills as well, students taught to read in their mother tongue acquire such skills more quickly". (86.0 per cent) Parents/students stated that teachers discuss about writing and reading material with children in the class.

Table 4.54: Discussion about Writing and Reading Material

Discussion	*Respondents*	
	Teacher (n=50)	*Parent/Student (n=50)*
	per cent	*per cent*
Yes	91.0	86.0
No	9.0	14.0

4.1.51 Evaluation of the Children and Student Profile

The study reveals that a majority number of the teachers (85.5 per cent) stated that they evaluated children and student profile. (78.0 per cent) parents/students opined that teachers discuss the evaluation of student and children and rest (22.0 per cent) avoid this.

Table 4.55: Evaluation of Student and Children

Discussion	*Respondents*	
	Teacher (n=50)	*Parent/Student (n=50)*
	per cent	*per cent*
Yes	85.5	78.0
No	14.5	22.0

4.1.52 Discussion on Co-conscious Activity

The data reveals that (81.0 per cent) of the teachers stated they discussed about coconscious activity and the rest of the teachers negated. Majority of the parents/students (89.0 per cent) stated that teachers discussed coconscious activity of children.

Table 4.56: Discussion Co-conscious Activity

Discussion	*Respondents*	
	Teacher (n=50)	*Parent/Student (n=50)*
	per cent	*per cent*
Yes	81.0	89.0
No	19.0	11.0

4.1.53 Discussion on Participation of Parent Teacher Association

The data portrayed that a majority of the teacher (92.0 per cent) discussed about the participation of parent teacher association and its functions. (64.0 per cent) parents/students agreed that teachers discussed on participation and rest (36.0 per cent) did not participated.

Table 4.57: Discussion Participation

Discussion	*Respondents*	
	Teacher (n=50)	*Parent/Student (n=50)*
	per cent	*per cent*
Yes	92.0	64.0
No	8.0	36.0

4.1.54 Discussion on Time Table of the School

As per teachers opinion 95.0 per cent of the teachers discussed about the time table in the school and a small sample (5.0 per cent) negated. (55.0 per cent) parents/students stated that teachers discuss on time table in the class and rest (45.0 per cent) negated.

Table 4.58: Discussion on Time Table

Discussion	*Respondents*	
	Teacher (n=50)	*Parent/Student (n=50)*
	per cent	*per cent*
Yes	95.0	55.0
No	5.0	45.0

4.1.55 Discussion on Expectation of Every Children

As per opinion of teachers that (92.0 per cent) of the teachers discussed about the expectation of every children in the schools. The teacher is a reflective practitioner who systematically collects, synthesises, and evaluates student-achievement data in order to accurately identify his or her own professional strengths and weaknesses and to gain professional insight and vision regarding ways to enhance student learning. As a result of this self-assessment, the teacher collaborates with his or her supervisors to develop an appropriate individualised professional growth plan. Additionally, the teacher regularly seeks out, participates in, and contributes to activities that promote collaboration and that support his or her continued professional growth (i.e., participation in professional associations, courses, conferences, workshops, and seminars). (65.0 per cent) Parents/students opined that teachers discussed on expectation of every child and (35.0 per cent) did not discussed.

Table 4.59: Discussion on Children

Discussion	Respondents	
	Teacher (n=50)	Parent/Student (n=50)
	per cent	per cent
Yes	92.0	65.0
No	8.0	35.0

4.1.56 Discussion about the Book

The study revealed that a majority of the teachers (92.0 per cent) discussed about book. The teacher's expectations are appropriately challenging for the grade and/or ability levels of the particular students. The teacher communicates the learning objectives so that students clearly understand what they are expected to know and be able to do. The teacher reviews and/or clarifies the objectives as necessary. (92.0 per cent) Parents/ students reveal that teachers discuss about the book with children.

Table 4.60: Discussion about the Book

Discussion	Respondents	
	Teacher (n=50)	Parent/Student (n=50)
	per cent	per cent
Yes	95.0	92.0
No	5.0	8.0

4.1.57 Discusson Regarding the Good Work which is done

The data accentuated that (81.5 per cent) of the teachers discussed about the good work done by them and as well as by the children. The teacher's expectations are appropriate for the grade and/or ability levels of the particular students and for the subject area. The teacher effectively communicates these expectations so that his or her students will readily apply them to instructional activities and events during the lessons and to assignments and tasks both in and out of the classroom. (85.0 per cent) Parents/students accepted that teachers discussed regarding good work and rest (15.0 per cent) did not discussed.

Table 4.61: Discussion Regarding Good Work

Discussion	*Respondents*	
	Teacher (n=50)	*Parent/Student (n=50)*
	per cent	*per cent*
Yes	81.5	85.0
No	18.5	15.0

4.1.58 Solving of Problem Regarding the Teaching and Learning Method

Majority of the teachers (88.0 per cent) stated that they solved the problems regarding the teaching and learning methods. The teacher clearly communicates the importance and relevance of the academic standards and learning objectives as well as the way the standards and objectives relate to the students' previous and/or future learning. The teacher encourages the students to become the active agents of their own learning and to take the initiative to follow through with their work. The teacher provides appropriate opportunities for the students to engage in self-assessment and reflection on their learning and to develop a meta-cognitive awareness of their own strengths and weaknesses. The teacher assists the students in developing strategies to compensate for their weaknesses when it is necessary. Majority of the parents/students (82.0 per cent) reveal that teachers actively participate into solving problems regarding the teaching and learning method.

Table 4.62: Solving of Problems

Solving of Problems	*Respondents*	
	Teacher (n=50)	*Parent/Student (n=50)*
	per cent	*per cent*
Yes	88.0	82.0
No	12.0	18.0

4.1.59 Regarding Professional Experiences

The data revealed that 85.5 per cent of the teachers opined that they had professional experience and rest of the teachers negated. The teacher's strategies are appropriate for the particular objectives and content and the particular students' grade, developmental, and ability levels. The strategies build on the students' interests and prior learning and are appropriate for the students' stage of learning (i.e., initial, application, practice, review) with regard to the particular material. The teacher's strategies promote higher levels of thinking and/or performance. (86.0 per cent) parents/students stated that teachers have professional experience of teaching and rests (14.0 per cent) are in experienced.

Table 4.63: Professional Experience

Professional Experience	*Respondents*	
	Teacher (n=50)	*Parent/Student (n=50)*
	per cent	*per cent*
Yes	85.5	86.0
No	14.5	14.0

4.1.60 Following of Guidelines Regarding RTE

The data revealed that (89.0 per cent) of the teachers stated that they are following the Right to Education act guidelines and rest of the teachers negated. (70.0 per cent) parents/ students opined that teachers follow the guidelines of teaching. For many children, the schooling experience is a nightmare. Studies have shown that teachers frequently beat children, terrorise them, and humiliate them publicly. Many forms of discrimination and biases enter the classroom. A recent survey of rural schools, for example, carried out in Chhattisgarh found disturbing evidence of primary school teachers showing much less regard for the interests of children belonging to Scheduled Castes. Teachers tended to perceive themselves as belonging to a different and higher class, often the result of earning much higher incomes than most parents. They rebuked children for not coming properly dressed to school, for being obviously dirty, for being stupid because they belonged to a certain community. Children were ridiculed for their eating habits. In some instances, they were made to sit separately.

Table 4.64: Following of Guidelines

Following of Guidelines	*Respondents*	
	Teacher (n=50)	*Parent/Student (n=50)*
	per cent	*per cent*
Yes	89.0	70.0
No	11.0	30.0

4.1.61 Special Essential Help and Co-operation to Children on Teaching

The data revealed that 96.0 per cent of the teachers cooperated with children by teaching. The teacher's instruction goes beyond the simple presentation of factual knowledge. The teacher aligns the content with the learning objectives and ensures that students are provided with opportunities to acquire the knowledge and to use the cognitive processes that are necessary for successful problem solving. The teacher is able to identify and to explain and/or demonstrate key concepts and skills as well as their broader relationships and applications. The teacher guides student learning by presenting concepts and/or procedures in a logical sequence and in clear and sufficient detail. The teacher uses appropriate examples to make the content relevant, meaningful, and applicable to the students. When students experience difficulties in mastering the content, the teacher is able to identify and address the sources of the problems. On the other hand (52 per cent) parents/students accept that teachers help and co-operate with children by teaching.

Table 4.65: Co-operation to Children on Teaching

Teaching	*Respondents*	
	Teacher (n=50)	*Parent/Student (n=50)*
	per cent	*per cent*
Yes	96.0	52.0
No	4.0	48.0

4.1.62 Evaluation of Ability of Every Children

The data accentuated that 89.0 per cent of the teachers stated that they evaluated the ability of every children. The teacher systematically collects, analyses, and summarises assessment data to monitor students' progress. On the basis of formal and informal assessment information, the teacher makes appropriate decisions regarding instruction. When his or her students have difficulty in answering questions, the teacher provides appropriate response, time, rephrases the question, and provides and prompts such other assistance. The teacher provides additional explanations, demonstrations, or assistance, and modifies the content and/or the instructional strategies when necessary. The teacher adjusts the pace of the lessons to conform to the needs of the students. The teacher promotes student retention of the content by actively engaging the students in reviews of the key elements, steps, or procedures as necessary. The teacher extends students' learning and development through appropriate enrichment activities. (90.0 per cent) parents/students reveal that teachers evaluate the ability of every child of the class.

Table 4.66: Evaluation of Ability of Every Child

Professional Experience	*Respondents*	
	Teacher (n=50)	*Parent/Student (n=50)*
	per cent	*per cent*
Yes	89.0	90.0
No	11.0	10.0

4.1.63 Identification of Problems and Solutions of Children

The data revealed that a majority of the teachers (89.0 per cent) identified problems and give solutions to children. The teacher conveys confidence in his or her ability to teach the lesson content and to work with diverse groups of students. The teacher exhibits the enthusiasm necessary to generate interest in the subject matter and the patience and sensitivity necessary to assist and support all students, regardless of their social and cultural backgrounds or intellectual abilities. The teacher shows respect for the feelings, ideas, and contributions of all students and encourages the students to do likewise. (80.0 per cent) parents/students stated that teachers identify the problems of learning and give solution to children.

Table 4.67: Identification of Problems

Professional Experience	*Respondents*	
	Teacher (n=50)	*Parent/Student (n=50)*
	per cent	*per cent*
Yes	89.0	80.0
No	11.0	20.0

4.1.64 Special Help to Every Children as per their Demand

The data portrayed that 85.0 per cent of the teachers give special help to children and rest of the teachers negated. The teacher provides feedback to the students throughout the lesson.

The teacher also provides feedback on all significant student work. The teacher's feedback—whether oral, written, or nonverbal—is equitable (i.e., provided to all students) and individualised. The feedback is accurate, constructive, substantive, specific, and timely. The feedback is effective in helping correct students' misunderstandings or errors, reinforcing their knowledge and skills, and/or extending their learning. (74.0 per cent) parents/students opined that teachers give special help to children for learning and rest 26.0 per cent parents/students avoid the preparation.

Table 4.68: Special Help to Children

Special help to children	*Respondents*	
	Teacher (n=50)	*Parent/Student (n=50)*
	per cent	*per cent*
Yes	85.0	74.0
No	15.0	26.0

4.1.65 Maximum Evaluation and Construction of Material: Preparation of Evaluation Format

The study revealed that a majority of the teachers (77.0 per cent) prepared evaluation format and rest of the teachers (23.0 per cent) they did not prepare. (74.0 per cent) parents/students opined that teachers prepare evaluation format to evaluate children for learning and rest (26.0 per cent) avoid the preparation.

Table 4.69: Preparation of Evaluation Format

Preparation of Evaluation Format	*Respondents*	
	Teacher (n=50)	*Parent/Student (n=50)*
	per cent	*per cent*
Yes	77.0	74.0
No	23.0	26.0

4.1.66. Conduct of Survey for Utilisation

The data revealed that 71.0 per cent of the teachers stated that they conducted the survey for their utilisation purpose and rest of the teachers (29.0 per cent) they did not conduct it. The data is quite similar as parents/students opinion. The teacher ensures that his or her students are engaged in meaningful academic learning throughout the instructional period. Instructional materials, resources, and technologies are useable, well organised, and accessible. In general, instruction is characterised by a smooth flow of activity.

Table 4.70: Conduct of Survey of Utilisation

Conduct of Survey of Utilisation	*Respondents*	
	Teacher (n=50)	*Parent/Student (n=50)*
	per cent	*per cent*
Yes	71.0	69.0
No	29.0	31.0

4.1.67 Implementation of Good Things which was Evaluated by other School

The data revealed that a majority of the teachers (85.5 per cent) opined that they used good things which were evaluated by the other schools. The teacher exemplifies and emphasises initiative, industriousness, inquisitiveness, and excellence and, by doing so, encourages the students to do likewise. The teacher facilitates cooperation and teamwork among students and provides them with appropriate incentives and rewards for learning. The teacher works to ensure that every student can feel a sense of belonging in the classroom. To the extent appropriate, the teacher invites student input and suggestions when designing instructional activities and events. Majority of the parents/students (65.0 per cent) reveal that teachers always implemented good things for the progress of children while (35.0 per cent) do not implement any things.

Table 4.71: Implementation of Good Things

Implementation of good things	*Respondents*	
	Teacher (n=50)	*Parent/Student (n=50)*
	per cent	*per cent*
Yes	85.5	65.0
No	14.5	35.0

A special scale was designed for the study to know the status and knowledge levels of the informants regarding the Right to Education Act. The following five point scale depicts the same.

Table 4.72: Teachers/Parents/Students Opinions on RTE Impact

Statement	*Respondents (n=100)*				
	per cent				
	Strongly Agree	*Agree*	*Undecided*	*Disagree*	*Strongly Disagree*
RTE can reduce the illiteracy among disadvantaged groups	20.00	60.00	5.00	10.00	5.00
RTE can promote the social change	10.00	56.00	18.00	10.00	6.00
Through RTE we can establish empowered childhood	19.00	61.00	11.00	3.00	6.00
RTE promotes sustainable development	18.00	26.00	26.00	11.00	19.00
Child labour can be addressed through RTE	23.00	47.00	14.00	11.00	5.00
Girl child education can be increased through RTE	35.00	48.00	1.00	9.00	7.00
Quality education can achieve through RTE	23.00	59.00	2.00	5.00	11.00
RTE can build knowledge based societies	29.00	59.00	1.00	8.00	3.00
RTE Promotes inclusive growth in near future	15.00	64.00	10.00	9.00	2.00
Systems and structures in the society can be changed by RTE	19.00	59.00	11.00	4.00	7.00

4.1.67.1 Bastar District Primary Schools Responses on Statements Regarding RTE Impact

It can be observed from the above table that a significant number of the respondents were either strongly agree or agreed to the statements related to Right to Education. As regards to the sustainable development, most of the respondents negated. As per the opinions, of the respondents, there is no significant realation between Right to education and development. However, most of the respondents stated that RTE promotes social change and change in the systems and structure and builds knowledge based societies. The respondents either strongly agree or agreed that the RTE can reduce child labour, improve girl child education and empower childhood. Moreover, the respondents strongly agreed or agree that RTE can reduce the illiteracy among the disadvantaged communities and promote quality education.

4.1.67.2 Implementation Status of Primary Schools in Bastar District

The following table describes about the time schedule which is implemented by the teachers under the RTE in 45 hours schedule. The data revealed that the school authorities are following the 45 hours schedule effectively and systematically.

4.1.67.3 Major Findings from Primary Schools in Bastar District

- 40.5 per cent teachers were in the age group of 32-41. 14.5 per cent of the respondents were in the age group of 42-46 and the rest of the respondents are in different age groups. 43.0 per cent Parents/Student were in the age group of 32-41.13.0 per cent of the respondents were in the age group of 22-26 while 7.0 per cent of the respondents were in the age group of 27-31 and rest of the respondents were in different age group.
- 55.6 per cent of the teachers have completed Higher Middle and 18.5 per cent of the teachers were in metric. 36.5 per cent parents/students were matriculated, (12.0 per cent) were B.A. (15.0 per cent) B.Sc (21.5.1) higher secondary with D.Ed and rest (12.5 per cent) were higher Secondary and (2.5 per cent) were M.A. only.
- 40.7 per cent teachers belonged to Schedule Tribe and one fourth of the respondents (25.9 per cent) were in

Table 4.73: Implementation Status

Sl. No.	Name of the Activity	Approved Targets as per RTE act. up to the time of study (Hours/ Minute/ per day/ per week)	Progress against the targets shown in column.3 at the time of Study	
			Average achievement	per cent of actual achievement (4/3x100)
1	Prayer and Attendance	20 minutes/per day	18 minutes/per day	90.0 per cent
2	Teaching	4 hours/per day	3.4 hours/per day	84.5 per cent
3.	Mid-day meal	40 minutes/per day	35 minutes/per day	88.5 per cent
4.	Preparation of action plan for teaching and evaluation	1 hours/per day	52 hours/per day	87.5 per cent
5.	Student Portfolio	30 minutes/per day	26 minutes/per day	85.0 per cent
6.	Discussion with parent and Community	1 hour/per week	31 hours/per week	52.0 per cent
7.	Staff meeting	30 minutes/per week	23 minutes/per week	78.0 per cent
8.	Special need to help the Children	40 minutes/per day	32 minutes/per day	81.0 per cent
9.	Tools/format fixed for evaluation	30 minutes/per week	23 minutes/per week	78.0 per cent
Total Time		**45 hours/week**		

General Category. Other Backward Classes (18.5 per cent) and Schedule Caste (14.8 per cent) were in that order. (52.5 per cent) parents/students were schedule caste while (15.0 per cent) were OBC and (7.0 per cent) were general caste.

- (52.0 per cent) teachers were staying in the village and rest of the teachers (48.0 per cent) were staying outside the village where the school is located.
- (41.0 per cent) teachers are staying less than five kilometers away and (37.0 per cent) of the teachers staying between 6-10 kms 11-15 kms (14.5 per cent), 16-20 kms. (3.5 per cent) and > 20 km are in that order.
- (34.0 per cent) of teachers stated that their school is less than 10 km away from Block Resource Centre and (26.0 per cent) schools 10-20 km away. The data indicate that the distance from BRC is less than 10 km (33.0 per cent), (25.0 per cent) schools 10-20 km away, (18.0 per cent) schools away are in between 21-30 km away, (15.0 per cent) school 31-40 km away, (5.77 per cent) schools were situated in between 41-50 km and rest (3.23 per cent) schools were more than 51 km away.
- (18.5 per cent) of the schools were situated between 31-40 and (11.0 per cent) schools were between 21-30 kms. away.
- An overwhelming fact was that (7.0 per cent) of the schools were situated more than 51 kms away from BRC.
- (81.5 per cent) teachers stated that the schools does not have electricity facility and the rest of the schools (18.5 per cent) have the electricity facility. (50.5 per cent) parents/students accepted that there was no electricity facility in the school and rest (19.5 per cent) parents / student accepted that electricity was present in school.
- (49.0 per cent) of the teachers stated that schools have two rooms and (44.0 per cent) schools have three rooms. According to parents/students, in primary level the whole classes are going in single class room (68.75 per cent), (15.25 per cent) in two class room and rest (1.0 per cent) are in four class room.
- (74.0 per cent) of the schools have toilet facility and rest of the schools (26.0 per cent) have no toilet facility. (71.0

per cent) of the schools have drinking water facility and rest of the schools (29.0 per cent) has no that facility. (85.7 per cent) parents/students reveals that they have toilet and drinking water facility in their school.

- (40.0 per cent) of the schools were connected with the road and a majority of the schools (60.0 per cent) have not connected with the road while (46.5 per cent) parents/students stated that schools are connected with road and rest (54.5 per cent) schools are not connected.
- (37.0 per cent) of the schools have two teachers and (30.0 per cent) schools have three teachers. (64.0 per cent) primary school has only one permanent teacher, (18.0 per cent) school going through two permanent teacher and rest school have three (11.0 per cent), four (3.5 per cent) and five (2.5 per cent) permanent teacher.
- (18.0 per cent) schools have one teacher as such. (64.0 per cent) primary school has only one permanent teacher, (18.0 per cent) school going through two permanent teacher and rest school have three (11.0 per cent) , four (3.5 per cent) and five (2.5 per cent) permanent teacher.
- (92.6 per cent) have no temporary teachers and (5.0 per cent) of the schools have two temporary teachers.
- (78.0 per cent) of the teachers stated that schools are allocating 20 minutes for prayer and (12.0 per cent) of the schools are taking 30 minutes to complete the prayer. (75.0 per cent) parents/students opinion is that prayer timing is 30 minutes but teachers depicted it has taking only 20 minutes. The data depicted that (15.0 per cent) school have taking less than 20 minutes time for prayer and (10.0 per cent) are taking 20 minutes for prayer.
- (63.0 per cent) are of the teachers stated that teachers are teaching four for hours and (21.5 per cent) are teaching above four hours. As per parents/students that (12.5 per cent) of the teachers are taking class up to four hours and (42.0 per cent) are teaching four hours and rest (45.5 per cent) are teaching above four hrs.
- (74.0 per cent) of the school teachers stated that teachers were allocated 40 minutes and 14.5 per cent of the schools allocated more than 40 minutes for midday meal.

On the other hand, as per the parents/students stated that midday meal had taken more than 40 minutes (75.0 per cent) and rest had taken 40 minutes (15.0 per cent).

- 63.0 per cent of the teachers, whereas according to parents/students (72.5 per cent) stated that teachers had taken one hour per day for preparation of action plan and 24.5 per cent of the teachers have taken more than one hour. In this case similar trend it also observed among parents/students opinion.
- According to parents/ students (50.5 per cent) stated that teachers (66.5 per cent) had allocated 30 minutes time for student portfolio and (18.5 per cent) of the teachers allocated more than 30 minutes for the same activity. According to parents/students; data reveals that majority of the teachers (50.5 per cent) took 30 minutes time to make student portfolio and (14.0 per cent) teachers took less than 30 minutes time and rest (35.5 per cent) took more than 30 minutes time for preparation.
- (48.0 per cent) of the teachers opined that, teachers spared less than one hour for discussion with parents and (41.0 per cent) of the respondents spared one hour. Whereas 69.0 per cent parents/students opined that teachers take at least one hour for discussion with parents.
- (74.0 per cent) of the teachers stated that teachers had given 30 minutes time for staff meeting and (22.0 per cent) of the teachers allocated less than 30 minutes for the same. The parent/student data reveals that (68.0 per cent) teachers took more than 30 minutes, (22.0 per cent) took 30 minutes and (10.0 per cent) teacher took less than 30 minutes time for staff meeting.
- (70.5 per cent) of the teachers stated that they had given 40 minutes time to address the special needs of the children and (19.0 per cent) of the teachers opined that they had allocated less than 40 minutes time for the same activity. The opinion of parents/students indicate that (38.5 per cent) teachers spend 40 minutes to help the children for their special need in study (26.0 per cent) teachers took less than 40 minutes and (35.5 per cent), took more than 40 minutes time.

- (70.0 per cent) of the teachers stated that they allocated 30 minutes for tools or formats evaluation and (22.0 per cent) of the teachers opined that less than 30 minutes spared for the same. Majority of the parent/student opinion is that (54.5 per cent) take more than 30 minutes time for tools/format fixed for evaluation, (35.5 per cent) take 30 minutes and rest had taken less than 30 minutes.
- (90.0 per cent) of the teachers stated that they were present during the prayer along with students and rest of the teachers negated. Parent/student accepted that (92.0 per cent) teachers were present at the time of prayer and rest (8.0 per cent) were absent at that time.
- (47.0 per cent) of the teachers opined that they observed national song, national anthem and prayer and national anthem alone (14.5 per cent), group song, national song, national anthem and prayer (14.0 per cent) were observed in the prayer. The data reveals that majority of the (parents/students) stated (68.0 per cent) that they do national song anthem and prayer, (25.0 per cent) accentuated that they do group song, national song, anthem and prayer and rest were do only national song (2.0 per cent) or anthem (3.0 per cent) and both national song and anthem (2.0 per cent).
- (45.0 per cent) of the teachers stated that they used lecture method, 32.5 per cent of the teachers used *Mahapurus* thought and (22.5 per cent) used both variables as teaching model. Parents/students data indicate that (65.0 per cent) teachers gave lecture only, while (25.0 per cent) teachers gave lecture and *Mahapurus* thought also.
- Majority of the teachers (92.0 per cent) stated that they had taken attendance after assembly and rest of the teachers negated. According to parents/students the data reveals that (98.0 per cent) teachers had taken attendance after assembly and rest (2.0 per cent) said that they were absent.
- (75.5 per cent) teachers stated that they used cognitive teaching for class I-II and rest of the teachers negated. (85.0 per cent) of the teachers stated they taught Class III-V through cognitive mode. Majority of the parents/students stated that teachers used cognitive teaching for class I-II (65.0 per cent), (III-V) (60.5 per cent) and rest of them negated.

- Majority of the teachers (81.5 per cent) opined they adopted whole class approach and rest of the teachers negated. Parents/students indicate that more than (90.0 per cent) teacher adopted whole class approach.
- (89.5 per cent) of the teachers stated that they adopted group based activity and rest of the sample despised. (72.5 per cent) parents/students opined that teachers adopted group based activities and rest of the teachers negated.
- (41.0 per cent) of the teachers opined that they adopted oral, (25.5 per cent) used written and (33.5 per cent) used both for continuous evaluation. The study of parents/students opinion revealed that (46.0 per cent) teacher have been addressing oral and written evaluation while (32.0 per cent) had taken written examination only.
- (70.5 per cent) teachers opined that they adopted Co-cognitive technique for teaching of class I-V and rest of the teachers negated. Parents/students stated that (82.0 per cent) teachers doing co-cognitive teaching in primary school.
- (37.0 per cent) of the teachers stated that they have given chance for drawing and (21.0 per cent) of the teachers adopted drawing, music and dance. (17.5 per cent) of the teachers used drawing, music, dance, art and craft, literary and cultural activities and (14.5 per cent) of the teachers used drawing and dance. Majority of the parents and students stated that (65.0 per cent) school has organised drawing, music, dance, art and craft literary and cultural activities, (17.0 per cent) school has given chance for drawing and dance, (3.0 per cent) adopted drawing only and the rest have organised other kind of art activities.
- (56.5 per cent) teachers stated that they have given project and (29.0 per cent) opined that they have displayed creative work and (14.5 per cent) of the teachers opined they adopted both for work experience. Majority of the parents/students stated that (49.5 per cent) teachers display creative work (16.0 per cent) have given project work and display creative work both and (34.0 per cent) have given only project work.

- (33.5 per cent) of the teachers stated that they adopted sports and games, (18.5 per cent) of the teachers adopted yoga and (15.5 per cent) of the teachers used yoga, sports and games, nutritional food, knowledge about diseases and cleanliness about the surrounding for physical education and health. Majority of the parents/students (42.0 per cent) addressing sports and games as a physical education, (30.0 per cent) used sports games and cleanliness, (11.5 per cent) used yoga, (7.0 per cent) used yoga sports and games and rest (37.5 per cent) used yoga sports, games, nutritional food knowledge about the surroundings.
- (35.5 per cent) teachers opined that they adopted attitude, life skill and awareness towards environment and (29.0 per cent) of the respondents used attitude, life skill, awareness towards environment and value system for improvement of social/personal attitudes and values. (48.5 per cent) parents/students stated that teachers addressing knowledge about attitude, life skill, awareness towards environments, (10.0 per cent) parents/students accepted only attitude, (11.0 per cent) learning life skill, and rest (30.0 per cent) accepted attitude, life skill, awareness towards environment and value system.
- (37.0 per cent) of the teachers stated that they could complete midday meal distribution between 31-40 minutes. (30.5 per cent) of the teachers had taken 10-21 minutes, (14.5 per cent) of the teachers had taken 41-50 minutes for the same. Majority of the parents/students (35.0 per cent) opined that distribution of mid day meal completed between 41-50 minutes, (10.0 per cent) had taken 21-30 minutes and (25.0 per cent) had taken more than 50 minutes respectively.
- (90.5 per cent) teachers opined that they prepared action plan for teaching and evaluation and rest of the teachers (9.5 per cent) negated. The parents/students data was quite similar as teachers opinion.
- (97.0 per cent) of the teachers stated that they prepared activities for class room teaching. Majority of parents/students stated that (92.0 per cent) teacher prepare activities plan for school/children.

- (85.5 per cent) of teachers stated that they prepared Teaching and Learning material and rest of the respondents (14.5 per cent) negated. 86.4 per cent) parents/students reveal that teachers prepare TLM for teaching students while (13.6 per cent) negated.
- (85.0 per cent) of the teachers opined that they applied techniques for teaching and rest of the respondents negated. On the other hand (82.0 per cent) parents/students opined that the teacher applied technique for teaching and rest negated.
- Three fourths of the teachers (76.0 per cent) stated they planned for group work and 24.0 per cent of the teachers negated. Majority of the parents/students stated that (80.0 per cent) teachers were creating plan for group work and rest (20.0 per cent) were not participating in it.
- (92.0 per cent) of the teachers opined that they were planned for action plan for teaching and learning. (70.0 per cent) parents/students revealed that teacher planned for teaching and learning.
- (89.0 per cent) of the teachers opined that they were learned and followed teaching and learning material and rest of the teachers negated. Majority of the parents/students (91.0 per cent) stated that teacher followed teaching learning material and rest (9.0 per cent) of the respondents negated.
- (67.0 per cent) of the teachers opined that they planned useful books for the library and (25.0 per cent) of the teachers were using books and Book Corner for the use of library. (72.0 per cent) parents/students opined that teachers used books, (10.0 per cent) used books corner and (18.0 per cent) used books and Books Corner only.
- (92.0 per cent) of the teachers stated that they have developed new information and new techniques for the class rcom. (90 per cent) students/parents opined that teachers gather new information and technique for the classroom and rest (10.0 per cent) negated.
- (86.0 per cent) of the teachers opined that they prepared portfolio for individual children and rest of the teachers (14.0 per cent) have not prepared. (84.0 per cent)

parents/students stated that teachers make portfolio for individual children and (16.0 per cent) parents/students did not agree with this. On the basis of these analyses, the teacher determines the impact of instruction on student learning and makes appropriate decisions about the need to modify his or her instructional plans.

- (52.0 per cent) of the teachers stated that they take name only. One fifths of the teachers (22.0 per cent) have taken name, weight, height, blood group, other physical and family background. (55.0 per cent) parents/students reveals that teachers take their name only as a information of children, (12.0 per cent) take family background also, (25.0 per cent) take name weight and height, (3.0 per cent) take family background, name, other, height and weight and rest 5.0 per cent take name, weight, height, blood group, other physical and family background also.
- (92.0 per cent) of the teachers stated that they find out the areas of interests of the children. Whereas (91.0 per cent) parents/students opined that teachers find out the areas of interests of the children.
- (78.0 per cent) of the teachers stated that they measured the learning status and improvement and rest of the teachers (22.0 per cent) negated. On the other hand, (63.0 per cent) parents/students reveled that teachers measured learning status and improvement of children and rest (37.0 per cent) negated.
- (82.0 per cent) teachers opined that they had collected information regarding special work. (72.0 per cent) parents/students stated that teachers collect information about children.
- (89.0 per cent) of the teachers stated that they are assessing the past and present status of the students. Less than three forth of parents/students (72.0 per cent) reveal that teachers collect information about the assessment of past and present status of students.
- Majority of the teachers (79.0 per cent) were stated that they discussed with the students parents to solve the problems and rest of the teachers negated. The data indicate (25.0 per cent) parents/students opined that

teachers discuss with parents and (75.0 per cent) negated.

- (71.0 per cent) of the teachers stated that they were contacted with the parents and parent teacher association and (29.0 per cent) of the teachers did not contact. It's clear from the data as per opinion of parents/ students that only (28.0 per cent) teachers contact with parents and rest (72.0 per cent) avoid communication.
- (43.5 per cent) of the teachers stated that they discussed with the parent teacher association regarding quality of education, educational survey, school activity/ programme, health awareness and (27.0 per cent) of the teachers stated they discussed about quality education and (18.0 per cent) of the teachers were discussed social activity and other programmes.
- (92.5 per cent) of the teachers stated that they discussed about dropout and un-enrolled children. A large number of school going children are not even able to access schools. (84.0 per cent) parents/students stated that teachers discuss about dropouts and un-enrolled children and rest (16.0 per cent) were not done this.
- Discussion about the regular attendance is very vital to improve the standards and quality education. The study revealed that all the respondents stated that they were discussed about the regular attendance. School performance is marked by absenteeism, inadequately trained teachers with indifferent attitudes, non-availability of teaching materials, inadequate supervision, and little support. Many poor families, have lost faith in Government schools, are forced to send their children to private schools even when they have access to 'free' public schools. Several cases of discrimination are reported-against girls, against children belonging to socially disadvantaged and minority communities, and against the poor. Corporal punishment is common and many children are afraid of going to school for fear of being beaten, if not publicly ridiculed or rebuked by teachers and other students.
- (59.5 per cent) of the teachers stated that they had discussed about the school plan only. (17.0 per cent) of

the teachers opined that they discussed school plan and unit plan. (42.0 per cent) parents/students stated that teachers discuss on school plan, (16.0 per cent) discuss on unit plan, (12.0 per cent) discuss on TLM and its uses and (30.0 per cent) discuss on school plan and unit plan.

- (93.0 per cent) teachers stated that they discussed about particular activity in the classroom. (59.0 per cent) parents/students opined that teachers discuss about particular activity in the class and rest (41.0 per cent) were avoiding discussion.
- (91.0 per cent) of the teachers stated that they discussed about writing and reading material. (86.0 per cent) parents/students stated that teachers discuss about writing and reading material with children in the class.
- (85.5 per cent) teachers stated that they evaluated children and student profile. (78.0 per cent) parents/students opined that teachers discuss and evaluate of student and children profile and rest 22.0 per cent avoids this.
- (81.0 per cent) of the teachers stated they discussed about coconscious activity and the rest of the teachers negated. Majority of the parents/students (89.0 per cent) stated that teachers discussed coconscious activity of children.
- (92.0 per cent) teachers opined that they discussed about the participation of parent teacher association and its functions. (64.0 per cent) parents/students agreed that teachers discussed on participation and rest (36.0 per cent) negated.
- (95.0 per cent) of the teachers stated that they discussed about the time table in the school and a small sample (5.0 per cent) negated. (55.0 per cent) parents/students stated that teachers discussed on time table in the class and the rest (45.0 per cent) negated.
- (92.0 per cent) of the teachers opined that they discussed about the expectation of every children in the schools. (65.0 per cent) parents/students opined that teachers discussed on expectation of every child and (35.0 per cent) did not discuss.

- Majority of the teachers (95.0 per cent) discussed about book. Whereas (92.0 per cent) parents/students reveal that teachers discussed about the book with children
- (81.5 per cent) of the teachers stated that they discussed about the good work done by them and as well as by the children. (85.0 per cent) parents/students accepted that teachers discussed regarding good work and rest (15.0 per cent) did not discuss.
- Majority of the teachers (88.0 per cent) stated that they solved the problems regarding the teaching and learning methods. Majority of the parents/students (82.0 per cent) also reveal that teachers actively participate in solving problems regarding the teaching and learning method.
- (85.5 per cent) of the teachers opined that they had professional experience and rest of the teachers negated. (86.0 per cent) parents/students stated that teachers have professional experience of teaching and rest (14.0 per cent) were not experienced.
- (89.0 per cent) of the teachers stated that they are following the Right to Education act guidelines and rest of the teachers negated. (70.0 per cent) parents/students opined that teaching follow the guidelines of Right to Education Act.
- (96.0 per cent) of the teachers opined that they were cooperating the children by while teaching. On the other hand only (52 per cent) parents/students accept that teachers help and co-operate with children while teaching.
- (89.0 per cent) of the teachers stated that they evaluated the ability of every child. (90.0 per cent) parents/students reveal that teachers evaluate the ability of every child of class.
- (89.0 per cent) stated that they identified problems and give solutions to children. (80.0 per cent) parents/students stated that teachers identify the problems of learning and give solution to children.
- (85.0 per cent) of the teachers stated that they give special help for to the children and rest of the teachers negated. (74.0 per cent) parents/students opined that teachers

give special help to children for learning and rest (26.0 per cent) parents/students avoid to give help.

- (77.0 per cent) teachers stated that they prepared evaluation format and rest of the teachers (23.0 per cent) did not prepare. (74.0 per cent) parents/students opined that teachers prepare evaluation format to evaluate children for learning and rest (26.0 per cent) avoid the preparation.
- (71.0 per cent) of the teachers stated that they conducted the survey for their utilisation purpose and rest of the teachers (29.0 per cent) did not conduct it. The data is quite similar of parents/students opinion as of the teachers.
- (85.5 per cent) teachers opined that they used good things which were evolved by the other schools. The teacher exemplifies and emphasises initiative, industriousness, inquisitiveness, and excellence and, by doing so, encourages the students to do likewise. Majority of the parents/students (65.0 per cent) reveal that teachers always implemented good things for the progress of children while (35.0 per cent) do not implement any things.

4.2 Middle Schools in Bastar District

4.2.1 Social Characteristics

The data revealed that a majority of the teachers (81.5 per cent) participated in the study and the rest of the teachers (18.5 per cent) were female. As regarding the age (41.5 per cent) of the teachers were in the age group of 32-38 and (22.0 per cent) of the teachers were in more than 52 age group. (37.0 per cent) of the teachers belonged to Schedule Tribe and (33.5 per cent) of the teachers belonged to OBC. General (18.5 per cent) and SC (11.0 per cent) were in that order. The social class of parents/ student depicted that (11.0 per cent) are schedule caste, (37.0 per cent) schedule Tribe while (33.5 per cent) were OBC and (18.5 per cent) were general caste. The parents/student data revealed that majorities (40.0 per cent) were in the age group of 32-38. (8.0 per cent) parents/students were in the age group of 27-31 while (10.0 per cent) of the parents/students were in the age group of 37-51 and rest (22.0 per cent) of the parents/ students were more than 52 years age group.

Table 4.74: Social Characteristics

Variable	Respondents	
	Teacher (n=50)	*Parent/Student (n=50)*
	per cent	*per cent*
Gender		
Male	81.5	80.0
Female	18.5	20.0
Age		
27-31	7.5	8.0
32-38	41.5	40.0
37-41	11.0	10.0
42-46	11.0	10.0
57-51	7.0	10.0
> 52	22.0	22.0
Caste		
SC	11.0	11.0
ST	37.0	37.0
OBC	33.5	33.5
General	18.5	18.5

4.2.2 Residence and Distance

The data revealed that (78.0 per cent) of the teachers were staying outside the village and the rest of the teachers (22.0 per cent) were staying in the same village, where the school is located. A majority of the teachers (48.0 per cent) staying less than 5 kms and (37.0 per cent) of the teachers were staying 6-10 km away from the school. As regard to the distance from Block Resource Centre was more than one fourths, (26.0 per cent) stated that 10-20 kms and (22.5 per cent) of the teachers stated 31-40 kms away and (22.0 per cent) of the teachers stated that they stayed less than 10 kms away. Locations of a school and its connectivity with the outer world have a greater influence in the academic performance of the students. If a school is located in an urban set up or at any roadside point having bus communication facility, the teachers face less difficulty to access it. Similarly, the students also have less difficulty to attend such a school but in tribal areas many school are situated in hilly sites within the forest and the students fear to attend such school as they are to approach those through forest roads where they are susceptible to face feral animals while coming to school in morning and returning home at evening hours.

Whatever, may be the distance of school from the district headquarters and local towns, the distance can easily be covered by bus or any other motor vehicle, but the distance of school is situated at a significant distant place from the local bus stop, such teachers have to cover the distance by walk or some other means. Covering the distance by walk and by bus are very time consuming and physically strenuous test and therefore it create a major impact on the classroom teaching process. The data indicate that the distance from BRC is less than 10 kms. (28.0 per cent), (22.0 per cent) school 10-20 kms. away, (14.0 per cent) school away in between 21-30 kms, (15.0 per cent) school 31-40 kms away, (11.0 per cent) school were situated in between 41-50 kms and rest (10.0 per cent) school were away more than 51 kms.

Table 4.75: Residence and Distance

Variable	Respondents	
	Teacher (n=50)	*Parent/Student (n=50)*
	per cent	*per cent*
Residence		
Same Village	22.0	15.0
Other Village	78.0	85.0
Distance from School		
> 5	48.0	52.0
6-10	37.0	15.0
11-15	4.5	10.0
16-20	7.0	13.0
> 20	3.5	10.0
Distance from BRC		
> 10 KM	22.0	28.0
10-20	26.0	22.0
21-30	11.5	14.0
31-40	22.5	15.0
41-50	7.0	11.0
> 51	11.0	10.0

4.2.3 Facilities in the School

The study revealed that 40.5 schools have electricity facility and rest of the schools (59.5 per cent) did not have such facility. As regards the class rooms 85.5 per cent of the teachers stated that these are three class rooms in their school. A majority of the teachers (89.0 per cent) stated that they have toilet facility in the school. (45.0 per cent) of the schools were connected with roads. (90.0 per cent) of the schools have drinking water facility. Majority of the parents/students (65.0 per cent) reveals that they have no toilet and drinking water facility in their school. (52.0 per cent) parents/students stated that schools are not connected with road and rest (48.0 per cent) schools are connected. When data gathered from parents/students it's observed that (65.0 per cent) responding accepted that there was no electricity facility in the school and rest (35.0 per cent) parents/student accepted that electricity was present in school. In middle school level the (90.0 per cent) parents/students stated that there were three class rooms, (3.0 per cent) stated that two class rooms and rest (7.0 per cent) stated that there were five/ six class rooms.

Table 4.76 Facilities in the School

Variable	*Respondents*	
	Teacher (n=50)	*Parent/Student (n=50)*
	per cent	*per cent*
Electricity		
Yes	40.5	35.0
No	59.5	65.0
No of Class Rooms		
2.	7.0	3.0
3.	85.5	90.0
5.	4.0	5.0
6.	3.5	2.0
Toilet Facility		
Yes	89.0	35.0
No	11.0	65.0
Road Connected		
Yes	45.0	48.0
No	55.0	52.0
Drinking Water Facility		
Yes	90.0	74.0
No	10.0	26.0

4.2.4 Staffing

The data revealed that (36.5 per cent) of the teachers stated that there were two teachers, (29.0 per cent) of the teachers opined that one teacher and 25.5 per cent of the teachers opined that three permanent teachers in their schools. As regarding the temporary teachers (81.5 per cent) of the teachers stated that they don't have such teachers. However, (11.5 per cent) of the teachers stated that they have two teachers in their schools. As per opinion of parents/students the data reveals that (42.0 per cent) middle school have only two permanent teacher followed by (30 per cent) of school having one permanent teacher and (20.0 per cent) school going through three permanent teacher.

Table 4.77: Staffing

Variable	*Respondents*	
	Teacher (n=50)	*Parent/Student (n=50)*
	per cent	*per cent*
Permanent Teachers		
1.	3.0	3.0
2.	29.0	30.0
3.	36.5	42.0
4.	25.5	20.0
5.	3.0	3.0
6.	3.0	2.0
Temporary Teachers		
1.	81.5	82.0
2.	11.5	16.0
3.	4.0	1.0
4.	3.0	1.0

4.2.5 Prayer and Teaching Time

The study revealed that a majority of the teachers (70.5 per cent) stated that they took 20 minutes to complete prayer and 18.5 per cent of the teachers opined that they took 30 minutes for the same. As regards the teaching hours (90.0 per cent) of the teachers stated that they taught more than 4.35 hours per day. As per opinion of parents/students (78 per cent) stated that they took 30 minutes to complete prayer and 93 per cent stated that they taught more than 4.35 hours per day.

Table 4.78: Prayer and Teaching Time

Prayer and Teaching Time	*Respondents*	
	Teacher (n=50)	*Parent/ Student (n=50)*
	per cent	*per cent*
Prayer		
Less than 20 Minutes	11.0	3.0
20 Minutes	70.5	19.0
30 Minutes	18.5	78.0
Teaching Hours		
Less than 4.35 Hrs	3.0	3.0
4.35 Hrs	7.0	4.0
Above 4.35 Hrs	90.0	93.0

4.2.6 Mid-day Meal

The study revealed that (90.0 per cent) of the teachers opined that they have taken 40 minutes for mid-day meal. The data of parents/students, indicate that (3.0 per cent) teacher spend 40 minutes to help the children for their special need in study, (7.0 per cent) teachers take less than 40 minutes and (90.0 per cent) took more than 40 minutes time.

Table 4.79: Mid-day Meal

Midday Meal	*Respondents*	
	Teacher (n=50)	*Parent/ Student (n=50)*
	per cent	*per cent*
< 40 Minutes	3.0	7.0
40 Minutes	90.0	3.0
> 40 Minutes	7.0	90.0

4.2.7 Preparation of Action Plans

The data accentuated that 85.0 per cent of the teachers had taken 40 minutes per day for preparation of action plans. Parents/students data indicate that (78.0 per cent) teachers take up to one hr per day for preparation of action plan, and rest have taken less than one hrs per day.

Table 4.80: Preparation of Action Plans

Preparation of Action Plans	*Respondents*	
	Teacher (n=50)	*Parent/Student (n=50)*
	per cent	*per cent*
< 1 hour per day	11.5	78.0
40 Minutes per day	85.0	12.0
> 40 Minutes per day	3.5	10.0

4.2.8 Student Portfolio

The data portrayed that (81.5 per cent) of the teachers stated that they have taken 30 minutes for student portfolio and 11.0 per cent of the teachers have taken more than 30 minutes for the same. Parents/students data reveals that the (20.0 per cent) teachers take 30 minutes time to make student portfolio and (4.0 per cent) teachers take less than 30 minutes time and rest (76.0 per cent) take more than 30 minutes time for preparation.

Table 4.81: Student Portfolio

Student Portfolio	*Respondents*	
	Teacher (n=50)	*Parent/Student (n=50)*
	per cent	*per cent*
< 30 Minutes	7.5	4.0
30 Minutes	81.5	20.0
> 30 Minutes	11.0	76.0

4.2.9 Discussion with Parent

The data portrayed that a majority of the teachers (81.5 per cent) have taken one hour for discussion with parents and (11.5 per cent) of the teachers have taken less than one hour for the same. As per opinion of parents/students, generally (10.0 per cent) teachers take one hour for discussion with parents, (18.0 per cent) take less than one hour and only (72.0 per cent) take more than one hours.

Table 4.82: Discussion with Parent

Discussion	Respondents	
	Teacher (n=50)	Parent/Student (n=50)
	per cent	per cent
< 1 hour	11.5	18.0
1 hour	81.5	10.0
> 1 hour	7.0	72.0

4.2.10 Staff Meeting

The data revealed that 86.0 per cent of the teachers stated that they spared 30 minutes for staff meeting per week. The data of parents/students revealed that (80.0 per cent) teachers take more than 30 minutes, (15.0 per cent) take 30 minutes and (5.0 per cent) teacher take less than 30 minutes time for staff meeting.

Table 4.83: Staff Meeting

Discussion	Respondents	
	Teacher (n=50)	Parent/Student (n=50)
	per cent	per cent
< 30 Minutes	7.0	5.0
30 Minutes	86.0	15.0
> 30 Minutes	7.0	80.0

4.2.11 Special Need to Help the Children

The data accentuated that (75.0 per cent) of the teachers opined that they allocated 40 minutes for children those who are in special need and (14.0 per cent) of the teachers stated that they spared less than forty minutes per day. The data of parents/students indicate that (11.0 per cent) teacher expand 40 minutes to help the children for their special need in study, (20.0 per cent) teachers take less than 40 minutes and (69.0 per cent) take more than 40 minutes time.

Table 4.84: Special Help to Needy Children

Discussion	*Respondents*	
	Teacher (n=50)	*Parent/Student (n=50)*
	per cent	*per cent*
< 40 Minutes	14.0	20.0
40 Minutes	75.0	11.0
More Than 40 Minutes	11.0	69.0

4.2.12 Tools/Format Fixed for Evaluation

The study revealed that the (86.0 per cent) of the teachers stated that they allocated 30 minutes per week for tools and formats evaluation. Majority of the Parents/students stated that (87.0 per cent) take more than 30 minutes time for tools/format fixed for evaluation, (10.0 per cent) take 30 minutes and rest have taken less than 30 minutes.

Table 4.85: Tools/Format Fixed for Evaluation

Evaluation	*Respondents*	
	Teacher (n=50)	*Parent/Student (n=50)*
	per cent	*per cent*
< 30 Minutes	7.0	3.0
30 Minutes	86.0	10.0
> 30 Minutes	7.0	87.0

4.2.13 Attendance of Teachers and Students during Prayer

The data revealed that 86.0 per cent of the teachers have participated during prayer and rest of the teachers was negated. As regarding the pattern 48.5 per cent of the teachers stated that they used only prayer and 33.5 per cent of the teachers stated that they used group song, national song, national anthem and prayer during the prayer. As regarding the motivational activities 37.0 per cent of the teachers used *Mahapurus thought,* (33.0 per cent) of the teachers used lecture and (30.0 per cent) of the teachers used both. All the teachers stated that they have taken attendance after assembly. (90.0 per cent) parents/ students stated that all ware present at the time of prayer and rest (10.0 per cent) were absent at that time. The data reveals that majority of the respondents stated (80.0 per cent) that they do national song, anthem and prayer, (10.0 per cent) accentuated that they do group song, national song, national anthem and prayer and rest done only national song or anthem or both national song and anthem.

Table 4.86: Teacher and Students during Prayers

Variable	*Respondents*	
	Teacher (n=50)	*Parent/Student (n=50)*
	per cent	*per cent*
Present at the time of Prayer		
Yes	86.0	90.0
No	14.0	10.0
Pattern		
National Song	11.0	5.0
National Anthem	7.0	10.0
Group Song, National Song, National Anthem and Prayer	33.5	80.0
Prayer	48.5	5.0
Motivational Activities		
Lecture	33.0	45.0
Mahaparus Thought	37.0	25.0
Lecture + Mahapurus Thought	30.0	30.0

4.2.14 Teaching: Cognitive Teaching (Class VI-VIII)

The data revealed that all the respondents adopted cognitive teaching for class VI-VIII in the class room.

4.2.15 Whole Class Approach and Group Based Activity

The data revealed that (96.0 per cent) of the teachers adopted whole class approach and (95.0 per cent) of the teachers adopted group based activity. Parents/students indicate that (86.0 per cent) teacher adopted whole class approach. (70.0 per cent) parents/students opined that teachers adopted group based activities.

Table 4.87: Whole Class Approach and Group Activity

Variables	Respondents	
	Teacher (n=50)	*Parent/ Student (n=50)*
	per cent	*per cent*
Whole Class Approach		
Yes	96.0	86.0
No	4.0	14.0
Group Based Activity		
Yes	95.0	70.0
No	5.0	30.0

4.2.16 Mode of Continuous Evaluation and Co-cognitive Teaching

The data revealed that a majority of the teachers stated that they evaluated the oral and (37.5 per cent) of the teachers stated that they evaluated the oral and writing. As regarding the co-cognitive teaching (78.0 per cent) of the teachers they used and (22.0 per cent) of the teachers did not use it. Parents/ students stated that (65.0 per cent) teachers doing co-cognitive teaching in primary school. The study revealed that (25.0 per cent) teacher addressing oral and (64.0 per cent) written evaluation while (11.0 per cent) taking written and oral examination.

Table 4.88: Mode of Continuous Evaluation and Co-cognitive Teaching

Evaluation	Respondents	
	Teacher (n=50)	*Parent/ Student (n=50)*
	per cent	*per cent*
Evaluation Oral	59.5	25.0
Written	3.0	64.0
Oral and Written	37.5	11.0
Co-cognitive Teaching		
Yes	78.0	65.0
No	22.0	35.0

4.2.17 Art

The study revealed that (52.0 per cent) of the teachers conducted drawing and (20.0 per cent) of the teachers conducted drawing, music, dance, literary and cultural activities for the children. The parents and students stated that (35.0 per cent) school has organised drawing, music, dance, art and craft literary and cultural activities, (12.0 per cent) school given chance for music and rest haveorganised other kind of art activities.

Table 4.89: Art

Art	*Respondents*	
	Teacher (n=50)	*Parent/Student (n=50)*
	per cent	*per cent*
Drawing	52.0	35.0
Music	14.0	12.0
Drawing, Dance, Art and Craft, Literary and cultural Activities	14.0	23.0
Drawing, Music, Dance, Literary and cultural Activities	20.0	30.0

4.2.18 Work Experience

The data revealed that (63.0 per cent) of the teachers stated that they had given project work and (22.0 per cent) of the teachers stated that they display creative work. Majority of the parents/students stated that (20.0 per cent) teacher display creative work, (70.0 per cent) given project work and display creative work both and (10.0 per cent) given only project work.

Table 4.90: Work Experience

Work Experience	*Respondents*	
	Teacher (n=50)	*Parent/Student (n=50)*
	per cent	*per cent*
Project Work	63.0	10.0
Display Creative Work	22.0	20.0
Project Work and Display Creative Work	15.0	70.0

4.2.19 Physical Education and Health

The study revealed that (37.0 per cent) of the teachers stated that they conducted sports and games and (33.0 per cent) of the respondents stated they conducted yoga, sports and games, nutritional food, knowledge about diseases. Yoga (15.0 per cent), Yoga, Sports and Games (7.5 per cent) and Cleanliness (7.5 per cent) in that order. Majority of the parents/students (52.0 per cent) addressing yoga, sports and games, nutritional Food, Knowledge about Diseases, (15.0 per cent) used sports and games, (15.0 per cent) used yoga, (5.0 per cent) used yoga sports and games and rest used Cleanliness.

Table 4.91: Physical Education and Health

Physical Education and Health	*Respondents*	
	Teacher (n=50)	*Parent/Student (n=50)*
	per cent	*per cent*
Yoga	15.0	15.0
Sports and Games	37.0	15.0
Yoga, Sports and Games	7.5	5.0
Cleanliness	7.5	13.0
Yoga, Sports and Games, Nutritional Food, Knowledge about Diseases	33.0	52.0

4.2.20 Social/Personal Attitudes and Values

The data revealed that (34.0 per cent) of the teachers stated that they adopted attitude, life skill, awareness towards Environment and Value System and 26.0 per cent of the teachers opined that attitude, life skill, and awareness towards Environment. (22.0 per cent) of the teachers stated that Life skill and (18.0 per cent) of the teachers stated attitude. (21.0 per cent) parents/students stated that teacher addressing knowledge about attitude, life skill, awareness towards environments, (10.0 per cent) respondents accepted only attitude, (9.0 per cent) learning life skill and rest (60.0 per cent) accepted attitude, life skill, awareness towards environment and value system.

Table 4.92: Social/Personal Attitudes and Values

Social and Personal Attitude	Respondents	
	Teacher (n=50)	Parent/Student (n=50)
	per cent	per cent
Attitude	18.0	10.0
Life Skill	22.0	9.0
Attitude + Life Skill+ Awareness towards Environment	26.0	21.0
Attitude + Life Skill+ Awareness towards Environment + Value System	34.0	60.0

4.2.21 Mid-day Meal Distribution

The data portrayed that 60.0 per cent of the teachers stated they have taken 31-40 minutes per day for midday meal distribution. Majority of the parents/students stated that (89.0 per cent) distributed mid day meal in between 31-40 minutes, (6.0 per cent) of the parents/students had taken 21-30 minutes, (5.0 per cent) parents/students had taken 10-21 minutes for the same.

Table 4.93: Mid-day Meal Distribution

Mid-day Meal	Respondents	
	Teacher (n=50)	Parent/Student (n=50)
	per cent	per cent
10-21	7.0	5.0
21-30	33.0	6.0
31-40	60.0	89.0

4.2.22 Preparation of Action Plan for Teaching and Evaluation

The data accentuated that 81.5 per cent of the teachers stated that they prepared action plans and rest of the teachers (18.5 per cent) negated. A majority of the teachers (89 per cent) stated that they prepared activities for class room teaching. Majority of parents/students stated that (90.0 per cent) teacher prepare activities plan for school/children.

Table 4.94: Preparation of Action Plan

Variables	*Respondents*	
	Teacher (n=50)	*Parent/ Student (n=50)*
	per cent	*per cent*
Preparation of Action Plan		
Yes	81.5	90.0
No	18.5	10.0
Preparation of Activities for Class Room Teaching		
Yes	89.0	60.0
No	11.0	40.0

4.2.23 Preparation of TLM and Application of Techniques for Active Participation

The data portrayed that (89.0 per cent) of the teachers stated that they prepared teaching learning material. (81.5 per cent) of the teachers adopted techniques to activate participation. (92.0 per cent) parents/students reveal that teachers prepare TLM for teaching students while (8.0 per cent) were neglected. (76.0 per cent) parents/students opined that the teacher applied technique for teaching and rest were negated.

Table 4.95: Preparation of TLM and Techniques

Variables	*Respondents*	
	Teacher (n=50)	*Parent/ Student (n=50)*
	per cent	*per cent*
Preparation of TLM		
Yes	89.0	92.0
No	11.0	8.0
Technique to active participation		
Yes	81.5	76.0
No	18.5	14.0

4.2.24 Plan for Group Work of the Children

The data portrayed that (89.0 per cent) of the teachers stated that they planned for group work for the children. Majority of the parents/teacher stated (69.0 per cent) that teachers creating plan for group work and rest (31.0 per cent)did not participated in it.

Table 4.96: Plan for Group Work

Plan for Group Work	*Respondents*	
	Teacher (n=50)	*Parent/Student (n=50)*
	per cent	*per cent*
Yes	89.0	69.0
No	11.0	31.0

4. 2.25 Preparation for Action Plan for Teaching and Learning

The data portrayed that a majority of the teachers (78.0 per cent) stated that they prepared for Action Plan for Teaching and learning and rest of the respondents (22.0 per cent) were negated. On the other hand (54 per cent) parents/students stated that teacher prepared for Action Plan for Teaching and learning.

Table 4.97: Plan for Teaching and Learning

Plan Action Plan and TLM	*Respondents*	
	Teacher (n=50)	*Parent/Student (n=50)*
	per cent	*per cent*
Yes	78.0	54.0
No	22.0	46.0

4.2.26 Learn and Follow Teaching and Learning Material

The data revealed that 92.0 per cent of the teachers stated that they learned and followed teaching and learning material. Majority of the parents/students (82.0 per cent) stated that teacher followed teaching learning material and rests (18.0 per cent) of the respondents were negated.

Table 4.98: Learn and Follow Teaching and Learning

Learn and Follow TLM	*Respondents*	
	Teacher (n=50)	*Parent/Student (n=50)*
	per cent	*per cent*
Yes	92.0	82.0
No	8.0	18.0

4. 2.27 Collect New Information and Portfolio for Individual Children

The data revealed that a majority of the teachers stated that they give information by books and followed portfolio of children (78.0 per cent). Whereas (65.0 per cent) parents/students accepted that the teachers make portfolio for individual children and (35.0 per cent) parents/students did not agree with this. (90 per cent) students/parents opined that they gather new information and technique from the teachers and rest of them negated.

Table 4.99: Information and Portfolio

Variable	*Respondents*	
	Teacher (n=50)	*Parent/Student (n=50)*
	per cent	*per cent*
Information and Portfolio		
Books	89.0	51.0
Book Corner	11.0	49.0
Portfolio for Individual Children		
Yes	78.0	65.0
No	22.0	35.0

4.2.28 General Information of Children

The data portrayed that (46.0 per cent) of the teachers stated that they have taken name and (33.0 per cent) of the teachers have taken name, weight, height, blood group, other physical and family background as part of the general information of the children. (14.0 per cent) parents/students reveals that teachers take their name only as an information of children, (80.0 per cent) take name, weight and height, (2.0 per cent) take other physical health and rest (4.0 per cent) take name, weight, height, blood group, other physical and family background also.

Table 4.100: General Information of Children

Information of Children	*Respondents*	
	Teacher (n=50)	*Parent/ Student (n=50)*
	per cent	*per cent*
Name	46.0	14.0
Name, Weight and Height	7.0	80.0
Other Physical Health	14.0	2.0
Name, Weight, Height, Blood Group, Other Physical and Family Background	33.0	4.0

4.2.29 Identification of Interests and Measuring Improvement

The data revealed that (96.0 per cent) of the teachers stated that they identified the problems. (92.0 per cent) of the teachers stated that they measured the improvement of the students. When the date gathered from parents/students (74.0 per cent) respondents opined that teachers found areas of interest of the children and (80 per cent) of the parents/students stated that they measured the improvement of the students.

Table 4.101: Interests and Improvement

Variable	*Respondents*	
	Teacher (n=50)	*Parent/ Student (n=50)*
	per cent	*per cent*
Identification of Interests		
Yes	96.0	74.0
No	4.0	26.0
Measuring Improvement		
Yes	92.0	80.0
No	8.0	20.0

4.2.30 Collection of Information Regarding Special Work

The data revealed that (89.0 per cent) of the teachers stated that they collected information regarding the special work. (59.0 per cent) parents/students stated that teachers collected information about the special work of children.

Table 4.102: Collection of Information Regarding Special Work

Variable	*Respondents*	
	Teacher (n=50)	*Parent/Student (n=50)*
	per cent	*per cent*
Yes	89.0	59.0
No	11.0	41.0

4.2.31 Assessment of Past and Present Status

The data revealed that (81.5 per cent) of the teachers stated that they assessed the past and present status of the student. Majority of the parents/students (59.0 per cent) reveal that teachers collect information about the assessment of past and present status of students.

Table 4.103: Assessment of Past and Present Status

Variable	*Respondents*	
	Teacher (n=50)	*Parent/Student (n=50)*
	per cent	*per cent*
Yes	81.5	59.0
No	18.5	41.0

4.2.32 Solving the Problems and Contact Parent Teacher Association

The data portrayed that 89.0 per cent of the teachers stated that they solved problems of the children. A majority of the teachers (92.0 per cent) stated that they contacted the parents and parent teacher association. Whereas (65.0 per cent) Parents/ students stated that teachers identify the problems of learning and give solution to children. It's clear from the data that only (80.0 per cent) teachers contact with parents and rest (20.0 per cent) avoid communication.

Table 4.104: Contact Parent Teacher Association

Variable	Respondents	
	Teacher (n=50)	Parent/Student (n=50)
	per cent	per cent
Solve the Problem		
Yes	89.0	65.0
No	11.0	35.0
Contact Parent Teacher Association		
Yes	92.0	80.0
No	8.0	20.0

4.2.33 Discuss with Parents and PTAs

The data portrayed that (55.0 per cent) of the teachers stated that they discussed about the quality education and (27.0 per cent) of the teachers stated that they discussed quality of education, educational survey, school activity/programme, health awareness with the parents and parent teacher association. Majority of the parents/students (40 per cent) stated that they discussed with teachers regarding school activity/programme followed by only (35 per cent) parents/students discussed regarding quality of education.

Table 4.105: Discussion

Discussion	Respondents	
	Teacher (n=50)	Parent/Student (n=50)
	per cent	per cent
Quality of Education	55.0	35.0
Educational Survey	7.0	5.0
School Activity/Programme	11.0	40.0
Quality of Education, Educational Survey, School Activity/Programme, Health Awareness	27.0	20.0

4.2.34 Discussion about Dropout, Un-enrolled and Regular Attendance

The data accentuated that (85.0 per cent) teachers discussed about dropouts and un-enrolled children. (93.0 per cent) of the teachers discussed about the regular attendance. A majority of the teachers (48.0 per cent) discussed about school plan, and unit plan (33.5 per cent) about TLM and its uses (11.0 per cent) were in that order. On the other hand (74.0 per cent) parents/ students stated that teachers discuss about dropouts and un-enrolled children and rest (26.0 per cent) did not discuss this. (32.0 per cent) parents/students stated that teachers discuss on school plan, (13.0 per cent) discuss on unit plan (15.0 per cent) discuss on TLM and its uses and (40.0 per cent) discuss on school plan and unit plan. (82.0 per cent) parents/students opined that teachers discuss about particular activity in the class and rest (18.0 per cent) avoided discussion.

Table 4.106: Discussion

	Respondents	
Variable	*Teacher (n=50)*	*Parent/Student (n=50)*
	per cent	*per cent*
Dropout and un-enrolled		
Yes	85.0	74.0
No	14.0	26.0
Regular attendance		
Yes	93.0	82.0
No	7.0	18.0
Discuss regarding		
School Plan	48.0	32.0
Unit Plan	7.5	13.0
TLM and its uses	11.0	15.0
School plan and Unit Plan	33.5	40.0

4.2.35 Discussion on Practical Activity, Writing and Reading Material

The data accentuated that (86.0 per cent) of the teachers discussed about the practical and rest of the teachers (14.0 per cent) negated. As regarding the writing and reading material (96.0 per cent) of the teachers followed. Whereas (98.0 per cent) parents/students stated that teachers discuss about writing and reading material with children in the class.

Table 4.107: Discussion

Variable	Respondents	
	Teacher (n=50)	*Parent/Student (n=50)*
	per cent	*per cent*
Practical Activity		
Yes	86.0	80.0
No	14.0	20.0
Writing and Reading Material		
Yes	96.0	98.0
No	4.0	2.0

4.2.36 Evaluation for the Children and Student Profile Co-conscious Activity

The data revealed that a majority of the teachers (88.0 per cent) stated that they discussed about evaluation for the children and student profile. (90.0 per cent) of the teachers stated that they discussed about the coconscious activity. On the other hand (90.0 per cent) parents/students opined that teachers discussed the evaluation of student and children and rest (10.0 per cent) avoided this.

Table 4.108: Evaluation and Co-Conscious Activity

Variable	Respondents	
	Teacher (n=50)	*Parent/Student (n=50)*
	per cent	*per cent*
Evaluation		
Yes	88.0	90.0
No	12.0	10.0
Co-conscious Activity		
Yes	90.0	90.0
No	10.0	10.0

4.2.37 Participation of Parent Teacher Association and Time Table

The data portrayed that a majority of the teachers (93.0 per cent) discussed about the participation of parent teacher association. (95.0 per cent) of the teachers stated that they discussed about the time table of the school. (75.0 per cent) Parents/students agreed that teachers discussed on Participation and rest (25.0 per cent) of them did not participate. (80.0 per cent) Parents/students stated that teachers discussed on time table in the class and rest of them(20.0 per cent) negated.

Table 4.109: Parent Teacher Association and Time Table

Variable	Respondents	
	Teacher (n=50)	Parent/Student (n=50)
	per cent	per cent
Parent Teacher Association		
Yes	93.0	75.0
No	7.0	25.0
Time Table		
Yes	95.0	80.0
No	5.0	20.0

4.2.38 Expectation of Every Children and Discuss on Book

The data revealed that a majority of the teachers (89.0 per cent) opined that they discussed about the expectations of every child. (93.0 per cent) of the teachers stated that they discussed about the books. Whereas (75.0 per cent) Parents/students opined that teachers discuss on expectation of every child and (25.0 per cent) did not discussed. (60.0 per cent) Parents/ students revealed that teachers discussed about the book with children

Table 4.110: Expectation of Every Children

Variable	Respondents	
	Teacher (n=50)	Parent/Student (n=50)
	per cent	per cent
Yes	89.0	75.0
No	11.0	25.0
Discuss on Books		
Yes	93.0	60.0
No	7.0	40.0

4.2.39 Discussion on Regarding the Good Work and Problem Solving

The data accentuated that (96.0 per cent) of the teachers discussed about the good work. A majority of the teachers stated (95.0 per cent) that they solved the problems regarding the teaching and learning method. (65.0 per cent) parents/students accepted that teachers discuss regarding good work and rest (35.0 per cent) did not discussed. Majority of the parents/ students (70.0 per cent) revealed that teachers actively participated in solving the problem regarding the teaching and learning method.

Table 4.111: Good Work and Problem Solving

Variable	*Respondents*	
	Teacher (n=50)	*Parent/Student (n=50)*
	per cent	*per cent*
Good Work		
Yes	96.0	65.0
No	4.0	35.0
Problem Solving		
Yes	95.0	70.0
No	5.0	30.0

4.2.40 Professional Experience of Teachers and Guideline of RTE

The study revealed that (85.5 per cent) of the teachers stated that they have professional experiences. A majority of the teachers (85.0 per cent) stated that they followed the all guideline of Right to Education Act. (70.0 per cent) parents/students stated that teachers have professional experience of teaching and rest (30.0 per cent) were not experienced. (69.0 per cent) parents opined that teaching followed the guidelines of teaching.

4.2.41 Teaching and Ability of Every Children

The data revealed that a majority of the teachers (92.0 per cent) opined that they have given special essential help regarding teaching. (75.0 per cent) of the teachers stated that they evaluated the ability of every child. (78.0 per cent) parents/ students revealed that teachers evaluated the ability of every child of the class.

Table 4.112: Professional Experience and Guideline of RTE

Variable	Respondents	
	Teacher (n=50)	Parent/Student (n=50)
	per cent	per cent
Professional Experience		
Yes	85.5	70.0
No	14.5	30.0
Guidelines of RTE		
Yes	85.0	69.0
No	15.0	31.0

Table 4.113: Teaching and Ability of Every Children

Variable	Respondents	
	Teacher (n=50)	Parent/Student (n=50)
	per cent	per cent
Teaching		
Yes	92.0	78.0
No	8.0	22.0
Ability of Every Children		
Yes	75.0	55.0
No	25.0	45.0

4.2.42 Identify the Problems and give Solutions and Special Help

The data accentuated that (89.0 per cent) of the teachers stated that they identified the problems of the children and give solutions. A majority of the teachers (92.0 per cent) stated that they give special help to every children as per their demand. On the other hand, (69.0 per cent) parents/students stated that teachers identify the problems of learning and give solution to children. (59.0 per cent) parents/students opined that teachers give special help to children for learning and rest (41.0 per cent) respondents avoid to give the special help to children.

Table 4.114: Identify the Problems and Special Help

Variable	Respondents	
	Teacher (n=50)	Parent/Student (n=50)
	per cent	per cent
Identify the Problems		
Yes	89.0	69.0
No	11.0	31.0
Special Help		
Yes	92.0	59.0
No	8.0	41.0

4.2.43 Format for Evaluation, Survey for the Utilisation and Implemented Good Things

The data revealed that (88.0 per cent) of the teachers stated that they prepared format for evaluation of entire activity and material development. A majority of the teachers (82.0 per cent) stated that they conducted survey for the utilisation of material and its importance. (89.0 per cent) of the teachers stated that they implemented good things which were evolved by other school. Majority of the parents/students (60.0 per cent) reveal that teachers always implemented good things for the progress of children while (40.0 per cent) do not implement any thing. (71.0 per cent) teachers used format for evaluation and (80.0 per cent) conducted survey for the utilisation of material and its importance

Table 4.115: Format for Evaluation, Survey for the Utilisation and Implemented Good Things

Variable	Respondents	
	Teacher (n=50)	Parent/Student (n=50)
	per cent	per cent
Format for Evaluation		
Yes	88.0	71.0
No	12.0	29.0
Survey for the Utilisation		
Yes	82.0	80.0
No	18.0	20.0
Implemented Good Things		
Yes	89.0	60.0
No	11.0	40.0

Table 4.116: Teachers, Parents and Students Opinion on RTE Impact

Statement	*Respondents (n=100)*				
	per cent				
	Strongly Agree	*Agree*	*Undecided*	*Disagree*	*Strongly Disagree*
RTE can reduce the illiteracy among disadvantaged groups	30.00	55.00	2.00	8.00	5.00
RTE can promote the social change	36.00	42.00	5.00	14.00	3.00
Through RTE we can establish empowered childhood	29.00	49.00	5.00	10.00	7.00
RTE promotes sustainable development	25.00	62.00	10.00	2.00	1.00
Child labour can be addressed through RTE	23.00	68.00	3.00	3.00	3.00
Girl child education can be increased through RTE	60.00	20.00	3.00	9.00	8.00
Quality education can achieve through RTE	39.00	43.00	2.00	5.00	11.00
RTE can build knowledge based societies	29.00	62.00	1.00	6.00	2.00
RTE Promotes inclusive growth in near future	30.00	58.00	5.00	3.00	4.00
Systems and structures in the society can be changed by RTE	21.00	63.00	5.00	4.00	7.00

Table 4.117: Implementation Status

S. No.	Name of the Activity	Approved Targets as per RTE act. up to the time of study (Hours/ Minuites/per day/per week)	Progress against the targets shown in column.3 at the time of study	
			Total achievement	per cent of actual achievement (4/3×100)
1.	Prayer and Attendance	20 minutes/per day	18 minutes/per day	89.0 per cent
2.	Teaching	4 hours 35 minutes/ per day	4 hours 20 minutes/ per day	97.0 per cent
3.	Mid day meal	40 minutes/per day	39 minutes/ per day	97.0 per cent
4.	Preparation of action plan for teaching and evaluation	40 minutes/per day	35 minutes/per day	88.5 per cent
5.	Student Portfolio	30 minutes/per day (4 days)	37 minutes/per day (4 days)	92.5 per cent
6.	Discussion with parents and community	1 hour/per week	35 hours/ per week	88.5 per cent
7.	Staff meeting	30 minutes/per week	37 minutes/ per week	93.0 per cent
8.	Special need to help the Children	40 minutes/per day	34 minutes/ per day	86.0 per cent
9.	Tools/format fixed for evaluation	30 minutes/per week	37 minutes/ per week	93.0 per cent
Total Time		**45 ½ hours/week**		

4.2.43.1 Bastar District Middle Schools Responses on Statements regarding RTE Impact

The data accentuated that the RTE can reduce the illiteracy among disadvantaged groups. A majority of the respondents agreed that RTE can promote the social change. A significant number of the respondents either strongly agreed or agreed that through RTE we can establish empowered childhood. A majority of the respondents were agreed that RTE can promote sustainable development and will reduce the Child labour. A majority of the respondents strongly agreed that Girl child education can be increased through RTE. A majority of the respondents opined that through RTE, quality education can be achieved, it can build the knowledge based societies; it promotes inclusive growth and will change the systems and structures in the society.

4.2.43.2 Implementation Status of Middle Schools in Bastar District

The following table accentuates that the status of the time how the teachers utilising the time in allocated manner. The following schedule has been designed under the 45 hours schedule. The data revealed that the schools are following the schedule effectively and systematically.

4.2.43.3 Major Findings from Middle Schools in Bastar District

- (81.5 per cent) of the male teachers have participated in the study and the rest of the teachers (18.5 per cent) were female. (41.5 per cent) of the teachers were in the age group of 32-38 and (22.0 per cent) of the teachers were in more than 52 age group. (37.0 per cent) of the teachers belonged to Schedule Tribe and (33.5 per cent) of the respondents belonged to OBC. General (18.5 per cent) and SC (11.0 per cent) were in that order. (11.0 per cent) parents/students are Schedule Caste, (37.0 per cent) schedule Tribe while (33.5 per cent) were OBC and (18.5 per cent) were general caste. (40.0 per cent) parents/students were in the age group of 32-38. (8.0 per cent) of the parents/students were in the age group of 27-31 while (10.0 per cent) of the parents/students were in the age group of 37-51 and rest (22.0 per cent) of the parents/student were more than 52 years age group.

- (78.0 per cent) of the teachers were staying outside the village and the rest of the teachers (22.0 per cent) were staying in the same village where the school is located.
- (48.0 per cent) teachers were staying less than 5 kms away and (37.0 per cent) of the teachers were staying 6-10 km away from the school. As regards the distance form Block Resource Centre more than one fourths (26.0 per cent) stated that 10-20 and (22.5 per cent) of the respondents stated 31-40 km. away and (22.0 per cent) of the respondents stated that they stated less than 10 km. The data indicate that the distance from BRC is less then 10km. (28.0 per cent), (22.0 per cent) school 10-20 km. away, (14.0 per cent) school away in between 21-30 km., (15.0 per cent) school 31-40 km. away, (11.0 per cent) school were situated in between 41-50 km. and rest (10.0 per cent) school were away more than 51 km.
- (40.5 per cent) schools have electricity facility and rest of the schools (59.5 per cent) did not have such facility. 85.5 per cent of the teachers stated that 3 class rooms in their school. (89.0 per cent) stated that they have toilet facility in the school. (45.0 per cent) of the schools were connected with roads. (90.0 per cent) of the schools have drinking water facility. (90.0 per cent) of the schools have drinking water facility. Majority of the teachers (65.0 per cent) reveals that they have no toilet and drinking water facility in their school. (52.0 per cent) respondent stated that schools are connected with road and rest of the (48.0 per cent) schools are connected. On the other hand (65.0 per cent) parents/students respondant accepted that there were no electricity facility in the school and rest (35.0 per cent) parents/student accepted that electricity was in school. In middle school level the whole classes were going in three class room (90.0 per cent), (3.0 per cent) in two class rooms and rest (7.0 per cent) were in 5/6 class room.
- (36.5 per cent) of the respondents stated that there were two teachers, (29.0 per cent) of the respondents opined that one teacher was in school and (25.5 per cent) of the respondents opined that three permanent teachers were in their schools. The data reveals that (42.0 per cent) middle school has only two permanent teachers , (20.0 per cent) schools are going through three permanent

teachers and rest of the schools have one (30.0 per cent), four (3.0 per cent) and five (2.0 per cent) permanent teacher. As regarding the temporary teachers 81.5 per cent of the respondents stated that they don't have such teachers.

- (70.5 per cent) teachers stated that they took 20 minutes to complete prayer and 18.5 per cent of the teachers opined that they took 30 minutes for the same. As regards the teaching hours (90.0 per cent) of the teachers stated that they taught more than 4.35 hours per day. As per opinion of parents/students (78 per cent) stated that they took 30 minutes to complete prayer and 93 per cent stated that they taught more than 4.35 hours per day.
- (90.0 per cent) of the teachers opined that they have taken 40 minutes for midday meal. The data of parents/ students, indicate that (3.0 per cent) teachers spend 40 minutes to help the children for their special need in study, (7.0 per cent) teachers take less than 40 minutes and (90.0 per cent) take more than 40 minutes time.
- (85.0 per cent) of the teachers express their views that they had taken 40 minutes per day for preparation of action plans. Parents/students data indicate that (78.0 per cent) teachers take up to one hr per day for preparation of action plan, and rest have taken less than one hrs. per day.
- (81.5 per cent) of the teachers stated that they have taken 30 minutes for student portfolio and (11.0 per cent) of the teachers have taken more than 30 minutes for the same. Parents/students data reveals that the (20.0 per cent) teachers take 30 minutes time to make student portfolio and (4.0 per cent) teachers take less than 30 minutes time and rest (76.0 per cent) take more than 30 minutes time for preparation.
- (81.5 per cent) teachers stated that they have taken one hour for discussion with parents and (11.5 per cent) of the teachers have taken less than one hour for the same. As per opinion of parents/students, generally (10.0 per cent) teachers take one hour for discussion with parents, (18.0 per cent) take less than one hour and only (72.0 per cent) take more than one hour.

- (86.0 per cent) of the teachers stated that they spared 30 minutes for staff meeting per week. The data of parents/students revealed that (80.0 per cent) teachers take more than 30 minutes, (15.0 per cent) take 30 minutes and (5.0 per cent) teacher take less than 30 minutes time for staff meeting.
- (75.0 per cent) of the teachers opined that they allocated 40 minutes for children those who are in special need and (14.0 per cent) of the teachers stated that they spared less than forty minutes per day. The data of parents/ students indicate that (11.0 per cent) teacher spend 40 minutes to help the children for their special need in study, (20.0 per cent) teachers take less than 40 minutes and (69.0 per cent) take more than 40 minutes time.
- (86.0 per cent) of the teachers stated that they allocated 30 minutes per week for tools and formats evaluation. Majority of the parents/students stated that (87.0 per cent) take more than 30 minutes time for tools/format fixed for evaluation, (10.0 per cent) take 30 minutes and rest were take less than 30 minutes.
- (86.0 per cent) of the teachers stated that they were participated during prayer and rest of the teachers was negated. As regarding the pattern (48.5 per cent) of the teachers stated that they used only prayer and (33.5 per cent) of the teachers stated that they used group song, national song, national anthem and prayer during the prayer. As regarding the motivational activities (37.0 per cent) of the teachers used *Mahapurus* Thought, (33.0 per cent) of the teachers used lecture and (30.0 per cent) of the teachers used both. All the teachers stated that they have taken attendance after assembly. (90.0 per cent) parents/ students stated that all are present at the time of prayer and rest (10.0 per cent) were absent at that time. The data reveals that majority of the respondents stated (80.0 per cent) that they do national song, Anthem and prayer, (10.0 per cent) accentuated that they do group song, national song, anthem and prayer and rest did only national song or anthem or both national song and anthem.
- All the respondents (teachers, parents, students) stated

that teachers adopted cognitive teaching for class VI-VIII in the class room.

- (96.0 per cent) of the teachers opined that they adopted whole class approach and (95.0 per cent) of the teachers adopted group based activity. Parents/students indicate that (86.0 per cent) teacher adopted whole class approach. (70.0 per cent) parents/students opined that teachers adopted group based activities.
- Majority of the teachers stated that they evaluated the oral and (37.5 per cent) of the teachers stated that they evaluated the oral and writing. As regarding the co-cognitive teaching (78.0 per cent) of the teachers they used and (22.0 per cent) of the teachers they did not use it. Parents/students stated that (65.0 per cent) teachers did co-cognitive teaching in primary schools. The study revealed that (25.0 per cent) teachers addressed oral and (64.0 per cent) written evaluation while (11.0 per cent) had taken written and oral examination.
- (52.0 per cent) of the teachers stated that they conducted drawing and (20.0 per cent) of the teachers conducted drawing, music, dance, literary and cultural activities for the children. The parents and students stated that (35.0 per cent) school has organised drawing, music, dance, art and craft literary and cultural activities, (12.0 per cent) school have given chance for music and rest have organised other kinds of art activities.
- (63.0 per cent) of the teachers stated that they had given project work and (22.0 per cent) of the teachers stated that they displayed creative work. Majority of the parents/students stated that (20.0 per cent) teachers displayed creative work, (70.0 per cent) given project work and displayed creative work both and (10.0 per cent) gave only project work.
- (37.0 per cent) of the teachers stated that they conducted sports and games and (33.0 per cent) of the respondants stated they conducted yoga, sports and games, nutritional food, knowledge about diseases. Yoga (15.0 per cent), yoga, sports and games (7.5 per cent) and cleanliness (7.5 per cent) in that order. Majority of the parents/students (52.0 per cent) stated that teachers used addressing yoga, sports and games, nutritional food,

Knowledge about diseases, (15.0 per cent) used sports and games, (15.0 per cent) used yoga, (5.0 per cent) used yoga sports and games and rest used cleanliness.

- (34.0 per cent) of the teachers stated that they adopted attitude, life skill, awareness towards environment and value system and (26.0 per cent) of the teachers opined that attitude, life skill, and awareness towards environment. (22.0 per cent) of the teachers stated that life skill and (18.0 per cent) of the teachers stated attitude. (21.0 per cent) parents/students stated that they adopted teacher addressing knowledge about attitude, life skill, awareness towards environments, (10.0 per cent) respondents accepted only attitude, (9.0 per cent)accepted learning life skill and rest (60.0 per cent) accepted attitude, life skill, awareness towards environment and value system.
- (60.0 per cent) of the teachers stated they have taken 31-40 minutes per day for midday meal distribution. Majority of the parents/students stated that (89.0 per cent) distributed mid day meal in between 31-40 minutes, (6.0 per cent) of the parents/students had taken 21-30 minutes, (5.0 per cent) parents/students had taken 10-21 minutes for the same.
- (81.5 per cent) of the teachers stated that they prepared action plans and rest of the teachers (18.5 per cent) negated. A majority of the teachers (89 per cent) stated that they prepared activities for class room teaching. Majority of parents/students stated that (90.0 per cent) teacher prepared activities plan for school/children.
- (89.0 per cent) of the teachers stated that they prepared teaching learning material. (81.5 per cent) of the teachers adopted techniques to activate participation. (92.0 per cent) parents/students revealed that teachers prepare TLM for teaching students while (8.0 per cent) negated. (76.0 per cent) parents/students opined that the teacher applied technique for teaching and rest of them negated.
- (89.0 per cent) of the teachers stated that they planned for group work for the children. Majority of the parents/student stated (69.0 per cent) that teachers created plan for group work and rest (31.0 per cent) did not participate in it.

- (78.0 per cent) teachers stated that they prepared for Action Plan for teaching and learning and rest of the respondents (22.0 per cent) negated. On the other hand (54 per cent) parents/students stated that teacher prepared for Action Plan for teaching and learning.
- (92.0 per cent) of the teachers stated that they had learned and followed teaching and learning material. Majority of the parents/students (82.0 per cent) stated that teachers followed teaching learning material and rest (18.0 per cent) of the respondants negated.
- (78.0 per cent) teachers stated that they had given information by books and followed portfolio of children. Whereas (65.0 per cent) parents/students accepted that the teachers make portfolio for individual children and (35.0 per cent) parents/students did not agree with this. (90 per cent) students/parents opined that they gathered new information and technique from the teachers and rest of them negated.
- (46.0 per cent) of the teachers stated that they have taken name and (33.0 per cent) of the teachers have taken name, weight, height, blood group, other physical and family background as part of the general information of the children. (14.0 per cent) parents/students reveals that teachers take their name only as a information of children, (80.0 per cent) take name, weight and height, (2.0 per cent) take other physical health and rest (4.0 per cent) take name, weight, height, blood group, other physical and family background also.
- (96.0 per cent) of the teachers stated that they identified the problems. (92.0 per cent) of the teachers stated that they measured the improvement of the students. When the date gathered from parents/students (74.0 per cent) respondents opined that teachers found areas of interests of the children and (80 per cent) of the parents/students stated that they measured the improvement of the students.
- (89.0 per cent) of the teachers stated that they collected information regarding the special work. (59.0 per cent) parents/students stated that teachers collect information about children.

- (81.5 per cent) of the teachers stated that they assessed the past and present status of the student. Majority of the parents/students (59.0 per cent) reveal that teachers collect information about the assessment of past and present status of students.
- (89.0 per cent) of the teachers stated that they solved problems of the children. A majority of the teachers (92.0 per cent) stated that they contacted the parents and parent teacher association. Whereas (65.0 per cent) Parents/students stated that teachers identify the problems of learning and give solution to children. It's clear from the data that only (80.0 per cent) teachers contact with parents and rest (20.0 per cent) avoid communication.
- (55.0 per cent) of the teachers stated that they discussed about the quality education and (27.0 per cent) of the teachers stated quality of education, educational survey, school activity/programme and health awareness with the parents and parent teacher association. Majority of the parents/students (40 per cent) stated that they discuss with teachers regarding school activity/ programme followed by only (35 per cent) parents/ students discuss regarding quality of education.
- (85.0 per cent) teachers opined that they discussed about dropouts and un-enrolled children. (93.0 per cent) of the teachers discussed about the regular attendance. A majority of the teachers (48.0 per cent) discussed about school plan, school plan and unit plan (33.5 per cent) and TLM and its uses (11.0 per cent) were in that order. On the other hand (74.0 per cent) parents/students stated that teachers discussed about dropouts and un-enrolled children and rest (26.0 per cent) have not done this. (32.0 per cent) parents/students stated that teachers discussed on school plan, (13.0 per cent) discuss on unit plan (15.0 per cent) discussed on TLM and its uses and (40.0 per cent) discussed on school plan and unit plan. (82.0 per cent) parents/students opined that teachers discussed about particular activity in the class and rest of them (18.0 per cent) avoided discussion.
- (86.0 per cent) of the teachers revealed that they discussed about the practical and rest of the teachers

(14.0 per cent) negated. As regarding the writing and reading material (96.0 per cent) of the teachers followed. Whereas (98.0 per cent) parents/students stated that teachers discussed about writing and reading material with children in the class.

- (88.0 per cent) teachers stated that they discussed about evaluation for the children and student profile. (90.0 per cent) of the teachers stated that they discussed about the coconscious activity. On the other hand (90.0 per cent) parents/students opined that teachers discussed the evaluation of student and children and rest (10.0 per cent) avoided this.
- (93.0 per cent) teachers revealed that they discussed about the participation of parent teacher association. (95.0 per cent) of the teachers stated that they discussed about the timetable of the school. (75.0 per cent) parents/ students agreed that teachers discussed on participation and rest (25.0 per cent) did not participate. (80.0 per cent) parents/students stated that teachers discussed time table in the class and rest (20.0 per cent) of them negated.
- (89.0 per cent) teachers opined that they discussed about the expectations of every child. (93.0 per cent) of the teachers stated that they discussed about the books. Whereas (75.0 per cent) parents/students opined that teachers discussed on expectation of every child and (25.0 per cent) did not discuss. (60.0 per cent) Parents/ students reveal that teachers discuss about the book with children
- (96.0 per cent) of the teachers stated that they discussed about the good work. A majority of the teachers stated (95.0 per cent) that they solved the problems regarding the teaching and learning method. (65.0 per cent) parents/students accepted that teachers discussed regarding good work and rest (35.0 per cent) did not discuss. Majority of the parents/students (70.0 per cent) reveal that teachers actively participate in solving the problem regarding the teaching and learning method.
- (85.5 per cent) of the teachers stated that they have professional experiences. A majority of the teachers (85.0

per cent) stated that they followed the all guideline of Right to Education Act. (70.0 per cent) parents/students stated that teachers have professional experience of teaching and rest (30.0 per cent) have no experience. (69.0 per cent) parents opined that teachers follow the guidelines of teaching.

- Majority of the teachers (92.0 per cent) opined that they have given special essential help regarding teaching. (75.0 per cent) of the teachers stated that they evaluated the ability of every child. (78.0 per cent) parents/students reveal that teachers evaluate the ability of every child of class.
- (89.0 per cent) of the teachers stated that they identified the problems of the children and give solutions. A majority of the teachers (92.0 per cent) stated that they give special help to every child as per their demand. On the other hand (69.0 per cent) parents/students stated that teachers identify the problems of learning and give solution to children. (59.0 per cent) Parents/students opined that teachers give special help to children for learning and rest (41.0 per cent) respondants avoided all this.
- (88.0 per cent) of the teachers stated that they prepared format for evaluation of entire activity and material development. A majority of the teachers (82.0 per cent) stated that they conducted survey for the utilisation of material and its importance. (89.0 per cent) of the teachers stated that they implemented good things which were evolved by other school. Majority of the parents/ students (60.0 per cent) reveal that teachers always implemented good things for the progress of children while (40.0 per cent) do not implement any things. (71.0 per cent) teachers used format for evaluation and (80.0 per cent) conducted survey for the utilisation of material and its importance.

4.3 Primary Schools in Dhamtari District

4.3.1 Social Characteristics

The data revealed that a majority of the teachers (68.0 per cent) were male participated in the study and the rest of the respondents (32.0 per cent) were female. As regarding the age (52.0 per cent) of the teachers were in the age group of 22-36 and (20.0 per cent) of the teachers were in age group of more than 51 years group. A majority of the teachers (64.0 per cent) belonged to OBC community and (16.0 per cent) of the teachers belonged to Schedule Tribe and (12.0 per cent) of the teachers belonged to SC. The parents/student data reveal that majority of the parents/students (43.0 per cent) were in the age group of 37-46. (14.0 per cent) of the parents/students were in the age group of 22-26 while (16.0 per cent) of the parents/students were in the age group of 27-31 and rest of the parents/ students were in different age groups. The social class of parents/student depicted that (12.0 per cent) are Schedule Caste while (64.0 per cent) were OBC, (8.0 per cent) were General Caste and 16.0 per cent were Schedule Tribe.

Table 4.118: Social Characteristics

Variable	*Respondents*	
	Teacher (n=50)	*Parent/Student (n=50)*
	per cent	*per cent*
Gender		
Male	68.0	70.0
Female	32.0	30.0
Age		
22-26	12.0	14.0
27-31	24.0	16.0
32-36	16.0	12.0
37-41	16.0	18.0
42-46	4.0	25.0
47-51	8.0	10.0
> 51	20.0	5.0
Caste		
SC	12.0	12.0
ST	16.0	16.0
OBC	64.0	64.0
General	8.0	8.0

4.3.2 Educational Qualifications

The data revealed that (44.0 per cent) of the teachers have Post Graduation degree, (24.0 per cent), higher secondary, (24.0 per cent) have PG and B.Ed or D.Ed are in that order. The educational qualification of the parents/students indicates that majority of the respondents (20.0 per cent) have higher secondary, (5 per cent) B.A./B.Sc/B.Com degrees and some persons were only at PG level.

Table 4.119 Educational Qualifications

	Respondents	
Educational	*Teacher (n=50)*	*Parent/Student (n=50)*
	per cent	*per cent*
Higher Secondary	24.0	20.0
Degree	24.0	5.0
PG	44.0	1.0
PG + B.Ed or D.Ed	8.0	0.0

4.3.3 Residence and Distance

The data revealed that (88.0 per cent) of the teachers were staying outside the village and the rest of the teachers (12.0 per cent) were staying in the same village where the school is located. A majority of the teachers (60.0 per cent) were staying less than five kms and (32.0 per cent) of the teachers were staying between 6-10 kms away from the school. As regarding the distance form Block Resource Centre a majority of the teachers (48.0 per cent) stated that their school is between 6-10 kms away and (20.0 per cent) of the teachers opined that it is between 11-15 km away. The data of parents/students indicate that the distance from BRC is less then 5 kms (35.0 per cent), (29.0 per cent) school is 6-10 kms away, (16.0 per cent) school is in between 11-15 kms away, (15.0 per cent) school is16-20 kms away, (5.0 per cent) school is more than 21 kms away.

4.3.4 Facilities in the School

The study revealed that all schools have electricity facility and all the schools were connected with the road. As regards the class rooms 35.0 per cent of the teachers stated that these are three class rooms in their school and (32.0 per cent) of the teachers stated four rooms. A majority of the teachers (76.0 per cent) stated that they have toilet facility in the school and rest of the

Table 4.120: Residence and Distance

Variable	*Respondents*	
	Teacher (n=50)	*Parent/Student (n=50)*
	per cent	*per cent*
Residence		
Same Village	12.0	45.0
Other Village	88.0	55.5
Distance From School		
< 5	60.0	65.0
6-10	32.0	25.0
11-15	8.0	10.0
Distance From BRC		
> 5 KM	16.0	35.0
6-10	48.0	29.0
11-15	20.0	16.0
16-20	4.0	15.0
>21	12.0	5.0

teachers negated. (88.0 per cent) of the schools have drinking water facility. When data gathered from parents/students it's observed that the whole classes are going in single class room (58.0 per cent), (25.0 per cent) in 2 class room and rest (10.0 per cent) are in four class rooms in primary level. Majority of the parents/students (80.0 per cent) reveal that they have toilet facility and (85.0 per cent) said that they have drinking water facility in their school.

4.3.5 Staffing

The data revealed that (36.0 per cent) of the teachers stated that there were no permanent teachers, 64.0 per cent of the teachers opined that there was one permanent teacher in their school. As regarding the temporary teachers (28.0 per cent) of the teachers stated that there were three teachers and four teachers on temporary basis in their school. Five temporary teachers (20.0 per cent) and two temporary teachers (16.0 per cent) were in that order. The data of parents/students revealed that (90.0 per cent) primary school had only one permanent teacher.

Table 4.21: Facilities in the School

Variable	Respondents	
	Teacher (n=50)	Parent/Student (n=50)
	per cent	per cent
No of Class Rooms		
1.	16.0	58.0
2.	35.0	25.0
3.	32.0	10.0
4.	17.0	7.0
Toilet Facility		
Yes	76.0	80.0
No	24.0	20.0
Drinking Water Facility		
Yes	88.0	85.0
No	12.0	15.0

Table 4.122: Staffing

Variable	Respondents	
	Teacher (n=50)	Parent/Student (n=50)
	per cent	per cent
Permanent Teachers		
1.	36.0	10.0
2.	64.0	90.0
Temporary Teachers		
1.	4.0	14.0
2.	16.0	10.0
3.	28.0	16.0
4.	28.0	20.0
5.	20.0	25.0
6.	4.0	15.0

4.3.6 Prayer and Teaching Time

The study revealed that a majority of the teachers (60.0 per cent) stated that they took 20 minutes to complete prayer and (28.0 per cent) of the teachers opined that they took less than 20 minutes for the same. As regards the teaching hours (88.0 per cent) of the teachers stated that they taught more than 4.00 hours per day. The data of parents/students depicted that (10.0 per cent) school have taken less than 20 minutes time for prayer, (15.0) have taken 20 minutes and rest have taken 30 minutes (75.0 per cent) for prayer. The data reveals that (25.0 per cent) of the teacher are taking class up to four hours and (65.0 per cent) are teaching less than 4 hours and rest (10.0 per cent) are teaching above four hrs.

Table 4.123: Prayer and Teaching Time

Prayer and Teaching Time	*Respondents*	
	Teacher (n=50)	*Parent/Student (n=50)*
	per cent	*per cent*
Prayer		
Less than 20 Minutes	28.0	10.0
20 Minutes	60.0	15.0
30 Minutes	12.0	75.0
Teaching Hours		
Less Than four Hours	4.0	65.0
4 Hours	88.0	25.0
Above four Hrs	8.0	10.0

4.3.7 Mid-day Meal

The study revealed that (68.0 per cent) of the teachers opined that they have taken 40 minutes for midday meal per day and (28.0 per cent) have taken more than 40 minutes. The data accentuated from parents/students that time for midday meal is more than 40 minutes (87.0 per cent) and rest (13.0 per cent) said that it was 40 minutes.

Table 4.124: Mid-day Meal

Midday Meal	*Respondents*	
	Teacher (n=50)	*Parent/Student (n=50)*
	per cent	*per cent*
< 40 Minutes	4.0	3.0
40 Minutes	68.0	10.0
> 40 Minutes	28.0	87.0

4.3.8 Preparation of Action Plans

The data accentuated that (76.0 per cent) of the teachers had taken less than one hour per day for preparation of action plans. The data of parents/students indicate that (68.0 per cent) teacher took more than one hr per day for preparation of action plan and rest had taken less than one hours.

Table 4.125: Preparation of Action Plans

Preparation of Action Plan	*Respondents*	
	Teacher (n=50)	*Parent/Student (n=50)*
	per cent	*per cent*
< 1 hour per Day	76.0	20.0
1 hour per Day	12.0	12.0
> 1 hour per Day	12.0	68.0

4.3.9 Student Portfolio

The data portrayed that (68.0 per cent) of the teachers stated that they have taken 30 minutes for preparation of student portfolio and (16.0 per cent) of the teachers have taken more than 30 minutes and less than 30 minutes for the same. Data of parents/students reveals that the teachers (12.0 per cent) take 30 minutes time to make student portfolio and (80.0 per cent) teachers take less than 30 minutes time and rest (8.0 per cent) take more than 30 minutes time for preparation.

Table 4.126: Student Portfolio

Student Portfolio	*Respondents*	
	Teacher (n=50)	*Parent/Student (n=50)*
	per cent	*per cent*
< 30 Minutes	16.0	80.0
30 Minutes	68.0	12.0
> 30 Minutes	16.0	8.0

4.3.10 Discussion with Parent

The data portrayed that a majority of the teachers (84.0 per cent) have taken less than one hour for discussion with parents. Generally (8.0 per cent) teachers take one hour for discussion with parents. On the other hand (89.0 per cent) parents/students stated that teachers take less than one hour for discussion with parents and only (2.0 per cent) take more than one hour.

Table 4.127: Discussion with Parent

Discussion	*Respondents*	
	Teacher (n=50)	*Parent/Student (n=50)*
	per cent	*per cent*
< 1 hour	8.0	89.0
1 hour	84.0	8.0
> 1 hour	8.0	2.0

4.3.11 Staff Meeting

The data revealed that (72.0 per cent) of the teachers stated that they spared 30 minutes for staff meeting per week. The data of parents/students reveals that (79.0 per cent) teachers take more than 30 minutes, (19.0 per cent) take 30 minutes and (2.0 per cent) teacher take less than 30 minutes time for staff meeting.

Table 4.128: Staff Meeting

Discussion	Respondents	
	Teacher (n=50)	*Parent/Student (n=50)*
	per cent	*per cent*
< 30 Minutes	12.0	2.0
30 Minutes	72.0	19.0
> 30 Minutes	16.0	79.0

4.3.12 Special Need to Help the Children

The data accentuated that (44.0 per cent) of the teachers opined that they allocated less than 40 minutes for children those who are in special need and (32.0 per cent) of the teachers stated that they spared forty minutes per day. Parents/students data indicate that (12.0 per cent) teacher spend 40 minutes to help the children for their special need in study (68.0 per cent) teachers take less than 40 minutes and (20.0 per cent) take more than 40 minutes time.

Table 4.129: Special Help to Needy Children

Discussion	Respondents	
	Teacher (n=50)	*Parent/Student (n=50)*
	per cent	*per cent*
< 40 Minutes	44.0	68.0
40 Minutes	32.0	12.0
> More Than 40 Minutes	24.0	20.0

4.3.13 Tools/Format Fixed for Evaluation

The study revealed that the (84.0 per cent) of the teachers stated that they allocated 30 minutes per week for tools and formats evaluation. Whereas 67 per cent parents/students stated teachers allocated less than 30 minutes per week for tools and formats evaluation.

Table 4.130: Tools/Format Fixed for Evaluation

Evaluation	*Respondents*	
	Teacher (n=50)	*Parent/ Student (n=50)*
	per cent	*per cent*
< 30 Minutes	4.0	67.0
30 Minutes	84.0	13.0
> 30 Minutes	12.0	20.0

4.3.14 Attendance of Teachers and Students during Prayer

The data revealed that all the teachers stated that they were presented in during the prayer. As regarding the pattern (76.0 per cent) of the teachers stated that they used national anthem and national song. As regarding the motivational activities (96.0 per cent) of the teachers used lecture method. All the teachers stated that they have taken attendance after the assembly. The similar trend it also observed in case of parents/students opinion.

Table 4.131: Teacher and Students during Prayers

Variable	*Respondents*	
	Teacher (n=50)	*Parent/ Student (n=50)*
	per cent	*per cent*
Pattern		
National Song	12.0	8.0
National Anthem	12.0	10.0
National Anthem and National Song	76.0	82.0
Motivational Activities		
Lecture	96.0	98.0
Mahapurus Thought	4.0	2.0

4.3.15 Teaching

All the teachers/parents/students stated that they used cognitive teaching for class one to five.

4.3.16 Whole Class Approach and Group Based Activity

The data revealed that (96.0 per cent) of the teachers stated that they adopted whole class approach and (52.0 per cent) of the teachers adopted group based activity and rest of the teachers (48.0 per cent) negated. Parents/students stated that (55 per cent) teachers followed the whole class approach and (30 per cent) teachers adopted group based activity.

Table 4.132: Whole Class Approach and Group Activity

Variable	*Respondents*	
	Teacher (n=50)	*Parent/Student (n=50)*
	per cent	*per cent*
Whole Class Approach		
Yes	96.0	55.0
No	4.0	45.0
Group Based Activity		
Yes	52.0	30.0
No	48.0	70.0

4.3.17 Mode of Continuous Evaluation and Co-cognitive Teaching

The data portrayed that (72.0 per cent) of the teachers and (20 per cent) of the parents/students stated that teachers evaluated oral and writing capacity of the student. The data revealed that a majority of the teachers (92.0 per cent) and parents/students (65 per cent) stated that teachers used Co-cognitive teaching for class first to fifth.

Table 4.133: Mode of Continuous Evaluation

Evaluation	*Respondents*	
	Teacher (n=50)	*Parent/Student (n=50)*
	per cent	*per cent*
Oral	16.0	74.0
Written	12.0	6.0
Oral and Written	72.0	20.0
Co-cognitive Teaching (Class 1-5)		
Yes	92.0	65.0
No	8.0	35.0

4.3.18 Art

The data reveals that (44.0 per cent) of the teachers and (45 per cent) of the parents/students stated that teachers had given chance for drawing, music, dance, art and craft, literary and cultural activities and (40.0 per cent) of the teachers and 30 per cent of the parents/students opine that students adopted Drawing, Music and Dance. (16.0 per cent) of the teachers and (25 per cent) of parents/students stated that teachers conducted Drawing for the children.

Table 4.134: Art

Variable	*Respondents*	
	Teacher (n=50)	*Parent/Student (n=50)*
	per cent	*per cent*
Drawing	16.0	25.0
Drawing, Music and Dance	40.0	30.0
Drawing, Music, Dance, Art and Craft, Literary and cultural Activities	44.0	45.0

4.3.19 Work Experience

The data accentuated that a majority of the teachers (72.0 per cent) stated that they have given project work and (16.0 per cent) opined that they have displayed creative work and (12.0 per cent) of the parents/students opined they adopted both project and creative for work experience. Majority of parents/students (45 per cent) stated that teachers displayed creative work and (35 per cent) stated that teachers have given project work.

Table 4.135: Work Experience

Work	*Respondents*	
	Teacher (n=50)	*Parent/Student (n=50)*
	per cent	*per cent*
Project Work	72.0	35.0
Display Creative Work	16.0	45.0
Project Work and Display Creative Work	12.0	20.0

4.3.20 Physical Education and Health

The data revealed that (49.0 per cent) of the teachers stated that they conducted sports and games, (16.0 per cent) of the teachers adopted yoga, sports and games. On the other hand, (47 per cent) parents/students stated that teachers look after sports, games and cleanliness and (23 per cent) only stress on sports and games.

Table 4.136: Physical Education and Health

Variable	*Respondents*	
	Teacher (n=50)	*Parent/Student (n=50)*
	per cent	*per cent*
Sports and Games	49.0	23.0
Sports and Games and Cleanliness	9.5	47.0
Yoga, Sports and Games	16.0	10.0
Yoga, Sports and Games, Nutritional Food, Knowledge about Diseases	8.0	3.0
Yoga, Sports and Games and Knowledge about Diseases	9.5	3.0
Yoga, Sports and Games and Knowledge about Diseases	8.0	4.0

4.3.21 Social/Personal Attitudes and Values

The data reveals that a majority of the teachers (36.0 per cent) stated that they adopted attitude, life skill and awareness towards environment and 29.0 per cent of the teachers used attitude, life skill, awareness towards environment and value system, 20.0 per cent of the teachers stated that they measured attitude of the children for improvement of social/personal attitudes and values. On the other hand majority of parents/ students 35 per cent stated that maximum focus on awareness towards environment, 35 per cent on attitude, life skill, awareness towards environment and value system.

Table 4.137: Social/Personal Attitudes and Values

Variable	*Respondents*	
	Teacher (n=50)	*Parent/ Student (n=50)*
	per cent	*per cent*
Attitude	20.0	15.0
Life Skill	10.5	15.0
Awareness Towards Environment	4.5	35.0
Attitude + Life Skill+ Awareness towards Environment	36.0	25.0
Attitude + Life Skill+ Awareness towards Environment + Value System	29.0	10.0

4.3.22 Mid-day Meal Distribution

The data accentuated that (52.0 per cent) of the teachers stated that they could complete mid-day meal distribution between 31-40 minutes. (18.0 per cent) of the teachers had taken 21-30 minutes, for the same. Majority of the parents/students stated that (65 per cent) of the teachers had taken more than 51 minutes.

Table 4.138: Mid-day Meal Distribution

Time	*Respondents*	
	Teacher (n=50)	*Parent/ Student (n=50)*
	per cent	*per cent*
10-21	8.5	5.0
21-30	18.0	4.0
31-40	52.0	11.0
41-50	10.5	15.0
> 51	11.0	65.0

4.3.23 Preparation of Action Plan for Teaching and Evaluation

The data reveals as per teachers that (76.0 per cent) of the teachers stated that they prepared action plan for teaching and evaluation and rest of the teachers (24.0 per cent) negated. Whereas (60 per cent) of parents/students stated that teachers prepared action plan for teaching and evaluation and rest of the teachers (40.0 per cent) negated.

Table 4.139: Preparation of Action Plan

Preparation	*Respondents*	
	Teacher (n=50)	*Parent/Student (n=50)*
	per cent	*per cent*
Yes	76.0	60.0
No	24.0	40.0

4.3.24 Preparation of Activities for Class Room Teaching

The study revealed that (84.0 per cent) of the teachers stated that they prepared activities for class room teaching and rest of the teachers (16.0 per cent) negated. On the other hand parents/students opined that (45 per cent) teachers prepared activities for class room teaching and rest of the teachers (55.0 per cent) negated.

Table 4.140: Preparation of Activities

Preparation of Activities	*Respondents*	
	Teacher (n=50)	*Parent/Student (n=50)*
	per cent	*per cent*
Yes	84.0	45.0
No	16.0	55.0

4.3.25 Preparation of Teaching and Learning Material

The data revealed that a majority of the teachers (92.0 per cent) stated that they prepared teaching and learning material and rest of the teachers (8.0 per cent) negated. As per opinion of parents/teachers only (35.0 per cent) teachers prepared teaching and learning material.

Table 4.141: Preparation of TLM

Preparation of TLM	*Respondents*	
	Teacher (n=50)	*Parent/ Student (n=50)*
	per cent	*per cent*
Yes	92.0	35.0
No	8.0	65.0

4.3.26 Application of Techniques

The data accentuated that (76.0 per cent) of the teachers opined that they applied techniques for teaching and rest of the teachers (24.0 per cent) negated. More or less similar trend it also observed in case of parents/teachers opinion.

Table 4.142: Application of Techniques

Application of Techniques	*Respondents*	
	Teacher (n=50)	*Parent/ Student (n=50)*
	per cent	*per cent*
Yes	76.0	75.0
No	24.0	25.0

4.3.27 Plan for Group Work of the Children

The study revealed that three fourths of the teachers (84.0 per cent) and parents/students (82.0 per cent) stated teachers planned for group work and 16.0 per cent of teachers and (18.0 per cent) of parents/students opined that the teachers negated.

Table 4.143: Plan for Group Work

Plan for group work	*Respondents*	
	Teacher (n=50)	*Parent/ Student (n=50)*
	per cent	*per cent*
Yes	84.0	82.0
No	16.0	18.0

4.3.28 Action Plan for Teaching and Learning

The study reveals that (88.0 per cent) of the teachers and (80.0 per cent) of parents/students stated that teachers were designed action plan for teaching and learning.

Table 4.144: Action Plan for Teaching and Learning

Teaching and Learning	*Respondents*	
	Teacher (n=50)	*Parent/Student (n=50)*
	per cent	*per cent*
Yes	88.0	80.0
No	12.0	20.0

4.3.29 Learned/Followed Teaching Learning Material

The data revealed that a majority of the teachers (76.0 per cent) and (60.0 per cent) of the parents/students stated that teachers were learned and followed teaching and learning material.

Table 4.145: Learned/Followed Teaching Learning Material

Followed Teaching Learning Material	*Respondents*	
	Teacher (n=50)	*Parent/Student (n=50)*
	per cent	*per cent*
Yes	76.0	60.0
No	24.0	40.0

4.3.30 Plan for the Uses of Library

The study revealed that (72.0 per cent) of the teachers opined that they planned useful books for the library and (20.0 per cent) of the teachers used Book Corner for the purpose of children. On the other hand, parents/students stated that (62.0 per cent) of teachers planned useful books for the library (20.0 per cent) of the teachers used book and (20.0 per cent) books and book corners for the purpose of children.

Table 4.146: Plan for the Uses of Library

Plan for use of Library	*Respondents*	
	Teacher (n=50)	*Parent/Student (n=50)*
	per cent	*per cent*
Books	72.0	62.0
Book Corner	20.0	18.0
Books and Book Corner	8.0	20.0

4.3.31 New Information and New Technique for the Class Room

The data accentuated that (96.0 per cent) of the teachers and (69.0 per cent) of parents/students stated that teachers were developed new information and new techniques for the class room.

Table 4.147: New Information and New Technique

New Information and New Technique	*Respondents*	
	Teacher (n=50)	*Parent/Student (n=50)*
	per cent	*per cent*
Yes	96.0	69.0
No	4.0	31.0

4.3.32 Preparation of Portfolio for Individual Children

The data accentuated that all the teachers prepared portfolio for individual children.

4.3.33 General Information of Children

The data revealed that (37.0 per cent) of the teachers stated that they collected family background, name, other details and height weight and Height. One fifth of the teachers (20.0 per cent) have taken name, weight, height, blood group, other physical and family background. On the other hand, (62.0 per cent) of the parents/students stated that teachers only collected name, weight and height.

Table 4.148: Information of Children

Information of Children	*Respondents*	
	Teacher (n=50)	*Parent/Student (n=50)*
	per cent	*per cent*
Name	12.0	10.0
Other Physical Health	11.5	10.0
Family Background	8.5	8.0
Name, Weight and Height	11.0	62.0
Family Background, Name, other details and Height Weight and Height	37.0	5.0
Name, Weight, Height, Blood Group, Other Physical and Family Background	20.0	5.0

4.3.34 Area of Interest of Children

The data revealed that (88.0 per cent) of the teachers (65.0 per cent) of the parents/students stated that teachers have identified areas of interests of the children.

Table 4.149: Area of Interest of Children

Area of Interest of Children	*Respondents*	
	Teacher (n=50)	*Parent/Student (n=50)*
	per cent	*per cent*
Yes	88.0	65.0
No	12.0	35.0

4.3.35 Measuring of Learning Improvement

The data portrayed that (84.0 per cent) of the teachers (80.0 per cent) of the parents/students stated that teachers measured the learning capacity and improvement capacity of the children.

Table 4.150: Measuring of Learning Improvement

Measurement	*Respondents*	
	Teacher (n=50)	*Parent/Student (n=50)*
	per cent	*per cent*
Yes	84.0	80.0
No	16.0	20.0

4.3.36 Collection of Information Regarding Special Work

The data portrayed that a majority of the teachers (72.0 per cent) opined that they had collected information regarding special work and rest of the teachers (28.0 per cent) negated. Almost similar trend is also observed in case of parents/students opinion.

Table 4.151: Collection of Information

Collection of Information	*Respondents*	
	Teacher (n=50)	*Parent/Student (n=50)*
	per cent	*per cent*
Yes	72.0	70.0
No	28.0	30.0

4.3.37 Assessing the Past and Present Status

The study reveals that (76.0 per cent) of the teachers and (70.0 per cent) of the parents/students stated that teachers assessed the past and present status of the students and rest of the teachers did not do the same.

Table 4.152: Assessing the Past and Present Status

Collection of Information	*Respondents*	
	Teacher (n=50)	*Parent/Student (n=50)*
	per cent	*per cent*
Yes	76.0	70.0
No	24.0	30.0

4.3.38 Discussion with Parents to Solve the Problems

The data reveals that a majority of the teachers (80.0 per cent) stated that they discussed with the student's parents to solve the problems and rest of the teachers (20.0 per cent) negated. Just opposite trend it also observed in case of parents/ students opinion.

Table 4.153: Discussion with Parents

Discussion with Parents	*Respondents*	
	Teacher (n=50)	*Parent/Student (n=50)*
	per cent	*per cent*
Yes	80.0	20.0
No	20.0	80.0

4.3.39 Contact with the Parents and Parent Teacher Association

The data portrayed that (84.0 per cent) of the teachers stated that they were contacted with the parents and parent teacher association and (16.0 per cent) of the teachers did not contact. As per opinion of parents/students shows that opposite trend.

Table 4.154: Contact with the Parents

Contact with the Parents	Respondents	
	Teacher (n=50)	Parent/Student (n=50)
	per cent	per cent
Yes	84.0	20.0
No	16.0	80.0

4.3.40 Discussion with Parents and PTAs

The data depicts that (56.0 per cent) of the teachers and (45.0 per cent) of the parents/students stated that teachers discussed with the parent teacher association regarding quality of education, (24.0 per cent) of the teachers and (28.0 per cent) of the parents/students stated that teachers discussed about the quality of education, educational survey, school activity and health awareness.

Table 4.155.: Discussion

Discussion with Parents	Respondents	
	Teacher (n=50)	Parent/Student (n=50)
	per cent	per cent
Quality of Education	56.0	45.0
Educational Survey	4.0	5.0
School Activity/ Programme	16.0	22.0
Quality of Education, Educational Survey, School Activity/ Programme, Health Awareness	24.0	28.0

4.3.41 Discussion about Dropout and Un-enrolled Children

The data revealed that (72.0 per cent) of the teachers stated that they discussed about dropout and un-enrolled children and rest of the teachers (28.0 per cent) did not discuss. As per opinion of parents/students show the more or less opposite trend.

Table 4.156: Discussion about Dropout and Un-enrolled Children

Discussion	Respondents	
	Teacher (n=50)	*Parent/Student (n=50)*
	per cent	*per cent*
Yes	72.0	25.0
No	28.0	75.0

4.3.42 Discussion about the Regular Attendance

Discussion about the regular attendance is very vital to improve the standards and quality education. The study revealed that (88.0 per cent) of the teachers stated that they discussed about the regular attendance and (22.0 per cent) of the teachers did not. The similar trend it also observed in case of parents/ students opinion.

4.3.43 Discussion Regarding School Plan and Unit Plan

The data accentuated that (38.0 per cent) of the teachers whereas (85.0 per cent) of parents/students stated that teachers had discussed about the school plan and (28.0 per cent) of the teachers and (9.0 per cent) of parents/students opined that teachers discussed on unit plan.

Table 4.157: Discussion Regarding School Plan and Unit Plan

Discussion	Respondents	
	Teacher (n=50)	*Parent/Student (n=50)*
	per cent	*per cent*
School Plan	38.0	85.0
Unit Plan	28.0	9.0
TLM and its uses	12.0	2.0
School plan and Unit Plan	12.0	2.0
School plan, unit plan and TLM and its uses	10.0	2.0

4.3.44 Discussion about Particular Activity in the Classroom

The data reveals that a majority of the teachers (84.0 per cent) whereas (45.0 per cent) of parents/students stated that teachers only discussed about particular activity in the classroom.

Table 4.158: Discussion about Particular Activity

Discussion	Respondents	
	Teacher (n=50)	Parent/Student (n=50)
	per cent	per cent
Yes	84.0	45.0
No	16.0	55.0

4.3.45 Discussion about Writing and Reading Material

The data revealed that all the teachers/parents/students stated that teachers had discussed about the writing and reading material.

4.3.46 Evaluation of the Children and Student Profile

The study reveals that a majority number of the teachers (96.0 per cent) and (89.0 per cent) of parents/students stated that teachers evaluated children and student profile.

Table 4.159: Evaluation of Student and Children

Discussion	Respondents	
	Teacher (n=50)	Parent/Student (n=50)
	per cent	per cent
Yes	96.0	89.0
No	4.0	11.0

4.3.47 Discussion on Co-conscious Activity

The data reveals that (96.0 per cent) of the teachers and only (40.0 per cent) of the parents/students stated teachers discussed about coconscious activity and as per opinion of (4.0 per cent) teachers and a large number of parents/students i.e., (60.0 per cent) neglected.

Table 4.160: Discussion Coc-onscious Activity

Discussion	Respondents	
	Teacher (n=50)	Parent/Student (n=50)
	per cent	per cent
Yes	96.0	40.0
No	4.0	60.0

4.3.48 Discussion on Participation of Parent Teacher Association

The data portrayed that a majority of the teachers (96.0 per cent) stated that they discussed about the participation of parent teacher association and its functions and as per opinion of (40.0 per cent) parents/students stated that teachers were discussed about the participation and a large number of parents/students i.e., (60.0 per cent) negated.

Table 4.161: Discussion Participation

Discussion	*Respondents*	
	Teacher (n=50)	*Parent/Student (n=50)*
	per cent	*per cent*
Yes	96.0	4.0
No	40.0	60.0

4.3.49 Discussion on Time Table of the School

The data revealed that (95.0 per cent) of the teachers and (50.0 per cent) of the parents/students stated that teachers discussed about the time table in the school and a small sample (5.0 per cent) of teachers and (50.0 per cent) of parents/students stated that teachers negated about this.

Table 4.162: Discussion on Time Table

Discussion	*Respondents*	
	Teacher (n=50)	*Parent/Student (n=50)*
	per cent	*per cent*
Yes	95.0	50.0
No	5.0	50.0

4.3.50 Discussion on Expectation of Every Children

The data reveals that (92.0 per cent) of the teachers and (65.0 per cent) of the parents/students stated that teachers discussed about the expectation of every children in the schools.

Table 4.163: Discussion on Children

Discussion	Respondents	
	Teacher (n=50)	*Parent/ Student (n=50)*
	per cent	*per cent*
Yes	92.0	65.0
No	8.0	35.0

4.3.51 Discussion about the Book

The study revealed that a majority of the teachers (96.0 per cent) and only (30.0 per cent) of parents/students stated that teachers discussed about book.

Table 4.164: Discussion about the Book

Discussion	Respondents	
	Teacher (n=50)	*Parent/ Student (n=50)*
	per cent	*per cent*
Yes	96.0	30.0
No	4.0	70.0

4.3.52 Discuss on Regarding the Good Work which is done

The data accentuated that (96.0 per cent) of the teachers and only (60.0 per cent) of parents/students stated that teachers discussed about the good work done by them and as well as by the children.

Table 4.165: Discuss on Regarding Good Work

Discussion	Respondents	
	Teacher (n=50)	*Parent/ Student (n=50)*
	per cent	*per cent*
Yes	96.0	60.0
No	4.0	40.0

4.3.53 Solving of Problem Regarding the Teaching and Learning Method

The data portrayed that a majority of the teachers (96.0 per cent) and (75.0 per cent) of parents/students stated that teachers solved the problems regarding the teaching and learning methods.

Table 4.166: Solving of Problems

Solvings of Problems	Respondents	
	Teacher (n=50)	Parent/Student (n=50)
	per cent	per cent
Yes	96.0	75.0
No	4.0	25.0

4.3.54 Regarding Professional Experiences

The data revealed that (92.0 per cent) of the teachers whereas only (55.0 per cent) of parents/students opinion that teachers had professional experience.

Table 4.167: Professional Experience

Professional Experience	Respondents	
	Teacher (n=50)	Parent/Student (n=50)
	per cent	per cent
Yes	92.0	55.0
No	8.0	45.0

4.3.55 Following of Guidelines Regarding RTE

The data revealed that (92.0 per cent) of the teachers and only (65.0 per cent) of parents/students stated that they are following the Right to Education act guidelines. As per opinion parents/students (35.0 per cent) of teachers did not follow the Right to Education act guidelines.

Table 4.168: Following of Guidelines

Following of Guidelines	Respondents	
	Teacher (n=50)	Parent/Student (n=50)
	per cent	per cent
Yes	92.0	65.0
No	8.0	35.0

4.3.56 Special Essential Help and Co-operation to Children Teaching

The data revealed that (92.0 per cent) of the teachers and only (65.0 per cent) of parents/students stated that teachers co-operated children by teaching.

Table 4.169: Teaching

Teaching	Respondents	
	Teacher (n=50)	Parent/Student (n=50)
	per cent	per cent
Yes	92.0	65.0
No	8.0	35.0

4.3.57 Evaluation of Ability of Every Children

The data accentuated that (92.0 per cent) of the teachers and only (45.0 per cent) of parents/students stated that teachers evaluated the ability of every children.

Table 4.170: Evaluation of Ability of Every Children

Professional Experience	Respondents	
	Teacher (n=50)	Parent/Student (n=50)
	per cent	per cent
Yes	92.0	45.0
No	8.0	55.0

4.3.58 Identification of Problems and Solutions of Children

The data revealed that a majority of the teachers (88.0 per cent) and only (45.0 per cent) of parents/students stated that teachers identified problems and give solutions to children.

Table 4.171: Identification of Problems

Professional Experience	Respondents	
	Teacher (n=50)	Parent/Student (n=50)
	per cent	per cent
Yes	92.0	45.0
No	8.0	55.0
Yes	88.0	45.0
No	12.0	55.0

4.3.59 Special Help to Every Child as per his/her Demand

The data portrayed that (96.0 per cent) of the teachers and very few numbers of parents/students stated that teachers give special help to children and as per opinion of parents/students (65.0 per cent) of the teachers negated.

Table 4.172: Special Help to Children

Special Help to Children	*Respondents*	
	Teacher (n=50)	*Parent/Student (n=50)*
	per cent	*per cent*
Yes	96.0	35.0
No	4.0	65.0

4.3.60 Maximum Evaluation and Construction of Material: Preparation of Evaluation Format

The study revealed that a majority of the teachers (92.0 per cent) and whereas only (50.0 per cent) of parents/students stated that teachers prepared evaluation format and as per opinion of parents/students (50.0 per cent) teachers did not prepared.

Table 4.173: Preparation of Evaluation Format

Preparation of Evaluation Format	*Respondents*	
	Teacher (n=50)	*Parent/Student (n=50)*
	per cent	*per cent*
Yes	92.0	50.0
No	8.0	50.0

4.3.61 Conduct of Survey for Utilisation

The data revealed that 92.0 per cent of the teachers and very few 28.0 per cent parents/students stated that teachers conducted the survey for their utilisation purpose and majority of parents/students (72.0 per cent) stated teachers did not conduct it.

Table 4.174: Conduct of Survey of Utilisation

Conduct of Survey of Utilisation	*Respondents*	
	Teacher (n=50)	*Parent/Student (n=50)*
	per cent	*per cent*
Yes	92.0	28.0
No	8.0	72.0

4.3.62 Implementation of Good Things which was Evaluated by Other School

The data revealed that a majority of the teachers (92.0 per cent) opined that they used good things which were evolved by the other schools. The more or less similar trend it also observed in case parents/students opinion.

Table 4.175: Implementation of Good Things

Implementation of good things	*Respondents*	
	Teacher (n=50)	*Parent/Student (n=50)*
	per cent	*per cent*
Yes	92.0	90.0
No	8.0	10.0

4.3.62.1 Dhamtari District Primary Schools Responses on Statements Regarding RTE Impact

The data accentuated that a majority of the respondents agreed that Right to Education (RTE) can reduce the illiteracy among disadvantaged groups and can promote the social change. A significant number of the respondents opined that through RTE we can establish empowered childhood and can promote sustainable development. The respondents agreed that child labour can be addressed through RTE. Moreover through RTE Girl child education can be increased and Quality education can be achieved. The RTE promotes knowledge based societies, inclusive growth and change in Systems and structures in the society.

4.3.62.2 Implementation Status of Primary Schools in Dhamtari District

The following table inferred that the actual implementation status of 45 hours schedule in the Dhamtari primary schools. The data revealed that the schools authorities are following the 45 hour schedule and they achieved good results in that particular schedule.

Table 4.176: Teachers, Parents and Students Opinion on RTE Impact

Statement	Respondents (n=100) per cent				
	Strongly Agree	Agree	Undecided	Disagree	Strongly Disagree
RTE can reduce the illiteracy among disadvantaged groups	5.00	42.00	10.00	15.00	28.00
RTE can promote the social change	15.00	49.00	13.00	10.00	13.00
Through RTE we can establish empowered childhood	19.00	52.00	9.00	11.00	9.00
RTE promotes sustainable development	5.00	49.00	19.00	18.00	9.00
Child labour can be addressed through RTE	9.00	59.00	15.00	8.00	9.00
Girl child education can be increased through RTE	10.00	69.00	14.00	5.00	2.00
Quality education can achieve through RTE	15.00	75.00	5.00	5.00	-
RTE can build knowledge based societies	10.00	82.00	5.00	3.00	-
RTE Promotes inclusive growth in near future	5.00	52.00	25.00	11.00	7.00
Systems and structures in the society can be changed by RTE	2.00	57.00	30.00	9.00	2.00

Table 4.177: Actual Implementation Status

Sl. No.	*Name of the Activity*	*Approved Targets as per RTE act up to the time of study (Hours/ Minute/ per day/ per week)*	*Progress against the targets shown in column.3 at the time of study*	
			Total achievement	*per cent of actual achievement (4/3×100)*
1.	Prayer and Attendance	20 minutes/per day	14 minutes/per day	72.0 per cent
2.	Teaching	4 hours/per day	3 hours 80 Minutes/ per day	96.0 per cent
3.	Mid day meal	40 minutes/per day	38 minutes/per day	96.0 per cent
4.	Preparation of action plan for teaching and evaluation	1 hours/per day	15 Minutes/per day	24.0 per cent
5.	Student Portfolio	30 minutes/per day	25 minutes/per day	84.0 per cent
6.	Discussion with parent and Community	1 hours/per week	55 minutes/per day	92.0 per cent
7.	Staff meeting	30 minutes/per week	26 minutes/per week	88.0 per cent
8.	Special need to help the Children	40 minutes/per day	22 minutes/per day	56.0 per cent
9.	Tools/format fixed for evaluation	30 minutes/per week	29 minutes/per week	96.0 per cent
Total Time		**45 hours/week**		

4.3.62.3 Major Findings from Primary Schools in Dhamtari District

- (68.0 per cent) teachers were male participated in the study and the rest of the respondents (32.0 per cent) were female.
- (52.0 per cent) of the teachers were in the age group of 22-36 and (20.0 per cent) of the teachers were in more than 51 age group.
- (64.0 per cent) of teachers belonged to OBC community and (16.0 per cent) of the teachers belonged to Schedule Tribe and (12.0 per cent) of the teachers belonged to SC.
- (44.0 per cent) of the teachers were having Post Graduation Degree (24.0 per cent), Higher Middle (24.0 per cent) have PG, B.Ed or D.Ed were in that order.
- (88.0 per cent) of the teachers were staying outside the village and the rest of the teachers (12.0 per cent) were staying in the same village where the school is located.
- (60.0 per cent) teachers were staying less than 5 km and (32.0 per cent) of the teachers were staying between six-ten km away from the school.
- Distance form Block Resource Centre a majority of the teachers (48.0 per cent) stated that their school is between 6-10 Kms away and (20.0 per cent) of the teachers opined that it is between 11-15 km away.
- All schools have Electricity facility and all the schools were connected with the road.
- As regarding the class rooms (35.0 per cent) of the teachers stated that there are three class rooms in their school and (32.0 per cent) of the teachers stated four rooms.
- (76.0 per cent) teachers stated that they have toilet facility in the school and rest of the teachers negated.
- (88.0 per cent) of the schools have drinking water facility.
- (36.0 per cent) of the teachers stated that there were no permanent teachers, (64.0 per cent) of the teachers opined that there is one permanent teacher in their school.

- (28.0 per cent) of the teachers stated that tgere were three teachers and four teachers on temporary basis in their school. Five temporary teachers (20.0 per cent) and two temporary teachers (16.0 per cent) were in that order.
- (60.0 per cent) teachers stated that they took 20 minutes to complete prayer and (28.0 per cent) of the teachers opined that they took less than 20 minutes for the same. As regarding the teaching hours (88.0 per cent) of the teachers stated that they taught more than 4.00 hours per day. The data of parents/students depicted that (10.0 per cent) school have taking less than 20 minutes time for prayer, (15.0) have taking 20 minutes and rest have taking 30 minutes (75.0 per cent) for prayer. The data reveals that (25.0 per cent) of the teachers ware taking class up to four hours and (65.0 per cent) ware teaching less than four hours and rest (10.0 per cent) teaching above four hrs.
- (68.0 per cent) of the teachers opined that they have taken 40 minutes for midday meal per day and (28.0 per cent) have taken more than 40 minutes. The data accentuated from parents/students that midday meal have taken more than 40 minutes (87.0 per cent) and rest (13.0 per cent) have taken 40 minutes.
- (76.0 per cent) of the teachers stated that they had taken less than one hour per day for preparation of action plans. The data of parents/students indicate that (68.0 per cent) teacher takes more than one hr per day for preparation of action plan and rest have taken less than one hour.
- (68.0 per cent) of the teachers stated that they have taken 30 minutes for preparation of student portfolio and (16.0 per cent) of the teachers have taken more than 30 minutes and less than 30 minutes for the same. Data of parents/students reveals that the teachers (12.0 per cent) take 30 minutes time to make student portfolio and (80.0 per cent) teachers take less than 30 minutes time and rest (8.0 per cent) take more than 30 minutes time for preparation.
- (84.0 per cent) teachers stated that they have taken less than one hour for discussion with parents. Generally

(8.0 per cent) teachers take one hour for discussion with parents. On the other hand (89.0 per cent) parents/students stated that teachers take less than one hour for discussion with parents and only (2.0 per cent) take more than one hour.

- (72.0 per cent) of the teachers stated that they spared 30 minutes for staff meeting per week. The data of parents/students reveals that (79.0 per cent) teachers take more than 30 minutes, (19.0 per cent) take 30 minutes and (2.0 per cent) teacher take less than 30 minutes time for staff meeting.
- (44.0 per cent) of the teachers opined that they allocated less than 40 minutes for children those who are in special need and (32.0 per cent) of the teachers stated that they spared forty minutes per day. Parents/students data indicate that (12.0 per cent) teachers spend 40 minutes to help the children for their special need in study (68.0 per cent) teachers take less than 40 minutes and (20.0 per cent) take more than 40 minutes time.
- (84.0 per cent) of the teachers stated that they allocated 30 minutes per week for tools and formats evaluation. Whereas (67 per cent) parents/students stated teachers allocated less than 30 minutes per week for tools and formats evaluation.
- (76.0 per cent) of the teachers stated that they used national anthem and national song. As regarding the motivational activities (96.0 per cent) of the teachers used lecture method. All the teachers stated that they have taken attendance after the assembly. The similar trend it also observed in case of parents/students opinion.
- All the teachers/parents/students stated that they used Cognitive teaching for class one to five.
- (96.0 per cent) of the teachers stated that they had adopted whole class approach and (52.0 per cent) of the teachers adopted group based activity and rest of the teachers (48.0 per cent) negated. Parents/students stated that (55 per cent) teachers followed the whole class approach and (30 per cent) teachers adopted group-based activity.

- (72.0 per cent) of the teachers and (20 per cent) of the parents/students stated that teachers evaluated oral and writing capacity of the student. The data revealed that a majority of the teachers (92.0 per cent) and parents/students (65 per cent) stated that teachers used Co-cognitive teaching for class first to fifth.
- (44.0 per cent) of the teachers and (45 per cent) of the parents/students stated that teachers had given chance for drawing, music, dance, art and craft, literary and cultural activities and (40.0 per cent) of the teachers and 30 per cent of the parents/students opined that students adopted drawing, music and dance. (16.0 per cent) of the teachers and (25 per cent) of parents/students stated that teachers conducted drawing for the children.
- (72.0 per cent) teachers stated that they have given project work and (16.0 per cent) opined that they have displayed creative work and (12.0 per cent) of the parents/students opined they adopted both creative and project work experience. Majority of parents/students (45 per cent) stated that teachers displayed creative work and (35 per cent) had given opinion for project work.
- (49.0 per cent) of the teachers stated that they conducted sports and games, (16.0 per cent) of the teachers adopted yoga, sports and games. On the other hand, (47 per cent) parents/students stated that teachers look after Sports, games and cleanliness and (23 per cent) only stress on sports and games.
- (36.0 per cent) teachers stated that they adopted attitude, life skill and awareness towards environment and (29.0 per cent) of the teachers used attitude, life skill, and awareness towards environment and value system, (20.0 per cent) of the teachers stated that they measured attitude of the children for improvement of social/personal attitudes and values. On the other hand, majority of parents/students (35 per cent) stated that maximum focus on awareness towards environment, (35 per cent) on attitude, life skill, awareness towards environment and value system.
- (52.0 per cent) of the teachers stated that they could complete midday meal distribution between 31-40

minutes. (18.0 per cent) of the teachers had taken 21-30 minutes, for the same. Majority of the parents/ students stated that (65 per cent) of the teachers had taken more than 51 minutes.

- (76.0 per cent) of the teachers stated that they prepared action plan for teaching and evaluation and rest of the teachers (24.0 per cent) negated. Whereas (60 per cent) of parents/students stated that teachers prepared action plan for teaching and evaluation and rest of the teachers (40.0 per cent) negated.
- (84.0 per cent) of the teachers stated that they prepared activities for class room teaching and rest of the teachers (16.0 per cent) negated. On the other hand, parents/ students opined that (45 per cent) teachers prepared activities for class room teaching and rest of the teachers (55.0 per cent) negated.
- (92.0 per cent) teachers stated that they prepared teaching and learning material and rest of the teachers (8.0 per cent) negated. As per opinion of parents/teachers only (35.0 per cent) teachers prepared teaching and learning material.
- (76.0 per cent) of the teachers opined that they applied techniques for teaching and rest of the teachers (24.0 per cent) were negated. More or less similar trend it was also observed in case of parents, teachers opinion.
- (84.0 per cent) teachers and parents/students (82.0 per cent) stated teachers planned for group work and (16.0 per cent) of teachers and (18.0 per cent) of parents/ students opined that the teachers negated.
- (88.0 per cent) of the teachers and (80.0 per cent) of parents/students stated that teachers had designed action plan for teaching and learning.
- (76.0 per cent) teachers and (60.0 per cent) of the parents/students stated that teachers were learned and followed teaching and learning material.
- (72.0 per cent) of the teachers opined that they planned useful books for the library and (20.0 per cent) of the teachers used Book Corner for the purpose of children. On the other hand parents/students stated that (62.0

per cent) of teachers planned useful books for the library (20.0 per cent) of the teachers used Book and (20.0 per cent) books and book corners for the purpose of children.

- (96.0 per cent) of the teachers and (69.0 per cent) of parents/students stated that teachers have developed new information and new techniques for the class room.
- All teachers, parents and students gave same opinion to prepare portfolio for individual children.
- (37.0 per cent) of the teachers stated that they collected family background, name, other details and height and weight and one fifths of the teachers (20.0 per cent) have taken name, weight, height, blood group, other physical and family background. On the other hand, (62.0 per cent) of the parents/students stated that teachers only collected name, weight and height.
- (88.0 per cent) of the teachers (65.0 per cent) of the parents/students stated that teachers have identified areas of interests of the children.
- (84.0 per cent) of the teachers (80.0 per cent) of the parents/students stated that teachers have measured the learning capacity and improvement capacity of the children.
- (72.0 per cent) teachers opined that they had collected information regarding special work and rest of the teachers (28.0 per cent) negated. Almost similar trend is also observed in case of parents/students opinion.
- (76.0 per cent) of the teachers and (70.0 per cent) of the parents/students stated that teachers assessed the past and present status of the students and rest of the teachers did not do the same.
- (80.0 per cent) teachers stated that they have discussed with the student's parents to solve the problems and rest of the teachers (20.0 per cent) negated. Just opposite trend it also observed in case of parents/students' opinion.
- (84.0 per cent) of the teachers stated that they were contacted with the parents and parent teacher

association and (16.0 per cent) of the teachers they did not contact. As per opinion of parents/students shows opposite trend.

- (56.0 per cent) of the teachers and (45.0 per cent) of the parents/students stated that teachers discussed with the parent teacher association regarding Quality of Education, (24.0 per cent) of the teachers and (28.0 per cent) of the parents/students stated that teachers discussed about the quality of education, educational survey, school activity and health awareness.

- (72.0 per cent) of the teachers stated that they discussed about dropout and un-enrolled children and rest of the teachers (28.0 per cent) did not discuss. As per opinion of parents/students show more or less opposite trend.

- (88.0 per cent) of the teachers stated that they had discussed about the regular attendance and (22.0 per cent) of the teachers did not. The similar trend it also observed in case of parents/students opinion.

- (38.0 per cent) of the teachers and (85.0 per cent) of parents/students stated that teachers had discussed about the school plan and (28.0 per cent) of the teachers and 9.0 per cent of parents/students opined that teachers discussed on unit plan.

- (84.0 per cent) teachers whereas only (45.0 per cent) of parents/students stated that teachers only discussed about particular activity in the classroom.

- All the teachers/parents/students stated that teachers had discussed about the writing and reading material.

- (96.0 per cent) teachers and (89.0 per cent) of parents/students stated that teachers evaluated children and student profile.

- (96.0 per cent) of the teachers and whereas only (40.0 per cent) of the parents/students stated that teachers discussed about coconscious activity and as per opinion of (4.0 per cent) teachers and a large number of parents/students i.e., (60.0 per cent) negated.

- (96.0 per cent) teachers stated that they discussed about the participation of parent teacher association and its functions and as per opinion of (40.0 per cent) parents/ students stated that teachers discussed about the participation and a large number of parents/students i.e., (60.0 per cent) negated.
- (95.0 per cent) of the teachers and (50.0 per cent) of the parents/students stated that teachers discussed about the time table in the school and a small sample (5.0 per cent) of teachers and (50.0 per cent) of parents/students stated that teachers negated about this.
- (92.0 per cent) of the teachers and (65.0 per cent) of the parents/students stated that teachers discussed about the expectation of every child in the schools.
- (96.0 per cent) teachers and only (30.0 per cent) of parents/students stated that teachers discussed about book.
- (96.0 per cent) of the teachers and only (60.0 per cent) of parents/students stated that teachers discussed about the good work done by them and as well as by the children.
- Majority of the teachers (96.0 per cent) and (75.0 per cent) of parents/students stated that teachers solved the problems regarding the teaching and learning methods.
- (92.0 per cent) of the teachers whereas only (55.0 per cent) of parents/students opined that teachers had professional experience.
- (92.0 per cent) of the teachers and only (65.0 per cent) of parents/students stated that they are following the Right to Education act guidelines. As per opinion parents/students (35.0 per cent) of teachers did not follow the Right to Education act guidelines.
- (92.0 per cent) of the teachers and whereas only (65.0 per cent) of parents/students stated that teachers co-operated children by teaching.
- (92.0 per cent) of the teachers and whereas only (45.0 per cent) of parents/students stated that teachers evaluated the ability of every child.

- (88.0 per cent) teachers and only (45.0 per cent) of parents/students stated that teachers identified problems and give solutions to children.
- (96.0 per cent) of the teachers and very few numbers of parents/students stated that teachers give special help to children and as per opinion of parents/students (65.0 per cent) of the teachers negated.
- (92.0 per cent) teachers and whereas only (50.0 per cent) of parents/students stated that teachers prepared evaluation format and as per opinion of parents/students (50.0 per cent) teachers did not prepare.
- (92.0 per cent) of the teachers and very few (28.0 per cent) parents/students stated that teachers conducted the survey for their utilisation purpose and majority of parents/students (72.0 per cent) stated teachers did not conduct it.
- (92.0 per cent) teachers opined that they used good things which were evolved by the other schools. The more or less similar trend it also observed in case of parents, students opinion.

4.4 Middle Schools in Dhamtari District

4.4.1 Social Characteristics

The data revealed that a majority of the teachers (89.0 per cent) participated in the study and the rest of the teachers (11.0 per cent) were female. As regarding the age (27.0 per cent) of the teachers were in the age group of more than 53 and (20.0 per cent) of the teachers were in 48-52 age group (37.0 per cent) of the teachers belonged to Schedule Tribe and (33.5 per cent) of the teachers belonged to OBC.

General (18.5 per cent) and SC (11.0 per cent) were in that order. The parents/student data revealed that majorities (26.0 per cent) of parents/students were in the age group of more than 53 years. (20.0 per cent) parents/students were in the age group of 48-52 while 14.0 per cent of the parents/students were in the age group of 28-32 years.

Table 4.178: Social Characteristics

Variable	Respondents	
	Teacher (n=50)	Parent/Student (n=50)
	per cent	per cent
Gender		
Male	89.0	90.0
Female	11.0	10.0
Age		
23-27	10.0	10.0
28-32	13.5	14.0
33-37	13.0	13.0
38-42	6.5	7.0
43-47	10.0	10.0
48-52	20.0	20.0
> 53	27.0	26.0
Caste		
SC	11.0	10.0
ST	37.0	38.0
OBC	33.5	34.0
General	18.5	18.0

4.4.2 Residence and Distance

The data revealed that (78.0 per cent) of the teachers were staying outside the village and the rest of the teachers (22.0 per cent) were staying in the same village where the school is located. A majority of the teachers (48.0 per cent) were staying less than five kms and (37.0 per cent) of the teachers were staying 6-10 kms away from the school. As regarding the distance form Block Resource Centre more than one fourth (26.0 per cent) stated that they reside away from school and (22.5 per cent) of the teachers stated school is 31-40 kms away and (22.0 per cent) of the teachers stated that they stayed less than 10 kms away. More or less similar trend is also observed following the distance from parents/students residence.

Table 4.179: Residence and Distance

Variables	Respondents	
	Teacher (n=50)	*Parent/Student (n=50)*
	per cent	*per cent*
Residence		
Same Village	22.0	30.0
Other Village	78.0	70.0
Distance from School		
> 5	48.0	47.0
6-10	37.0	37.0
11-15	4.5	5.0
16-20	7.0	7.0
> 20	3.5	4.0
Distance from BRC		
> 10 km	22.0	20.0
10-20	26.0	24.0
21-30	11.5	10.0
31-40	22.5	23.0
41-50	7.0	10.0
> 51	11.0	13.0

4.4.3 Facilities in the School

The study revealed that (46.5 per cent) schools have electricity facility and rest of the schools (53.5 per cent) did not have such facility. As regarding the class rooms (88.5 per cent) of the teachers stated that there are three class rooms in their school. A majority of the teachers (85.0 per cent) stated that they have toilet facility in the school. (69.0 per cent) of the schools were connected with roads. (92.0 per cent) of the schools have drinking water facility. More or less similar trend is observed in case of opinion of the parents/students.

Table 4.180: Facilities in the School

Variable	Respondents	
	Teacher (n=50)	*Parent/Student (n=50)*
	per cent	*per cent*
Electricity		
Yes	46.5	43.0
No	53.5	57.0
No of Class Rooms		
2.	5.0	2.0
3.	88.5	90.0
5.	3.0	2.0
6.	3.5	6.0
Toilet Facility		
Yes	85.0	75.0
No	15.0	25.0
Road Connected		
Yes	69.0	60.0
No	31.0	40.0
Drinking Water Facility		
Yes	92.0	95.0
No	8.0	5.0

4.4.4 Staffing

The data revealed that (39.5 per cent) of the teachers stated that there were two teachers, (29.0 per cent) of the teachers opined that there is one teacher and (25.5 per cent) of the teachers opined there is that one permanent teacher in their schools. As regarding the temporary teachers (89.5 per cent) of the teachers stated that they don't have such teachers. However, (5.5 per cent) of the teachers stated that they have two teachers in their schools. The similar data trend has been observed in case of parents/students opinion.

Table 4.181: Staffing

Variable	*Respondents*	
	Teacher (n=50)	*Parent/Student (n=50)*
	per cent	*per cent*
Permanent Teachers		
1.	1.0	1.0
2.	25.5	10.0
3.	39.5	45.0
4.	21.0	35.0
5.	3.0	5.0
6.	3.0	4.0
Temporary Teachers		
1.	89.5	90.0
2.	5.5	5.0
3.	2.0	3.0
4.	3.0	2.0

4.4.5 Prayer and Teaching Time

The study revealed that a majority of the teachers (62.5 per cent) and only (20.0 per cent) of parents/students stated that they took 20 minutes to complete prayer and (32.5 per cent) of the teachers and (70.0 per cent) of parents opined that they took 30 minutes for the same. As regarding the teaching hours 84.0 per cent of the teachers and (85.0 per cent) of parents/ students stated that they taught more than 4.35 hours per day and (15.0 per cent) of the teachers and (10 per cent) of parents/ students started that teachers have taken 4.35 hours per day.

Table 4.182: Prayer and Teaching Time

Prayer and Teaching Time	*Respondents*	
	Teacher (n=50)	*Parent/Student (n=50)*
	per cent	*per cent*
Prayer		
Less than 20 Minutes	5.0	10.0
20 Minutes	62.5	20.0
30 Minutes	32.5	70.0
Teaching Hours (per day)		
Less than 4.35 Hrs	1.0	5.0
4.35 Hrs	15.0	10.0
Above 4.35 Hrs	84.0	85.0

4.4.6 Mid-day Meal

The study revealed that (86.0 per cent) of the teachers, whereas only (12.0 per cent) of parents/students opined that they have taken 40 minutes and (11.0 per cent) of the teachers and majority of parents/students stated that teachers have taken more than 40 minutes for midday meal per day.

Table 4.183: Mid-day Meal

Mid-day Meal	*Respondents*	
	Teacher (n=50)	*Parent/Student (n=50)*
	per cent	*per cent*
< 40 Minutes	3.0	10.0
40 Minutes	86.0	12.0
> 40 Minutes	11.0	78.0

4.4.7 Preparation of Action Plans

The data accentuated that (77.0 per cent) of the teachers and (65.0 per cent) of parents' students stated that teachers had taken 40 minutes per day and (18.5 per cent) for the teachers and (30.0 per cent) of parents stated that teachers have taken more than 40 minutes for preparation of action plans.

Table 4.184: Preparation of Action Plans

Preparation of Action Plan	*Respondents*	
	Teacher (n=50)	*Parent/Student (n=50)*
	per cent	*per cent*
< 1 Hr Per Day	4.5	5.0
40 Minutes Per Day	77.0	65.0
> 40 Minutes Per Day	18.5	30.0

4.4. 8 Student Portfolio

The data portrayed that (91.5 per cent) of the teachers and only (30.0 per cent) of parents/students stated that teachers have taken 30 minutes for student portfolio. Most (65.0 per cent) of the parents/students stated that teachers have taken less than 30 minutes for student portfolio.

Table 4.185: Student Portfolio

Student Portfolio	*Respondents*	
	Teacher (n=50)	*Parent/Student (n=50)*
	per cent	*per cent*
< 30 Minutes	2.5	65.0
30 Minutes	91.5	30.0
> 30 Minutes	6.0	5.0

4.4.9 Discussion with Parents

The data portrayed that a majority of the teachers (90.5 per cent) and (85.0 per cent) of parents/students stated that teachers have taken one hour for discussion with parents per week.

Table 4.186: Discussion with Parents

Discussion	*Respondents*	
	Teacher (n=50)	*Parent/Student (n=50)*
	per cent	*per cent*
< 1 hour	6.5	2.0
1 hour	90.5	85.0
> 1 hour	3.0	13.0

4.4.10 Staff Meeting

The data revealed that (91.0 per cent) of the teachers and only (20.0 per cent) of parents/students stated that teachers had allocated 30 minutes for staff meeting per week. But majority (70.0 per cent) of parents/students stated that teachers had allocated more than 30 minutes for staff meeting per week.

Table 4.187: Staff Meeting

Staff Meeting	*Respondents*	
	Teacher (n=50)	*Parent/Student (n=50)*
	per cent	*per cent*
< 30 Minutes	2.0	10.0
30 Minutes	91.0	20.0
> 30 Minutes	7.0	70.0

4.4.11 Special Need to Help the Children

The data accentuated that (89.0 per cent) of the teachers and (82.0 per cent) of the parents/students opined that they allocated 40 minutes for children those who are in special need per day.

Table 4.188: Special Help to Needy Children

Special Help to Needy Children	*Respondents*	
	Teacher (n=50)	*Parent/Student (n=50)*
	per cent	*per cent*
< 40 Minutes per day	4.0	8.0
40 Minutes per day	89.0	82.0
More Than 40 Minutes per day	7.0	10.0

4.4.12 Tools/Format Fixed for Evaluation

The study revealed that the (81.0 per cent) of the teachers and (90.0 per cent) of parents/students stated that teachers allocated 30 minutes per week for tools and formats evaluation. However, (16.0 per cent) of the teachers and only (5.0 per cent) of parents/students expressed that teachers have taken more than 30 minutes per week.

Table 4.189: Tools/Format Fixed for Evaluation

Evaluation	*Respondents*	
	Teacher (n=50)	*Parent/Student (n=50)*
	per cent	*per cent*
< 30 Minutes per week	3.0	5.0
30 Minutes per week	81.0	90.0
> 30 Minutes per week	16.0	5.0

4.4.13 Attendance of Teachers and Students During Prayer

The data revealed that (77.0 per cent) of the teachers and 69.0 per cent of parents/students opined that they were participated during prayer and rest of the teachers (23.0 per cent) and parents/students (31.0 per cent) negated. As regarding the pattern (52.5 per cent) of the teachers and (65 per cent) of parents/students stated that they adopted group song, national song, national anthem and prayer and (31.5 per cent) of the teachers and only (15.0 per cent) of parents/students stated that they used prayer. As regarding the motivational activities (42.0 per cent) of the teachers and (52.5 per cent) of parents/ students stated that teachers used Lecture and *Mahapurush* thought, (37.0 per cent) of the teachers and only (11.0 per cent) of parents/students opined that teachers used *Mahapurush* thought only. All the teachers stated that they have taken attendance after assembly.

Table 4.190: Teacher and Students During Prayers

Variable	*Respondents*	
	Teacher (n=50)	*Parent/Student (n=50)*
	per cent	*per cent*
Present at the time of Prayer		
Yes	77.0	69.0
No	23.0	31.0
Pattern		
National Song	5.0	5.0
National Anthem	11.0	15.0
Group Song, National Song, National Anthem and Prayer	52.5	65.0
Prayer	31.5	15.0
Motivational Activities		
Lecture	21.0	5.0
Mahaparush Thought	37.0	11.0
Lecture + *Mahapurush* Thought	42.0	52.5

4.4.14 Training: Cognitive Teaching (Class VI-VIII)

The data revealed that all the teachers/parents/students stated that all teachers adopted cognitive teaching for class VI-VIII in the class room.

4.4.15 Whole Class Approach and Group Based Activity

The data revealed that (91.0 per cent) of the teachers and (91.0 per cent) of parents/students stated that teachers adopted whole class approach and (89.0 per cent) of the teachers and only (45.0 per cent) of parent/students opined that teachers adopted group based activity. Most of the (55.0 per cent) parents/student opined that teachers neglected group-based activity.

Table 4.191: Whole Class Approach and Group Activity

Variable	*Respondents*	
	Teacher (n=50)	*Parent/ Student (n=50)*
	per cent	*per cent*
Whole Class Approach		
Yes	91.0	95.0
No	4.0	5.0
Group based Activity		
Yes	89.0	45.0
No	11.0	55.0

4.4.16 Mode of Continuous Evaluation and Co-cognitive Teaching

The data revealed that (45.0 per cent) of teachers and (50.0 per cent) of parents/students stated that teachers evaluated the oral and (54.5 per cent) of the teachers and only (25.0 per cent) of parents/students stated that teachers evaluated the oral and writing and more than two fifth of the teachers stated that Oral for conscious evaluation. As regarding the co-cognitive teaching (75.0 per cent) of the teachers and (65.0 per cent) of parents/students and (25.0 per cent) of the teachers (35.0 per cent) of parents/students stated that teachers did not use it.

Table 4.192: Mode of Continuous Evaluation

Evaluation	*Respondents*	
	Teacher (n=50)	*Parent/ Student (n=50)*
	per cent	*per cent*
Oral	42.5	50.0
Written	3.0	25.0
Oral and Written	54.5	25.0
Co-cognitive Teaching		
Yes	75.0	65.0
No	25.0	35.0

4.4.17 Art

The study revealed that (40.0 per cent) of the teachers and (35.0 per cent) of parents/students stated that teachers conducted drawing, music, dance, literary and cultural activities and (32.0 per cent) of the teachers and (40.0 per cent) of parents/ students stated that teachers conducted drawing only.

Table 4.193: Art

Art	*Respondents*	
	Teacher (n=50)	*Parent/Student (n=50)*
	per cent	*per cent*
Drawing	32.0	40.0
Music	14.0	5.0
Drawing, Dance, Art and Craft, Literary and cultural Activities	14.0	20.0
Drawing, Music, Dance, Literary and cultural Activities	40.0	35.0

4.4.18 Work Experience

The data revealed that (76.0 per cent) of the teachers and (60.0 per cent) of the parents/students stated that teachers had given project work and (14.5 per cent) of the teachers and (20.0 per cent) of the teachers stated that teachers display creative work.

Table 1.194: Work Experience

Work Experience	*Respondents*	
	Teacher (n=50)	*Parent/Student (n=50)*
	per cent	*per cent*
Project Work	76.0	60.0
Display Creative Work	14.5	20.0
Project Work and Display Creative Work	9.5	20.0

4.4.19 Physical Education and Health

The study revealed that (47.0 per cent) of the teachers and

(50.0 per cent) of the parents/students stated that teachers conducted sports and games and (28.0 per cent) of the teachers and only (15.0 per cent) of the parents/students stated they conducted yoga, sports and games, nutritional food, knowledge about diseases.

Table 4.195: Physical Education and Health

Physical Education and Health	Respondents	
	Teacher (n=50)	Parent/Student (n=50)
	per cent	per cent
Yoga	10.0	8.0
Sports and Games	47.0	50.0
Yoga, Sports and Games	5.0	12.0
Cleanliness	10	15.0
Yoga, Sports and Games, Nutritional Food, Knowledge about Diseases	28.0	15.0

4.4.20 Social/Personal Attitudes and Values

The data revealed that (39.0 per cent) of the teachers and (25.0 per cent) of parents/students stated that teachers adopted attitude, life skill, awareness towards environment and (28.0 per cent) of the teachers and (20.0 per cent) of the parents/students opined that they taught life skills and (21.0 per cent) of the teachers and 30.0 per cent of the parents/students stated that Attitude + Life Skill + Awareness towards Environment + Value System.

Table 4.196: Social/Personal Attitudes and Values

Sccial and Personal Attitude	Respondents	
	Teacher (n=50)	Parent/Student (n=50)
	per cent	per cent
Attitude	12.0	25.0
Life Skill	28.0	20.0
Attitude + Life Skill+ Awareness towards Environment	39.0	25.0
Attitude + Life Skill+ Awareness towards Environment + Value System	21.0	30.0

4.4.21 Mid-day Meal Distribution

The data portrayed that (72.0 per cent) of the teachers and (80.0 per cent) of the parents/students stated teachers have taken 31-40 minutes per day for midday meal distribution.

Table 4.197: Midday Meal Distribution

Midday Meal	*Respondents*	
	Teacher (n=50)	*Parent/ Student (n=50)*
	per cent	*per cent*
10-21	7.0	5.0
21-30	21.0	15.0
31-40	72.0	80.0

4.4.22 Preparation of Action Plan for Teaching and Evaluation

The data accentuated that (91.5 per cent) of the teachers and (80.0 per cent) of parents/students stated that teachers prepared action plans and as per opinion of teachers (8.5 per cent) negated. A majority of the teachers (97.0 per cent) and parents/students (70.0 per cent) stated that teachers prepared activities for class room teaching.

Table 4.198: Preparation of Action Plan

Preparation and Action Plan	*Respondents*	
	Teacher (n=50)	*Parent/ Student (n=50)*
	per cent	*per cent*
Yes	91.5	84.0
No	8.5	16.0
Preparation of Activities for Class Room Teaching		
Yes	97.0	70.0
No	3.0	30.0

4.4.23 Preparation of TLM and Application of Techniques for Active Participation

The data portrayed that (92.0 per cent) of the teachers and (50.0 per cent) of parents/students stated that teachers prepared teaching learning material. (91.0 per cent) of the teachers and

(70.0 per cent) of parents/students stated that teachers adopted techniques to activate participation.

Table 4.199: Preparation of TLM and Techniques

Preparation of TLM	*Respondents*	
	Teacher (n=50)	*Parent/Student (n=50)*
	per cent	*per cent*
Yes	92.0	50.0
No	8.0	50.0
Technique to Activate Participation		
Yes	91.0	70.0
No	9.0	30.0

4.4.24 Plan for Group Work of the Children

The data portrayed that 73.0 per cent of the teachers stated that teachers planned for group work for the children. More or less similar trend have been observed in case of parents/ students opinion.

Table 4.200: Plan for Group Work

Plan for Group Work	*Respondents*	
	Teacher (n=50)	*Parent/Student (n=50)*
	per cent	*per cent*
Yes	73.0	70.0
No	27.0	30.0

4.4.25 Preparation for Action Plan for Teaching and Learning

The data portrayed that a majority of the teachers (76.0 per cent) and parents/students (65.0 per cent) stated that teachers prepared for action plan for teaching and learning and rest of the teachers (24.0 per cent) and parents/students (35.0 per cent) stated that teachers negated.

Table 4.201: Plan for Teaching and Learning

Plan for TLM	Respondents	
	Teacher (n=50)	Parent/Student (n=50)
	per cent	per cent
Yes	76.0	65.0
No	24.0	35.0

4.4.26 Learn and Follow Teaching and Learning Material

The data revealed that (87.0 per cent) of the teachers and (80.0 per cent) of the parents/students stated that teachers learned and followed teaching and learning material.

Table 4.202: Learn and Follow Teaching and Learning

Learn and Follow TLM	Respondents	
	Teacher (n=50)	Parent/Student (n=50)
	per cent	per cent
Yes	87.0	80.0
No	13.0	20.0

4.4.27 Collect New Information and Portfolio for Individual Children

The data revealed that (96.0 per cent) of the teachers and (80.0 per cent) of the parents/students stated that teachers give information by books and followed portfolio of children (82.0 per cent) and (65.0 per cent) were the opinion of teachers and parents/students respectively.

Table 4.203: Information and Portfolio

Information and Portfolio	Respondents	
	Teacher (n=50)	Parent/Student (n=50)
	per cent	per cent
Books	96.0	80.0
Book Corner	4.0	20.0
Portfolio for Individual Children		
Yes	82.0	65.0
No	18.0	35.0

4.4.28 General Information of Children

The data portrayed that (51.0 per cent) of the teachers and very negligible number i.e., (5.00 per cent) of parents/students stated that teachers have collected—name, weight, height, blood group, other physical and family background and (28.0 per cent) of the teachers and (10.0 per cent) of parents/students stated that teachers have taken only name as part of the general information of the children.

Table 4.204: General Information of Children

Information of Children	*Respondents*	
	Teacher (n=50)	*Parent/Student (n=50)*
	per cent	*per cent*
Name	28.0	10.0
Name, Weight and Height	7.0	80.0
Other Physical Health	14.0	5.0
Name, Weight, Height, Blood Group, Other Physical and Family Background	51.0	5.0

4.4.29 Identification of Interests and Measuring Improvement

The data revealed that all the teachers, parents and students stated that teachers have identified the interests of the children and measured the improvement of the children.

4.4.30 Collection of Information Regarding Special Work

The data revealed that (78.0 per cent) of the teachers and (55.0 per cent) of parents/students stated that teachers collected information regarding the special work.

Table 4.205: Collection of Information

Variable	*Respondents*	
	Teacher (n=50)	*Parent/Student (n=50)*
	per cent	*per cent*
Yes	78.0	55.0
No	22.0	45.0

4.4.31 Assessment of Past and Present Status

The data revealed that (91.0 per cent) of the teachers stated that they assessed the past and present status of the student. The opposite trend is observed in case of parents/students opinion.

Table 4.206: Assessment of Past and Present Status

Variable	*Respondents*	
	Teacher (n=50)	*Parent/Student (n=50)*
	per cent	*per cent*
Yes	91.0	10.0
No	9.0	90.0

4.4.32 Solving the Problems and Contact Parent Teacher Association

The data portrayed that (92.0 per cent) of the teachers and only (10.0 per cent) of parents/students stated that teachers solved problems of the children. A majority of the teachers (96.0 per cent) and very few parents/students (10.0 per cent) stated that teachers contacted with the parents and in parent teacher association.

Table 4.207: Contact Parent Teacher Association

Variable	*Respondents*	
	Teacher (n=50)	*Parent/Student (n=50)*
	per cent	*per cent*
Solve the problem		
Yes	92.0	10.0
No	2.0	90.0
Contact parent teacher association		
Yes	96.0	10.0
No	8.0	90.0

4.4.33 Discuss with Parents and PTAs Regarding Quality of Education

The data portrayed that (55.0 per cent) of the teachers and where as only (30.0 per cent) of parents/students stated that they discussed about the quality education and (27.0 per cent) of the teachers and (20.0 per cent) of the parents/students stated that teacher's contacted regarding quality of education, educational survey, school activity/programme, health awareness with the parents during Parent Teacher Association.

Table 4.208: Discussion Parents and PTAs

Discussion	*Respondents*	
	Teacher (n=50)	*Parent/Student (n=50)*
	per cent	*per cent*
Quality of Education	55.0	30.0
Educational Survey	7.0	10.0
School Activity /Programme	11.0	40.0
Quality of Education, Educational Survey, School Activity/Programme, Health Awareness	27.0	20.0

4.4.34 Discussion about Dropout, Un-enrolled and Regular Attendance

The data accentuated that (92.0 per cent) teachers and very insignificant number i.e., (10.0 per cent) of parents/students stated that teachers discussed about dropouts and un-enrolled children. (96.0 per cent) of the teachers and (90.0 per cent) of parents/students stated that teachers discussed about the regular attendance. A majority of the teachers (61.0 per cent) and parents students (70.0 per cent) stated that teachers discussed about school plan. Teachers opined for school plan and Unit Plan (20.5 per cent) and TLM and its uses (13.0 per cent) that teachers used them. Likewise school plan and unit plan (10.0 per cent) and TLM and its uses (5.0 per cent) were in the opinion of parents/students.

4.4.35 Discussion on Practical Activity, Writing and Reading Material

The data accentuated that (91.0 per cent) of the teachers and only (15.0 per cent) of parents/students stated that teachers discussed about the practical and rest of the teachers (9.0 per cent) and parents/students (85.0 per cent) were negated. As regarding the writing and reading material (89.0 per cent) of the teachers and (65.0 per cent) students/parents stated that teachers followed writing and reading material.

Table 4.209: Discussion about Dropout

Variable	*Respondents*	
	Teacher (n=50)	*Parent/ Student (n=50)*
	per cent	*per cent*
Dropout and un-enrolled		
Yes	92.0	10.0
No	8.0	90.0
Regular attendance		
Yes	96.0	90.0
No	4.0	10.0
Discuss regarding		
School Plan	61.0	70.0
Unit Plan	5.5	15.0
TLM and its uses	13.0	5.0
School plan and Unit Plan	20.5	10.0

Table 4.210: Discussion

Variable	*Respondents*	
	Teacher (n=50)	*Parent/ Student (n=50)*
	per cent	*per cent*
Practical Activity		
Yes	91.0	15.0
No	9.0	85.0
Writing and Reading Material		
Yes	89.0	65.0
No	4.0	35.0

4.4.36 Evaluation for the Children and Student Profile Co-conscious Activity

The data revealed that a majority of the teachers (92.0 per

cent) and parents/students (75.0 per cent) stated that teachers discussed about evaluation for the children and student profile. (89.0 per cent) of the teachers and only (30.0 per cent) of parents/ students stated that teachers discussed about the coconscious activity.

Table 4.211: Evaluation and Coconscious Activity

Variable	Respondents	
	Teacher (n=50)	*Parent/Student (n=50)*
	per cent	*per cent*
Evaluation		
Yes	92.0	75.0
No	8.0	25.0
Coconscious Activity		
Yes	89.0	30.0
No	11.0	70.0

4.4.37 Participation of Parent Teacher Association and Time Table

The data portrayed that a majority of the teachers (86.0 per cent) and parents/students only (35.0 per cent) stated that teachers discussed about the participation of parent teacher association. (97.0 per cent) of the teachers and only (35.0 per cent) of the parents/students stated that teachers discussed about the timetable of the school.

Table 4.212: Parent Teacher Association and Time Table

Variable	Respondents	
	Teacher (n=50)	*Parent/Student (n=50)*
	per cent	*per cent*
Parent Teacher Association		
Yes	86.0	35.0
No	14.0	65.0
Time Table		
Yes	97.0	35.0
No	5.0	65.0

4.4.38 Expectation of Every Children and Discussion on Book

The data revealed that a majority of the teachers (96.0 per cent) and parents/students (50.0 per cent) opined that teachers discussed about the expectations of every child. (88.0 per cent) of the teachers and (35.0 per cent) of parents/students stated that they discussed about the books.

Table 4.213: Expectation of Every Children

Variable	Respondents	
	Teacher (n=50)	*Parent/Student (n=50)*
	per cent	*per cent*
Expectation of Children		
Yes	96.0	50.0
No	4.0	50.0
Discuss on Books		
Yes	88.0	35.0
No	12.0	65.0

4.4.39 Discussion Regarding the Good Work and Problem Solving

The data accentuated that (89.0 per cent) of the teachers and (70.0 per cent) of parents/students stated that teachers discussed about the good work. A majority of the teachers (96.0 per cent) and parents/students only (35.0 per cent) stated that teachers solved the problems regarding the teaching and learning method.

Table 4.214: Good Work and Problem Solving

Variable	Respondents	
	Teacher (n=50)	*Parent/Student (n=50)*
	per cent	*per cent*
Good Work		
Yes	89.0	70.0
No	11.0	30.0
Problem Solving		
Yes	96.0	35.0
No	4.0	65.0

4.4.40 Professional Experience of Teachers and Guideline of RTE

The study revealed that (92.0 per cent) of the teachers and (45.0 per cent) of parents/students stated that teachers have professional experiences. A majority of the teachers (94.0 per cent) and parents/students only (39.0 per cent) stated that teachers followed the all guideline of Right to Education Act.

Table 4.215: Professional Experience and Guideline of RTE

Variable	*Respondents*	
	Teacher (n=50)	*Parent/Student (n=50)*
	per cent	*per cent*
Professional Experience		
Yes	92.0	45.0
No	8.0	55.0
Guidelines of RTE		
Yes	94.0	39.0
No	8.0	61.0

4.4.41 Teaching Ability of Every Children

The data revealed that a majority of the teachers (96.0 per cent) and more or less half (55.0 per cent) of the parents/students opined that teachers have given special essential help regarding teaching. (71.0 per cent) of the teachers and only (30.0 per cent) of parents/students stated that teachers evaluated the ability of every child.

Table 4.216: Teaching Ability of Every Children

Variable	*Respondents*	
	Teacher (n=50)	*Parent/Student (n=50)*
	per cent	*per cent*
Teaching		
Yes	96.0	55.0
No	4.0	45.0
Ability of Every Children		
Yes	71.0	30.0
No	29.0	70.0

4.4.42 Identification of Problems and Solutions and Special Help

The data accentuated that (92.0 per cent) of the teachers and less than half (45.0 per cent) of the parents/students stated that teachers identified the problems of the children and given solutions. A majority of the teachers (97.0 per cent) and only (30.0 per cent) of the parents/students stated that teachers sent child for special help and give help to every children as per their demand.

Table 4.217: Identification of Problems and Special Help

Variable	*Respondents*	
	Teacher (n=50)	*Parent/Student (n=50)*
	per cent	*per cent*
Identify of Problems		
Yes	92.0	45.0
No	8.0	55.0
Special Help		
Yes	97.0	30.0
No	3.0	70.0

4.4.43 Format for Evaluation, Survey for the Utilisation and Implemented Good Things

The data revealed that (93.0 per cent) of the teachers and (80.0 per cent) of parents/students stated that teachers prepared format for evaluation of entire activity and material development. A majority of the teachers (89.0 per cent) and parents/students (81.0 per cent) stated that teachers conducted survey for the utilisation of material and its importance. (94.0 per cent) of the teachers and (56.0 per cent) of parents/students stated that teachers implemented good things which were evolved by other school.

4.4.43.1 Dhamtari District Middle Schools Responses on Statements Regarding RTE Impact

The data revealed that a majority of the respondents strongly agreed that through RTE we can establish empowered childhood and majority of the respondents agreed that RTE can build knowledge based societies. A majority of the respondants agreed that RTE can reduce the child labour, increase girl child

Table 4.218: Format for Evaluation, Survey for the Utilisation and Implemented Good Things

Variable	Respondents	
	Teacher (n=50)	*Parent/Student (n=50)*
	per cent	*per cent*
Format for Evaluation		
Yes	93.0	80.0
No	7.0	20.0
Survey for the Utilisation		
Yes	89.0	81.0
No	11.0	19.0
Implemented Good Things		
Yes	94.0	56.0
No	6.0	44.0

education and quality education can be achieved. The respondents agreed that RTE can build knowledge based societies and it promotes inclusive growth in near future. A majority of the respondents agreed that through RTE quality education can be achieved and it promotes sustainable development.

4.4.43.2 Implementation Status of Middle Schools in Dhamtari District

The following data accentuated that the implementation status of 45 hours schedule in Middle schools in Dhamtari district. The data portrayed that all the schools are implementing the 45 hours schedule under RTE and the research revealed that the schools are performing well.

4.4.43.3 Major Findings from Middle Schools in Dhamtari District

- (46.5 per cent schools) have Electricity facility and rest of the schools (53.5 per cent) did not have such facility. The parents/students data revealed that only (15.0 per cent) schools have electricity facility.
- (88.5 per cent) of the teachers stated that there are three class rooms in their school. The data is quite similar as the data of parents/students.

Table 4.219: Teachers, Parents and Students Opinion on RTE Impact

Statement	*Respondents (n=100)*				
	per cent				
	Strongly Agree	*Agree*	*Undecided*	*Disagree*	*Strongly Disagree*
RTE can reduce the illiteracy among disadvantaged groups	25.00	58.00	2.00	11.00	4.00
RTE can promote the social change	36.00	62.00	2.00	—	—
Through RTE we can establish empowered childhood	54.00	38.00	4.00	3.00	1.00
RTE promotes sustainable development	28.00	35.00	12.00	16.00	9.00
Child labour can be addressed through RTE	39.00	59.00	2.00	—	—
Girl child education can be increased through RTE	29.00	68.00	3.00	—	—
Quality education can be achieved through RTE	15.00	79.00	2.00	4.00	—
RTE can build knowledge based societies	16.00	80.00	4.00	—	—
RTE Promotes inclusive growth in near future	15.00	59.00	15.00	9.00	2.00
Systems and structures in the society can be changed by RTE	19.00	61.00	12.00	8.00	—

Table 4.220: Actual Implementation Status

Sl. No.	*Name of the Activity*	*Approved Targets as per RTE act up to the time of study (Hours/ Minutes/per day/per week)*	*Progress against the targets shown in column.3 at the time of study*	
			Total achievement	*per cent of actual achievement (4/3×100)*
1	Prayer and Attendance	20 minutes/per day	19 minutes/per day	95.0 per cent
2	Teaching	4 hours 35 minutes/per day	4 hours 34 minutes/ per day	99.0 per cent
3.	Mid day meal	40 minutes/per day	39 minutes/per day	97.0 per cent
4.	Preparation of action plan for teaching and evaluation	40 minutes/per day	38 minutes/per day	95.5 per cent
5.	Student Portfolio	30 minutes/per day (4 days)	39 minutes/per day (4 days)	97.5 per cent
6.	Discussion with parent and Community	1 hours/per week	56 minutes/per week	93.5 per cent
7.	Staff meeting	30 minutes/per week	29 minutes/per week	98.0 per cent
8.	Special need to help the Children	40 minutes/per day	38 minutes/per day	96.0 per cent
9.	Tools/format fixed for evaluation	30 minutes/per week	29 minutes/per week	97.0 per cent
Total Time		**45 ½ hours/week**		

- (85.0 per cent) teachers stated that they have toilet facility in the school while parents/students data stated that only (35.0 per cent) schools have toilet facility.
- (69.0 per cent) of the teachers stated that schools were connected with roads whereas parents/students data show that (60.0 per cent) schools connected with road.
- (92.0 per cent) of the schools have drinking water facility. The data are quite similar as the data of parents/ students.
- (39.5 per cent) of the teachers stated that there were two teachers, (29.0 per cent) of the teachers opined that one teacher and (25.5 per cent) of the teachers opined that there is one permanent teacher in their schools while the data of parents/students stated that (45.0 per cent) schools going through two permanent teachers.
- (89.5 per cent) of the teachers stated that they don't have such temporary teachers.
- per cent of the teachers stated that they have two teachers in their schools.
- (62.5 per cent) teachers and only (20.0 per cent) of parents/ students stated that they took 20 minutes to complete prayer and (32.5 per cent) of the teachers and (70.0 per cent) of parents opined that they took 30 minutes for the same. As regarding the teaching hours (84.0 per cent) of the teachers and (85.0 per cent) of parents/ students stated that they taught more than 4.35 hours per day and (15.0 per cent) of the teachers and (10 per cent) of parents/students stated that teachers have taken 4.35 Hours per day.
- (86.0 per cent) of the teachers, whereas only (12.0 per cent) of parents/students opined that they have taken 40 minutes and (11.0 per cent) of the teachers and majority of parents/students stated that teachers have taken more than 40 minutes for midday meal per day.
- (77.0 per cent) of the teachers and (65.0 per cent) of parents students stated that teachers had taken 40 minutes per day and (18.5 per cent) for the teachers and (30.0 per cent) of parents stated that teachers have taken more than 40 minutes for preparation of action plans.

- (91.5 per cent) of the teachers and only (30.0 per cent) of parents/students stated that teachers have taken 30 minutes for student portfolio. (65.0 per cent) of the parents/students stated that teachers have taken less than 30 minutes for student portfolio.
- Majority of the teachers (90.5 per cent) and (85.0 per cent) of parents/students stated that teachers have taken one hour for discussion with parents per week.
- (91.0 per cent) of the teachers and only (20.0 per cent) of parents/students stated that teachers had allocated 30 minutes for staff meeting per week. But majority (70.0 per cent) of parents/students that teachers had allocated more than 30 minutes for staff meeting per week.
- (89.0 per cent) of the teachers and (82.0 per cent) of the parents/students opined that they allocated 40 minutes for children those who are in special needs per day.
- (81.0 per cent) of the teachers and (90.0 per cent) of parents/students stated that teachers allocated 30 minutes per week for tools and formats evaluation. However, (16.0 per cent) of the teachers and only (5.0 per cent) of parents/students expressed that teachers have taken more than 30 minutes per week.
- (77.0 per cent) of the teachers and (69.0 per cent) of parents/students opined that they participated during prayer and rest of the teachers (23.0 per cent) and parents/students (31.0 per cent) negated. As regarding the pattern (52.5 per cent) of the teachers and (65 per cent) of parents/students stated that they adopted group song, national song, national anthem and prayer and (31.5 per cent) of the teachers and only (15.0 per cent) of parents/students stated that they used prayer. As regarding the motivational activities (42.0 per cent) of the teachers and (52.5 per cent) of parents/students stated that teachers used lecture and *Mahapurush thought*, (37.0 per cent) of the teachers and only (11.0 per cent) of parents/students opined that teachers used *Mahapurush* thought only. All the teachers stated that they have taken attendance after assembly.
- All the teachers/parents/students stated that all teachers adopted cognitive teaching for class VI-VIII in the class room.

- (91.0 per cent) of the teachers and (91.0 per cent) of parents/students stated that teachers adopted whole class approach and (89.0 per cent) of the teachers and only (45.0 per cent) of parent/students opined that teachers adopted group based activity. Most of the (55.0 per cent) parents/student opined that teachers negated group based activity.
- (45.0 per cent) of teachers and (50.0 per cent) of parents/students stated that teachers evaluated the oral and (54.5 per cent) of the teachers and only (25.0 per cent) of parents/students stated that teachers evaluated the oral and writing and more than two fifths of the teachers stated oral for conscious evaluation. As regarding the co-cognitive teaching (75.0 per cent) of the teachers and 65.0 per cent of parents/students and (25.0 per cent) of the teachers (35.0 per cent) of parents/students stated that teachers did not use it.
- (40.0 per cent) of the teachers and (35.0 per cent) of parents/students stated that teachers conducted drawing, music, dance, literary and cultural activities and (32.0 per cent) of the teachers and (40.0 per cent) of parents/students stated that teachers conducted drawing only.
- (76.0 per cent) of the teachers and (60.0 per cent) of the parents/students stated that teachers had given project work and 14.5 per cent of the teachers and (20.0 per cent) of the teachers stated that teachers display creative work.
- (47.0 per cent) of the teachers and (50.0 per cent) of the parents/students stated that teachers conducted sports and games and 28.0 per cent of the teachers and only (15.0 per cent) of the parents/students stated they conducted yoga, sports and games, nutritional food, knowledge about diseases.
- (39.0 per cent) of the teachers and (25.0 per cent) of parents/students stated that teachers adopted attitude, life skill, awareness towards Environment and (28.0 per cent) of the teachers and (20.0 per cent) of the parents/students opined that they taught life skills and (21.0 per cent) of the teachers and (30.0 per cent) of the

parents/students stated that Attitude + Life Skill+ Awareness towards Environment + Value System.

- (72.0 per cent) of the teachers and (80.0 per cent) of the parents/students stated teachers have taken 31-40 minutes per day for midday meal distribution.
- (91.5 per cent) of the teachers and (80.0 per cent) of parents/students stated that teachers prepared action plans and as per opinion of teachers (8.5 per cent) negated. A majority of the teachers (97.0 per cent) and parents/students (70.0 per cent) stated that teachers prepared activities for class room teaching.
- (92.0 per cent) of the teachers and (50.0 per cent) of parents/students stated that teachers prepared teaching learning material. (91.0 per cent) of the teachers and (70.0 per cent) of parents/students stated that teachers adopted techniques to activate participation.
- (73.0 per cent) of the teachers stated that teachers planned for group work for the children. More or less similar trend have been observed in case of parents/ students opinion.
- (76.0 per cent) teachers and parents/students (65.0 per cent) stated that teachers prepared for action plan for Teaching and learning and rest of the teachers (24.0 per cent) and parents/students (35.0 per cent) stated that teachers negated.
- (87.0 per cent) of the teachers and (80.0 per cent) of the parents/students stated that teachers learn and follow teaching and learning material.
- (96.0 per cent) of the teachers and (80.0 per cent) of the parents/students stated that teachers give information by books and follow portfolio of children (82.0 per cent) and (65.0 per cent) were the opinion of teachers and parents/students respectively.
- (51.0 per cent) of the teachers and very negligible number, i.e., (5.00 per cent) of parents/students stated that teachers have collected name, weight, height, blood group, other physical and family background and (28.0 per cent) of the teachers and (10.0 per cent) of parents/ students stated that teachers have taken name are only names as part of the general information of the children.

- The data revealed that all the teachers, parents and students stated that teachers have identified the interests of the children and measured the improvement of the children.
- (78.0 per cent) of the teachers and (55.0 per cent) of parents/students stated that teachers collected information regarding the special work.
- (91.0 per cent) of the teachers stated that they assessed the past and present status of the student. The opposite trend it is observed in case of parents/students opinion.
- Majority (92.0 per cent) of the teachers and only (10.0 per cent) of parents/students stated that teachers solved problems of the children. A majority of the teachers (96.0 per cent) and very few parents/students (10.0 per cent) stated that teachers contacted the parents and parent teacher association.
- (55.0 per cent) of the teachers and where as only 30.0 per cent of parents/students stated that they discussed about the quality education and (27.0 per cent) of the teachers and (20.0 per cent) of the parents/students stated that regarding Quality of Education, Educational Survey, School Activity/Programme, Health Awareness with the parents and Parent Teacher Association.
- (92.0 per cent) teachers and very insignificant number i.e., (10.0 per cent) of parents/students stated that teachers discussed about dropouts and un-enrolled children. (96.0 per cent) of the teachers and (90.0 per cent) of parents/students stated that teachers discussed about the regular attendance. A majority of the teachers (61.0 per cent) and parents students (70.0 per cent) stated that teachers discussed about school plan. Teacher opined for school plan and Unit Plan (20.5 per cent) and TLM and its uses (13.0 per cent) that teachers used them. Likewise School plan and Unit Plan (10.0 per cent) and TLM and its uses (5.0 per cent) were in the opinion of parents/students.
- (91.0 per cent) of the teachers and only (15.0 per cent) of parents/students stated that teachers discussed about the practical and rest of the teachers (9.0 per cent) and parents/students (85.0 per cent) negated. As regarding

the writing and reading material (89.0 per cent) of the teachers and (65.0 per cent) students/parents stated that teachers followed writing and reading material.

- Majority of the teachers (92.0 per cent) and parents/ students (75.0 per cent) stated that teachers discussed about evaluation for the children and student profile. (89.0 per cent) of the teachers and only (30.0 per cent) of parents/students stated that teachers discussed about the coconscious activity.
- (86.0 per cent) teachers and parents/students only (35.0 per cent) stated that teachers discussed about the participation of parent teacher association. (97.0 per cent) of the teachers and only (35.0 per cent) of the parents/students stated that teachers discussed about the timetable of the school.
- Majority of the teachers (96.0 per cent) and parents/ students (50.0 per cent) opined that teachers discussed about the expectations of every child. (88.0 per cent) of the teachers and (35.0 per cent) of parents/students stated that they discussed about the books.
- (89.0 per cent) of the teachers and (70.0 per cent) of parents/students stated that teachers discussed about the good work. A majority of the teachers (96.0 per cent) and parents/students only (35.0 per cent) stated that teachers solved the problems regarding the teaching and learning method.
- 92.0 per cent of the teachers and 45.0 per cent of parents/students stated that teachers have professional experiences. A majority of the teachers (94.0 per cent) and parents/students only (39.0 per cent) stated that teachers followed the all guideline of Right to Education Act.
- Majority of the teachers (96.0 per cent) and more or less half (55.0 per cent) of the parents/students opined that teachers have given special essential help regarding teaching. (71.0 per cent) of the teachers and only (30.0 per cent) of parents/students stated that teachers evaluated the ability of the every child.
- (92.0 per cent) of the teachers and less than half (45.0 per cent) of the parents/students stated that teachers

identified the problems of the children and given solutions. A majority of the teachers (97.0 per cent) and only (30.0 per cent) of the parents/students stated that teachers sent child for special help and special help is given to every child as per his/her demand.

- (93.0 per cent) of the teachers and (80.0 per cent) of parents/students stated that teachers prepared format for evaluation of entire activity and material development. A majority of the teachers (89.0 per cent) and parents/students (81.0 per cent) stated that teachers conducted survey for the utilisation of material and its importance. (94.0 per cent) of the teachers and (56.0 per cent) of parents/students stated that teachers implemented good things which were evolved by other schools.

4.5 Comparative Analysis of Bastar and Dhamtari Primary Schools

Simply establishing school and enrolling students there in will not accrue any result unless other basic variables are taken into consideration Primary education depends upon a wide range of variables, like location of schools and their connectivity with the local urban centers, physical condition of school, availability of hostel for the students of the distant villages, sitting space available for students, classrooms infrastructure, availability of lavatory, drinking water facility, playground, teaching aids, sports material, numbers of teachers available per school, qualification and professional training of teachers and provision of Mid day meal schemes, provision of study book, school uniform etc. Apart from all these, there also many other variables, like motivation and level of awareness among the local people and the economic condition of parents, school management and supervision of school administration etc., on which the performance of a school is greatly dependable. Moreover, the medium of instruction, course contents and public holiday have greater relevance in influencing the performance of primary school operating in dominated tribal areas. The education of children is influenced by interplay of a range of factors at school, society and family, especially for the tribal children. For school participation, it is important that all the three factors should be positive or at least one or two factors should be strongly favourable.

The data accentuated that (22.0 per cent) of the respondents were in the age group of 37-41 in Bastar and (24.0 per cent) of the respondents were in the age group of 27-31 in Dhamtari district. As regards the Caste (42.0 per cent) of the respondents were in ST and (64.0 per cent) of the respondents were in OBC in Dhamtari region.

Table 4.221: Social Characteristics

	Respondents			
	Bastar		*Dhamtari*	
Variable	*Teacher* (*n=50*)	*Parent/ Student* (*n=50*)	*Teacher* (*n=50*)	*Parent/ Student* (*n=50*)
	per cent	*per cent*	*per cent*	*per cent*
Age				
22-26	10.0	13.0	12.0	14.0
27-31	12.0	7.0	24.0	16.0
32-36	18.5	25.5	16.0	12.0
37-41	22.0	17.5	16.0	18.0
42-46	14.5	14.0	4.0	25.0
47-51	12.0	11.0	8.0	10.0
> 51	11.0	12.0	20.0	5.0
Caste				
SC	14.0	25.5	12.0	12.0
ST	42.0	52.5	16.0	16.0
OBC	18.5	15.0	64.0	64.0
General	25.5	7.0	8.0	8.0

The data stated that (52.0 per cent) of the respondants were staying in same village in Bastar region, when we compare with same village in Dhamtari region (88.0 per cent) of the respondents were staying outside the village, where school exists. As regarding the distances (41.0 per cent) of the respondents are staying less than five km in Bastar and (60.0 per cent) of the respondents staying less than five kms in Dhamtari. Existing norms stipulate that a habitation (cluster of households) is entitled to have a primary school, if it has a population of 300 and more and has no school within a distance of one km. Upper primary schools are to be located at a distance of three kms from habitations with a population of 500 and more. These norms are often relaxed in case of hilly and tribal areas, difficult terrains and border districts.

Table 4.222: Distance

Variable	Respondents			
	Bastar		Dhamtari	
	Teacher (n=50)	Parent/ Student (n=50)	Teacher (n=50)	Parent/ Student (n=50)
	per cent	per cent	per cent	per cent
Staying in				
Same Village	52.0	81.73	12.0	45.0
Other Village	48.0	18.27	88.0	55.0
Other Village, Distance from School				
> 5	41.0	63.0	60.0	35.0
6-10	37.0	21.0	32.0	29.0
11-15	14.5	12.0	8.0	16.0
16-20	3.5	2.0	-	15.0
> 20	4.0	2.0	-	5.0

The data revealed that Dhamtari district have more facilities than Bastar district and the total percentages revealed that Dhamtari evincing greater than the Bastar district.

The data revealed that number of permanent teachers are high in Bastar and low in Dhamtari district. Whereas, number of temporary teachers are high in the Dhamtari. Ideally, there should be one specific classroom (68.75 per cent) for the students of each class it is very essentially required for the teachers to teach without being disturbed by the teaching noise' of other classes. Similarly, separate classrooms are also helpful for the students of each class so that they canbe attentive in classroom, but as Government have not yet been able to provide separate classrooms for each class for primary level schools. Another important aspect of primary education is not whether the space available for the students is sufficient or not, No matter, whether each has a specific classroom or not. Ordinarily the school which has less number of classrooms than the actual number of

Table 4.23: Facilities in the School

Variable	Respondents			
	Bastar		Dhamtari	
	Teacher (n=50)	Parent/ Student (n=50)	Teacher (n=50)	Parent/ Student (n=50)
	per cent	per cent	per cent	per cent
No of Class Rooms				
1.	4.0	68.75	—	—
2.	49.0	15.25	16.0	58.0
3.	44.0	15.0	35.0	25.0
4.	3.0	1.0	32.0	10.0
5.	00.0	00.0	17.0	7.0
Toilet Facility	74.0	85.74	76.0	80.0
Drinking Water Facility	71.0	85.74	88.0	20.0

classroom available should have more spacious classrooms to accommodate the students, in such cases the students must sit comfortably and there should be sufficient distance between classes. Moreover, there should also be good ventilation and lighting facility.

The STs Communities are least literate as in 2001 when the literacy rates for STs and SCs community were (37.37 per cent) and (55.53 per cent) respectively. The state aims to provide primary schools within one kilometer and upper primary schools within three kilometers having a population of more than 300 and 500 respectively. In 2008-09, 50,062 primary schools functioned with 1.25 lakh teachers and 44.87 lakh students. The annual growth rate of primary schools and teachers over this period were (2.36 per cent) and (1.16 per cent) respectively. During this year there was one primary school over an area of 3.1 sq km. The average teacher pupil ratio was 1:37, which was better than the national norm of 1:40. The dropout rate in this year was (4.95 per cent). Due to sustained Government efforts, the number of upper primary schools increased to 19,057, with 55,832 teachers and 21.28 lakh enrollment. The teacher pupil ratio for upper primary schools was 1:38; however the ratio was

Table 4.224: Teachers Availability

Variable	Respondents			
	Bastar		Dhamtari	
	Teacher (n=50)	Parent/ Student (n=50)	Teacher (n=50)	Parent/ Student (n=50)
	per cent	per cent	per cent	per cent
Permanent Teachers				
1.	4.0	2.0	36.0	10.0
2.	18.0	64.0	64.0	90.0
3.	37.0	18.0	—	—
4.	30.0	11.0	—	—
5.	7.5	3.5	—	—
6.	3.5	2.5	—	—
Temporary Teachers				
1.	92.0	76.0	—	—
2.	0.0	14.0	4.0	14.0
3.	5.0	10.0	16.0	10.0
4.	3.0	—	28.0	16.0
5.	—	—	28.0	20.0
6.	—	—	20.0	25.0
7	—	—	4.0	15.0

still away from the norm of 1:25. The most disturbing finding was that nothing has changed with respect to levels of teaching activity in the schools. Half of the Government schools had no teaching activity going on at the time of the unannounced visit because there is a serious shortage of teachers despite the large increase in the number of teachers appointed. The pupil-teacher ratio in the survey areas showed that therese was little improvement over the years. The survey found that contract teachers account for nearly (24 per cent) of all teachers in government primary schools. Local selection by the Gram Panchayats and the contractual nature of their appointment was expected to make these teachers more accountable. But this has clearly not happened. To begin with, many of them lack sufficient training and the requisite qualifications. They do not get the support they need to do a good job. A majority of contract teachers were from more privileged social groups and so establishing accountability was proving difficult. They were also not sufficiently motivated as their continuation in service depended very much on the local Panchayat, and not how well they performed in school.

The survey found that an additional (21 per cent) of schools were functioning as single teacher schools on the day of the investigators' unannounced visit due to teacher absenteeism. Even in schools where teaching was going on, children were not learning much of what the National Curriculum Framework (NCF) assures them. Classroom activity was dominated by mindless rote learning, senseless chanting, and blind copying from the board. The survey found that (80 per cent) of children in classes four or five could do simple addition, and (60 per cent) could do simple substraction. The analysis in the report argues that there are no quick fixes to the problem and that here major policy move remain deficient in several respects. The last decade has witnessed large-scale appointment of local 'contract teachers' (*shiksha karmis*, *shiksha mitras*, para-teachers, etc.,) at salaries far below those paid to permanent teachers in the same government schools.

The data revealed that in two locations the teachers are completed prayer 20 minutes but (78.0 per cent) of the Bastar schools are following and 60.0 per cent of the Dhamtari schools are following again (28.0 per cent) of the Dhamtari schools are completing prayer within 20 minutes. As regarding the teaching, Bastar is little behind and Dhamtari schools are able to teach in four hours and moreover (21.5 per cent) Bastar schools are teaching in more than four hours.

It can be inferred that both the schools from Bastar and Dhamtari are following the timing for midday meal in 40 minutes and whereas (28.0 per cent) of schools in Dhamtari are exceeding 40 minutes in this regard. As regarding the preparation of plan of action (76.0 per cent) of the schools in Dhamtari preparing in less than one hour and (63.0 per cent) of the schools in Bastar preparing in one hour per day and (24.5 per cent) of the schools are taking more than one hour in Bastar for the same. All the sample schools have a cook, who prepares the mid-day meal after obtaining the grain and other ingredients from the teacher or *Sarpanch*. Infrastructural facilities (cooking shed, water

Table 4.225: Prayer Timing Teaching Hours

	Respondents			
	Bastar		*Dhamtari*	
Variable	*Teacher* *(n=50)*	*Parent/ Student* *(n=50)*	*Teacher* *(n=50)*	*Parent/ Student* *(n=50)*
	percent	*percent*	*per cent*	*percent*
Prayer Timing				
Less than 20 Minutes	10.0	15.0	28.0	10.0
20 Minutes	78.0	14.0	60.0	15.0
30 Minutes	12.0	75.0	12.0	75.0
Teaching Hours				
Less Than four Hours	15.5	12.5	4.0	65.0
four Hours	63.0	42.0	88.0	25.0
Above four Hours	21.5	45.0	8.0	10.0

supply, utensils, and so on) vary a great deal between different schools. The mid-day meal is prepared in a soot-covered classroom using a makeshift stove, next to the swarming pupils. The cook struggles with inadequate utensils and takes help from young children for cutting the vegetables and cleaning the rice. All above kind of huddles take more than 40 minutes (75.0 per cent) for cooking. The teacher draws from a substantial repertoire of instructional strategies, varying his or her strategies both within and among lessons according to the particular objectives and content and the students' ability levels, learning styles, rates of learning, and special needs. The teacher conveys information in a variety of formats (e.g., lectures, videotapes, texts, DVDs) and approaches (e.g., demonstrations, guided practice, guided discovery, simulations). As appropriate to the learners and the learning, the teacher's instructional strategies include sharing instructional responsibilities with other teachers, guest speakers, and/or parents; varying and/or exchanging roles (e.g., instructor, facilitator, coach, and observer) with students; and creating opportunities for both independent and collaborative learning experiences.

Table 4.226: Timing for Midday Meal and Preparation of Action Plans

Variable	*Respondents*			
	Bastar		*Dhamtari*	
	Teacher (n=50)	*Parent/ Student (n=50)*	*Teacher (n=50)*	*Parent/ Student (n=50)*
	per cent	*per cent*	*per cent*	*per cent*
Timing for Mid-day Meal				
< 40 Minutes	11.5	10.0	4.0	3.0
40 Minutes	74.0	15.0	68.0	10.0
> 40 Minutes	14.5	75.0	28.0	87.0
Preparation of Action Plans				
< 1 Hr Per Day	12.5	2.0	76.0	20.0
1 Hr Per Day	63.0	72.5	12.0	12.0
> 1 Hr Per Day	24.5	25.5	12.0	68.0

The data revealed that majority of the schools in both the districts i.e., Bastar and Dhamtari are taking 30 minutes for student profile. In Dhamtari (84.0 per cent) of the schools are taking one hour for discussion with parent and (41.0 per cent) of the schools taking one hour in Bastar. The teacher begins the long-range planning process by gaining a thorough understanding of students' prior achievement levels, learning styles and needs, cultural and socio-economic backgrounds, and individual interests. The teacher gathers this information from a variety of sources, including student records (e.g., permanent records, individualised education programmes) and individuals such as other teachers, special-area professionals, administrators, service providers, parents, and the students themselves. From this information, the teacher identifies the factors that are likely to impact student learning. The teacher then uses this information to develop appropriate plans for meeting the diverse needs of his or her students. The teacher's goals are aligned with relevant federal, state, and local requirements and reflect the applicable grade-level academic standards. For preschool children and students with severe disabilities, the teacher's goals align with appropriate developmental and/or functional expectations. The teacher communicates with parents/guardians on a regular basis about goals and expectations for student learning, behavioural rules and consequences, assignments, suggestions for supporting student learning at home, assessment results, and student progress and performance. The teacher responds appropriately to parental concerns. The teacher uses a variety of formats (e.g., telephone contacts, meetings, conferences, letters/newsletters, Web sites, report cards, notes, e-mails, interactive journals) to maintain effective and ongoing communication with others.

Table 4.227: Student Portfolio and Discussion with Parent

Variable	*Respondents*			
	Bastar		*Dhamtari*	
	Teacher (n=50)	*Parent/ Student (n=50)*	*Teacher (n=50)*	*Parent/ Student (n=50)*
	per cent	*per cent*	*per cent*	*per cent*
Student Portfolio				
< 30 Minutes	15.0	14.0	16.0	80.0
30 Minutes	66.5	50.5	68.0	12.0
> 30 Minutes	18.5	35.5	16.0	8.0
Discussion with Parents				
< 1 Hour	48.0	21.0	8.0	89.0
1 Hour	41.0	69.0	84.0	8.0
> 1 Hour	11.0	10.0	8.0	2.0

The study revealed that a majority of the schools in Bastar and Dhamtari are sparing 30 minutes for staff meeting. As regards the special needs a majority of the schools in Bastar are sparing 40 minutes time to meet the students' special needs, whereas in Dhamtari there are some variations in addressing the needs of the children.

Table 4.228: Time Spared for Staff Meeting and Special Needs to Help the Children

Variable	Respondents			
	Bastar		Dhamtari	
	Teacher (n=50)	Parent/ Student (n=50)	Teacher (n=50)	Parent/ Student (n=50)
	per cent	per cent	per cent	per cent
Time Spared for Staff Meeting				
< 30 Minutes	22.0	10.0	12.0	2.0
30 Minutes	74.0	22.0	72.0	19.0
> 30 Minutes	4.0	68.0	16.0	79.0
Special Needs to Help the Children				
< 40 Minutes	19.0	26.0	44.0	68.0
40 Minutes	70.5	38.5	32.0	12.0
> 40 Minutes	10.5	35.0	24.0	20.0

It can be seen from the data the majority of the schools in both the districts are sparing 30 minutes time for staff meeting. In the educational institutions the atmosphere may be made conductive for the participation of the parents of the SC/ST children by organising functions, exhibitions, etc., so that linkage can be established. Further the students may be allowed to participate in the development programmes in the areas during summer vacations/holidays so that they can earn and learn. This would also instill a sense of awareness in them about the various developmental programmes being implemented for them. Emphasis may be laid for imparting vacation, training in Agriculture, Horticulture, etc., to the students in the school after the class hour so that they would be able to earn their livelihood in future. Voluntary services of the retired teachers of the area, senior students of the nearby schools may be availed of for extra coaching of the students. Training-Cum-Production Centres (TCPCs) could be started where the SC/tribal boys and girls could be given training in rural crafts. After their training is over, they could be given (in groups) production work on job order to be given by the State Corporations. These TCPCs could be integrated with higher secondary schools.

Table 4.229: Tools/Format Fixed for Evaluation

Tome Spared for Staff Meeting	Respondents			
	Bastar		Dhamtari	
	Teacher (n=50)	Parent/ Student (n=50)	Teacher (n=50)	Parent/ Student (n=50)
	per cent	per cent	per cent	per cent
< 30 Minutes	22.0	10.0	4.0	67.0
30 Minutes	70.0	35.5	84.0	13.0
> 30 Minutes	8.0	54.5	12.0	20.0

The study accentuated that a majority of the schools in Dhamtari evaluating students in oral and written mode, whereas in Bastar concentrating on Oral mode. The teacher maintains a constant awareness of student learning by engaging the students in classroom activities such as discussions, projects, performances, assignments, and quizzes. During these activities, the teacher uses effective questioning techniques to sample a representative cross section of students. The teacher's questions are appropriate to the content, the activities, and the students. The teacher determines the students' level of understanding of key concepts and skills by carefully observing/listening to and analysing students' verbal and nonverbal responses and reactions, inquiries, approaches to the task, performance, and final products.

Table 4.230: Mode of Continuous Evaluation

Mode of Continous Evaluation	Respondents			
	Bastar		Dhamtari	
	Teacher (n=50)	Parent/ Student (n=50)	Teacher (n=50)	Parent/ Student (n=50)
	per cent	per cent	per cent	per cent
Oral	41.0	22.0	16.0	74.0
Written	25.5	32.0	12.0	6.0
Oral and Written	33.5	46.0	72.0	20.0

The data inferred that a majority of the schools considering project work for evaluation in both the districts. But there is little variation in Bastar district regarding the modes of evaluation.

Table 4.231: Work Experience

Variable	Respondents			
	Bastar		Dhamtari	
	Teacher (n=50)	Parent/ Student (n=50)	Teacher (n=50)	Parent/ Student (n=50)
	per cent	per cent	per cent	per cent
Mode of Continuous Evaluation				
Project Work	56.5	34.5	72.0	35.0
Display Creative Work	29.0	49.5	16.0	45.0
Project Work and Display Creative Work	14.5	16.0	12.0	20.0

The data accentuated that a majority of the schools in both the districts are distributing midday meal within 31-40 minutes, but still Bastar is lagging behind with the Dhamtari for the same activity.

Table 4.232: Midday Meal Distribution

Variable	Respondents			
	Bastar		Dhamtari	
	Teacher (n=50)	Parent/ Student (n=50)	Teacher (n=50)	Parent/ Student (n=50)
	per cent	per cent	per cent	per cent
10-21	30.5	20.0	8.5	5.0
21-30	7.0	10.0	18.0	4.0
31-40	37.0	25.0	52.0	11.0
41-50	14.5	35.0	10.5	15.0
> 50	11.0	10.0	11.0	65.0

4.6 Comparative Analysis of Bastar and Dhamtari Middle Schools

The following data explains about the variations between same variables in Bastar and Dhamtari middle schools. Though, there are no major variations between these schools, the data accentuated that Bastar is lagging behind than Dhamtari district.

The data revealed that in both schools electricity facility is available but only less than (50.0 per cent) schools have that facility. As regards the class rooms in both the settings more than (80.0 per cent) of the schools having three rooms and more than (85.0 per cent) of the schools have toilet facility. As regards the Road connection Bastar is lagging behind of (45.0 per cent) whereas Damtari (69.0 per cent) of the schools have road facility. (90.0 per cent) of the schools have drinking water facility.

Table 4.233: Residence and Distance

Variable	*Respondents*			
	Bastar		*Dhamtari*	
	Teacher (n=50)	*Parent/ Student (n=50)*	*Teacher (n=50)*	*Parent/ Student (n=50)*
	per cent	*per cent*	*per cent*	*per cent*
Electricity	40.5	40.5	46.5	15.0
No of Class Rooms				
2.	7.0	7.0	5.0	2.0
3.	85.5	85.0	88.5	90.0
5.	4.0	4.0	3.0	2.0
6.	3.5	3.5	3.5	6.0
Toilet Facility	89.0	89.0	85.0	35.0
Road Connected	45.0	45.0	69.0	60.0
Drinking Water Facility	90.0	90.0	92.0	95.0

The data accentuated that there are lot of variations in permanent teachers in both the schools but more than 80.0 per cent of the schools don't have temporary teachers in both the schools.

Table 4.234: Staffing

Variable	Respondents			
	Bastar		Dhamtari	
	Teacher (n=50)	Parent/ Student (n=50)	Teacher (n=50)	Parent/ Student (n=50)
	per cent	per cent	per cent	per cent
Permanent Teachers				
1.	3.0	3.0	1.0	1.0
2.	29.0	30.0	25.5	10.0
3.	36.5	42.0	39.5	45.0
4.	25.5	20.0	21.0	35.0
5.	3.0	3.0	3.0	5.0
6.	3.0	2.0	3.0	4.0
Temporary Teachers				
1.	81.5	82.0	89.5	90.0
2.	11.5	16.0	5.5	5.0
3.	4.0	1.0	2.0	3.0
4.	3.0	1.0	3.0	2.0

The data portrayed that in both the schools more than 60.0 per cent are following 20 minutes time for prayers, but Bastar schools are little higher per cent following and (90.0 per cent) of the schools in Bastar teaching more than 4.35 hrs and in Dhamtari it is only 84.0.

Table 4.235: Prayer and Teaching Time

Variable	Respondents			
	Bastar		Dhamtari	
	Teacher (n=50)	Parent/ Student (n=50)	Teacher (n=50)	Parent/ Student (n=50)
	per cent	per cent	per cent	per cent
Prayer				
Less than 20 Minutes	11.0	3.	5.0	10.0
20 Minutes	70.5	19.0	62.5	20.0
30 Minutes	18.5	78.0	32.5	70.0
Teaching Hours				
Less than 4.35 Hrs	3.0	3.0	1.0	5.0
4.35 Hrs	7.0	4.0	15.0	10.0
Above 4.35 Hrs	90.0	93.0	84.0	85.0

The data inferred that (90.0 per cent) of the schools in Bastar taking 40 minutes for midday meal whereas (86.0 per cent) in Dhamtari for the same activity. As regards the preparation of action plan (85.0 per cent) of the Bastar schools are sparing 40 minutes per day for the same activity (77.0 per cent) of the schools of the Dhamtari allotted.

Table 4.236: Mid-day Meal

Variable	*Respondents*			
	Bastar		*Dhamtari*	
	Teacher (n=50)	*Parent/ Student* (n=50)	*Teacher* (n=50)	*Parent/ Student* (n=50)
	per cent	*per cent*	*per cent*	*per cent*
Mid-day meal				
< 40 Minutes	3.0	7.0	3.0	10.0
40 Minutes	90.0	3.0	86.0	12.0
> 40 Minutes	7.0	90.0	11.0	78.0
Preparation of Action Plans				
< 1 Hr Per Day	11.5	78.0	4.5	5.0
40 Minutes Per Day	85.0	12.0	77.0	35.0
> 40 Minutes Per Day	3.5	10.0	18.5	60.0

The data portrayed that (91.5 per cent) of the schools in Dhamtari are sparing 30 minutes for student portfolio whereas (81.5 per cent) of the schools are sparing the time for same activity. (90.5 per cent) of the schools are spared one hour for discussion with parents in Dhamtari and (81.5 per cent) of the schools spared for the same activity.

(91.0 per cent) of the schools were spared 30 minutes time for staff meeting in Dhamtari and (86.0 per cent) of the schools were followed the same thing. As regards the special need to help the children (89.0 per cent) of the schools spared 40 minutes time in Dhamtari and in Bastar (75.0 per cent) schools followed the same.

Table 4.237: Student Portfolio

Variable	Respondents			
	Bastar		Dhamtari	
	Teacher (n=50)	Parent/ Student (n=50)	Teacher (n=50)	Parent/ Student (n=50)
	per cent	per cent	per cent	per cent
Student Portfolio				
< 30 Minutes	7.5	4.0	2.5	65.0
30 Minutes	81.5	20.0	91.5	30.0
> 30 Minutes	11.0	76.0	6.0	5.0
Discussion with Parents				
< 1 hour	11.5	18.0	6.5	2.0
1 hour	81.5	10.0	90.5	13.0
> 1 hour	7.0	72.0	3.0	85.0

Table 4.238: Staff Meeting and Special Need to Help the Children

Variable	Respondents			
	Bastar		Dhamtari	
	Teacher (n=50)	Parent/ Student (n=50)	Teacher (n=50)	Parent/ Student (n=50)
	per cent	per cent	per cent	per cent
Staff Meeting				
< 30 Minutes	7.0	5.0	2.0	10.0
30 Minutes	86.0	15.0	91.0	20.0
> 30 Minutes	7.0	80.0	7.0	70.0
Special help to Children				
< 40 Minutes	14.0	20.0	4.0	8.0
40 Minutes	75.0	11.0	89.0	10.0
More Than 40 Minutes	11.0	69.0	7.0	82.0

The above table explains about the tools and formats fixed for evaluation for this purpose more than (80.0 per cent) schools in both the settings spared 30 minutes time for the same.

Table 4.239: Tools/Format Fixed for Evaluation

Variable	*Respondents*			
	Bastar		*Dhamtari*	
	Teacher (n=50)	*Parent/ Student (n=50)*	*Teacher (n=50)*	*Parent/ Student (n=50)*
	per cent	*per cent*	*per cent*	*per cent*
Tools/Format Fixed for Evaluation				
< 30 Minutes	7.0	3.0	3.0	5.0
30 Minutes	86.0	81.0	81.0	5.0
> 30 Minutes	7.0	16.0	61.0	90.0

The data revealed that for evaluation purpose (59.5 Per cent) schools in Bastar region are following Oral method and (78.0 per cent) of the respondents followed co cognitive teaching, whereas, (54.5 per cent) schools in Dhamtari were followed Oral and Written and (75.0 per cent) of the respondents adopted Co-cognitive teaching.

Table 4.240: Continuous Evaluation and Co-cognitive Teaching

Variable	*Respondents*			
	Bastar		*Dhamtari*	
	Teacher (n=50)	*Parent/ Student (n=50)*	*Teacher (n=50)*	*Parent/ Student (n=50)*
	per cent	*per cent*	*per cent*	*per cent*
Evaluation				
Oral	59.5	25.0	42.5	50.0
Written	3.0	64.0	3.0	25.0
Oral and Written	37.5	11.0	54.5	25.0
Co-cognitive Teaching	78.0		75.0	45.0

The data inferred that (72.0 per cent) of the respondents stated that they spared 31-40 minutes for midday meal distribution in Dhamtari schools, whereas it is (60.0 per cent) in Bastar schools.

Table 4.241: Mid-day Meal Distribution

Midday meal	Respondents			
	Bastar		Dhamtari	
	Teacher (n=50)	Parent/ Student (n=50)	Teacher (n=50)	Parent/ Student (n=50)
	per cent	per cent	per cent	per cent
10-21	7.0	5.0	7.0	5.0
21-30	33.0	6.0	21.0	15.0
31-40	60.0	89.0	72.0	80.0

(91.5 per cent) of the schools in Dhamtari ware preparing action plan where as schools (81.5 per cent) in Bastar. (97.0 per cent) of the respondents stated in Dhamtari that they prepared activities for class room teaching. In Dhamtari (92.0 per cent) of the respondents prepared TLM and (89.0 per cent) in Bastar schools. (91.0 per cent) of the respondents in Dhamtari stated that they used technique to take active participation whereas; it is (81.5 per cent) in the Bastar schools. (89.0 per cent) of the schools in Bastar planned for group work and whereas, in Dhamtari it is (73.0 per cent) for the same. More than (75.0 per cent) of the schools in both the settings planned for teaching and learning material. (92.0 per cent) of the respondents in Bastar schools implemented learn and follow teaching and learning whereas, it is (87.0 per cent) for the same.

(96.0 per cent of the schools in Dhamtari adopted Books for information and portfolio but it is (89.0 per cent) in Bastar. As regarding to portfolio (82.0 per cent) of the respondents adopted in Dhamtari schools, where as it is (78.0 per cent) in Bastar schools.

The data revealed that Dhamtari schools performed and achieved in regard to identification of interests and measuring of improvements of the children where as Bastar schools are

Table 4.242: Variables for Quality Enhancement

Variable	*Respondents*			
	Bastar		*Dhamtari*	
	Teacher (n=50)	*Parent/ Student (n=50)*	*Teacher (n=50)*	*Parent/ Student (n=50)*
	per cent	*per cent*	*per cent*	*per cent*
Preparation of Action Plan	81.5	90.0	91.5	84.0
Preparation of Activities for class room teaching	89.0	60.0	97.0	70.0
Preparation of TLM	89.0	92.0	92.0	50.0
Technique to active participation	81.5	76.0	91.0	70.0
Plan for group work	89.0	69.0	73.0	70.0
Plan for Teaching and Learning	78.0	54.0	76.0	65.0
Learn and follow Teaching and Learning	92.0	82.0	87.0	80.0

Table 4.243: Information and Portfolio

Variable	*Respondents*			
	Bastar		*Dhamtari*	
	Teacher (n=50)	*Parent/ Student (n=50)*	*Teacher (n=50)*	*Parent/ Student (n=50)*
	per cent	*per cent*	*per cent*	*per cent*
Books	89.0	51.0	96.0	80.0
Book Corner	11.0	49.0	04.0	20.0
Portfolio for individual children	78.0	65.0	82.0	65.0

lagging behind. (89.0 per cent) of the schools in Bastar collected information regarding the children and (78.0 per cent) schools were collected in Dhamtari. (91.0 per cent) of the schools assessed the past and present status of the children in Dhamtari whereas it was (81.5 per cent) in Bastar schools. As regarding the contact of parent teacher association and solving of the problems, Dhamtari is evincing better results than Bastar.

Table 4.244: Variables

Variable	*Respondents*			
	Bastar		*Dhamtari*	
	Teacher (n=50)	*Parent/ Student (n=50)*	*Teacher (n=50)*	*Parent/ Student (n=50)*
	per cent	*per cent*	*per cent*	*per cent*
Identification of Interests	96.0	74.0	100.0	85.0
Measuring Improvement	92.0	8.0	100.0	95.0
Collection of information	89.0	59.0	78.0	55.0
Assessment of Past and Present Status	81.5	59.0	91.0	10.0
Contact Parent Teacher Association	92.0	80.0	96.0	10.0
Solve the problem	89.0	65.0	92.0	10.0

The data revealed the schools in Dhamtari were performing well in dropout and un-enrolled, regular attendance and practical activity, where the Bastar schools are slightly lagging behind.

Table 4.245: Discussion

Variable	*Respondents*			
	Bastar		*Dhamtari*	
	Teacher (n=50)	*Parent/ Student (n=50)*	*Teacher (n=50)*	*Parent/ Student (n=50)*
	per cent	*per cent*	*per cent*	*per cent*
Dropout and un-enrolled	85.0	74.0	92.0	10.0
Regular attendance	93.0	82.0	96.0	90.0
Practical activity	86.0	80.0	91.0	15.0
Writing and reading material	96.0	98.0	89.0	65.0

The data revealed that the Bastar schools performed well in coconscious activity and parent teacher association whereas; the Dhamtari schools are slightly lagging behind.

Table 4.246: Performed Activity

Variable	*Respondents*			
	Bastar		*Dhamtari*	
	Teacher (n=50)	*Parent/ Student* (n=50)	*Teacher* (n=50)	*Parent/ Student* (n=50)
	per cent	*per cent*	*per cent*	*per cent*
Evaluation	88.0	90.0	92.0	75.0
Coconscious activity	90.0	90.0	89.0	30.0
Parent Teacher Association	93.0	75.0	86.0	30.0
Time Table	95.0	80.0	97.0	35.0

CHAPTER 5

Findings and Recommendations for Policy Making

This chapter deals with the recommendation for policy making. The study has evinced lot of findings that can be included in the policy for better implementation of the intervention. Always the intervention needs to be changed as per the evaluation. This impact assessment has given some necessary directions regarding some systemic changes and some findings are very qualitatively implemented by the education authorities.

The following problems were traced out through the Focused Group Discussion.

5.1 Identified Problems

During the process of the study we noticed lot of other problems which are directly or indirectly related to Right to Education Act. The problems are numerous and can be addressed with the active engagement of the local communities. Similarly, the administration should concentrate on the loop holes at the implementation stage. Some problems are related to demographic and the heritage which cannot be addressed but the policies need to align with the programmes to be carried.

5.1.1 Physical Location of Tribal Village

Maximum number of tribal villages are scattered especially in Chhattisgarh, it is more predominant in Bastar Region. Most of the villages have below population. So, it becomes impossible to open up separate schools in each village where the required student's strength is not available. So these physical barriers create a hindrance for the children to attend the school in a neighbouring village.

5.1.2 Economic Condition

Those who are attending the Government schools their economic conditions are very poor. So that their absenteeism is more high in the schools. This reason may be one of the contributing factors for low standards and low awareness among the children and the parents. The children of 10 to 14 years age group are found to be helping their parents in collection of forest products, chores and labour work. In this situation, parents do not desire to spare their children or their labour power and allow them to attend schools. In many tribal and non tribal areas in two districts i.e., Bastar and Dhamtari where community development programme have embarked on, ambitious programmes of economic development but the majority of the people do not come forward to take advantage of the schemes. In case where they do take up such schemes, they have come to grief or have been cheated out of their well earned income by middlemen. Thus, even though economic development puts more money in their hands; their standard of living does not show any appreciable improvement.

5.1.3 Parents Attitude

Majority of the parents are basically illiterate. Their illiteracy does not permit them to understand the long term values of education. As education does not yield them any immediate economic return, they prefer to engage their children in remunerative employment which supplements the family income and strengthens the family economy. Further a few parents, have become aware of the values of education.

5.1.4 Parents Education Committee (PEC)

The studies have revealed that the PECs existed in each school but they have poor knowledge on the RTE and its impact. PECs have been constituted to preserve and monitor the functioning of the schools. Till now people are not aware of the role of the VECs. Neither the villagers nor the members of the PECs take any active interest to enhance enrolment and attendance of children in primary and middle schools.

5. 1.5 Teachers Problem

There are significant problems between school teachers and the villagers, but they can be easily solved. The parent teachers meeting have to be conducted regularly. Maximum parents have virtually no relationships with the teachers. Teachers do not get any accommodation facility in the village, which makes them irregular which hampers the normal routine of a school. Further, the apathetic attitude among these communities and their simplicity provide ample scope to the teachers to act accordingly.

5.1.6 Concerns of the Students

The survey has been conducted in Primary and Middle Schools in Bastar and Dhamtari districts of the Chattisgarh. The study to the revealed many facts which are contributing to the children's poor attendance and low quality education, though the RTE rules and techniques are implementing. The reasons for poor quality of education and non-attendance are as follows:

(a) Helping parents at home

(b) Discharging sibling care responsibilities

(c) No positive environment or inspiration for students at home

(d) School environment is uncomfortable and horrifying

(e) Teachers impose punishments and do not help in studies

(f) No regular supply of study materials

(g) Parents have migrated from the villages to other towns to earn their livelihoods because of drought or other natural calamities

(h) Teachers do not bother whether the child comprehends the teaching or not

(i) No health care facilities for the children suffering from malaria, skin diseases and anaemia

(j) Tribal children contribute their physical power to supplement the family income

5.1.7 Teaching Learning Materials (TLM)

Though the TLM is available in all schools, its functions are not fruitful and not reaching to the students fully. The teachers need lot of training and knowledge to use the TLM for children's sake. The pedagogical methods are to be implemented in middle schools. So far as study TLM and other teaching materials are concerned, the following problems came to light:

(a) The language used in the books is beyond the understanding of the tribal children.

(b) Sometimes the local teachers also teach students by the bookish language and dòn't try to communicate in the tribal languages. As a result teaching seems to be artificial for the tribal children.

(c) The contents of the primary school books are less practice oriented and are more factual and abstract.

(d) Teaching at primary schools ignores the local nature, culture and environment.

(e) There is dearth of study materials and kits in the class rooms.

(f) The kits that have been provided to the schools under the RTE are not properly utilised by the teachers.

(g) Books are not supplied to the schools at the session beginning. This irregularity found in the supply of books creates problems both for the teachers and students.

(h) Further, stipends are not given in due time.

(i) School fails to work out the idea of utilising the services of the local architects, painters and artists at a low cost to prepare some of the educational kits for the children.

5.1.8 Condition of Schools

Maximum schools have buildings but some of them are in dilapidated condition. The teachers and parents reported that the class rooms are not sufficient at some locations. This reason is disrupting the learning capacity of the students and hindering the quality of education process. Lack of care and repair makes it difficult to sit in the collapsing class rooms. Neither the villagers nor the PEC take any active interest to preserve and protect the school building. They preserve the impression that it is the Government outlook and not theirs. No accommodation arrangement is being made for teachers either in the school or in the village.

5.1.9 Technical Education

The study revealed that many middle school students are

idle due to faulty educational strategies. The education doesn't have any technical values and not giving assurance for the employment opportunities. The education patterns need to change to address these kinds of problems. It is therefore, desirable that technical training institutes should be established in such areas to enable the students to secure skilled employment or a curriculum should be embedded in the middle school syllabus.

5.1.10 Lack of Inspection

(a) School inspectors (at the block and district level) are not active in solving problems associated with the primary schools in the tribal areas. (b) The surveys bring to notice that the block level inspectors have not inspected all the schools in their areas. (c) Inspectors do not provide equal importance to the schools of hill areas as they give to the schools of plain areas. (d) The tribal teachers remain indifferent to tribal education. They are also marked with some mental stress. (e) The non-tribal teachers adopt an apathetic attitude towards tribal school management.

5.1.11 Social and Cultural Problems

The community life, the economy, the life style, the traditions of the tribals and their outlook of the world is totally unique. All these have got their humanitarian values and cultural significance. But they have not found recognition in the ideas of local inspectors, teachers, parents and policy planners. The root cause of this can be attributed to the stratification system and the tribal and non-tribal attitude. Thus, a strong consciousness and pro-tribal attitude have not been built up among the people. The NGOs have no doubt taken some steps in this area. But how far the efforts of the NGOs will be successful in changing the institutionalised practices of society is still doubtful. The greatest problem is, the tribals have come to recognise the modernisation and the demands of time. But they are not coming forward to bring reforms in the educational status and economic standards. Now a strong campaign is needed for this. The voluntary agencies should try to launch this campaign on a long term basis with constructive ideas.

5.1.12 Quality of Teachers

There are number of temporary teachers in all schools who are not qualified and skill full to teach the subjects. This factor is also hindering the quality of education.

5.1.13 Duties Handling by Outsiders

The study revealed that a number of temporary teachers are engaging outsiders those who are not appointed by the education department, this is very predominant problem in the schools.

5.1.14 Apathy in Duties

Temporary teachers are not interested to conduct the classes effectively, this factor is hindering the quality of education.

5.1.15 Bad Environment Conditions

Both Physical and Social environment is not suitable to live in working place. The teachers are not staying in where they are working due to the environment and lack of other services like market, residence, transport and recreation facilities.

5.1.16 Poor Management

The data revealed that many schools are unable to manage the school management committee and unable to conduct the meetings. Moreover, the teachers are unable to prepare the action plans due to inefficiency.

5.1.17 Concerned Towards Students

It is observed that some teachers are taking adequate care of their students regarding nails cutting, combing and bathing. It is really a great concern towards the students. During the study the parents reported that some teachers are taking care of their children during games and sports.

5.1.18 Un-utilisation of Resources

It is observed and assessed that most of the teachers did not spend the teachers grant of Rs 50 for TLM. The data revealed that most of the schools don't have TLM and they are depending on the indigenous methods for teaching purpose.

5.1.19 Poor Sensitisation

The study accentuated that most of the teachers did not visit the villages to motivate and sensitise the dropouts to rejoin the schools.

5.1.20 No Participation in Parent Teachers Meeting

It is observed that in Parent Teachers meeting the student's parents are not participating properly due to their illiteracy, mobility and ignorance. This factor is promoting more dropout rate in the schools. The migration is very high in these two districts, the parents are moving here and there for bread winning. This factor is affecting the school attendance and parents are unable to not attend the parents' teachers meeting and they are unable to look after their children too.

5.2 Common Suggestion and Recommendation

The main aim of the research is to know the status of the programme implemented by the agency. The present study have brought major findings which are already discussed previously, but following suggestions and recommendations are very important for policy making and directions for future programmes and improvement.

- The government should concentrate on regular recruitment to enhance the standards of the education.
- Educational department have to include the likeminded people, NGOs and other civil societies to maintain the RTE standards.
- The government should appoint or hire a social scientist for improvement of the quality instead of depending on some agency.
- A strict and compulsory order or GO should be implemented for teachers those who are staying outside the working place. The study revealed that many teachers are coming outside the village, because of this reason the quality and schedule of the RTE is reducing.
- Vigilance is compulsory to keep up the standards of the RTE. The block level vigilance committee is needed. The vigilance committee should be constituted with the parents, teachers, Panchayat members and civil society members.
- Education department authorities should concentrate on the monitoring and evaluation of the school standards on regular basis.

- Weekly reports should be submitted by the teachers regarding the RTE act.
- Providing competency based training to teachers and others who are involved in imparting education and literacy; A wide range of community sensitisation is needed for the quality implementation of RTE.
- The education department should think of appointing the English, Mathematics and Science teachers for the quality education.
- The schools should perform the annual day, this should be mandatory to keep the health and hygiene of the students.

5.3 Specific Suggestion and Recommendation

Suggestion and recommendation have been devoted to the analysis of different educational facilities, problems and their impact on the communities, for their overall socio-economic upliftment. The analysis has also been made to ascertain their capabilities and constraints with regard to educational development programmes causing dissatisfaction among the communities. Inspite of various plans, programmes and projects taken up by the Government machinery, the result has been far from satisfactory. The reason as far as can be ascertained, is due to faulty scheme and the lack of warm support of the people in these educational development programmes. It is an established fact that this is necessary for development of communities, in general. Constitutional provisions and various educational developmental strategies adopted during the different plan periods clearly indicate the action pattern of the Welfare State of India. The following points are important in this respect:

5.3.1 Policy Interventions

- Minimising the barrier to literacy and educational related services for the tribal, physically, financially and culturally;
- Improving basic literacy and educational services, particularly for the tribal girl child, including formal and non-formal education;
- Orientation towards basic literacy and education for the tribal girl child by improved outreach activities, formally as well as non-formally;

- Providing competency based training to teachers and others involved in imparting education and literacy;
- Collaboration between public and private sector for management and delivery of services for education and literacy: (i) To supplement the logistic, finance and educational expertise of the private sector with that of the public sector so as to develop the required synergy to deal with the low level of tribal child education in Bastar district of Chattisgarh, and (ii) Building managerial capacity to address service delivery provision;
- Benefits should be taken from the frontier areas of technology, e.g., information and communication technologies;
- Policy development, financing, regulation, monitoring and evaluation of educational programmes.

5.3.2 Awareness Campaign

- Promote education campaigns aimed at improving knowledge, skills and attitudes. This training can augment future earning potential for these girls who will benefit from dual utility of basic education along with an initiation into some basic vocational practices (Chattopadhyay *et al.,* 2005);
- Professional groups should be involved like teaching communities, community groups, religious and philanthropic bodies in the promotion of education and literacy related issues. Media, both electronic and print media, play a vital role in the awareness campaigns which need to be channelised in the areas having a bearing on the tribal education.

5.3.3 Community Mobilisation

The issues like enrolment, education of girl children, retention of children in schools and school involvement should be carried out in tribal areas. The specific features of such mobilisation are:

- Use of local/folk art forms
- Meetings of mothers and family meetings and involvement of tribal youth volunteers

- Leaflets posters, Kalajathas, and video cassettes in local languages
- Organisation of meetings in 'haats'/ 'bazaars' and use of community fairs and festive occasions to discuss primary education issues.
- Involvement of traditional organisations in the mobilisation effort.
- Involvement of the community including VECs members in documentation of local folklore, history, traditional medicine, agricultural practices.

5.3.4 Community Partnership

Not only to encourage but also facilitate for the involvement of community and non-governmental organisations for the tribal child education and literacy. These organisations have some experience and operate at the field level and can be involved in an interactive mode of relationships with family and Government and private educational initiatives within the national educational policy framework.

5.4 Conclusion

RTE implementation is very complex and hard at grass root level. Government has enacted and implemented the Act in the right spirit towards providing quality elementary education to all. Most of the investigated schools are able to fulfill basic infrastructure except a few but with regard to curriculum, assessment, PTA and other related issues they are lagging behind. The observation and findings from the interview and questionnaire show a wide gap between what was expected and what has so far been done. The findings show that so far there has been some progress only in terms of enrollment/basic infrastructure but towards guaranteeing quality education in terms of student learning the state has to go a long way. Further, from the findings of the study, it can be concluded that most of the parents are aware about the free education provided to the students of elementary schools. But, many of them are not aware of the benefits provided to the children. Similarly students are also not aware of their rights. Therefore, as per the findings parents and children should be made aware about the benefits and provisions provided in the Act.

There is a need to forge partnerships among state, school functionaries, voluntary agencies, parents and other stakeholders. Concerted efforts are required at all levels since isolated efforts do not bring the desired results. Two years have been passed since the implementation of RTE Act in Chattisgarh but the study reveals, still there is long road ahead before all stakeholders even become aware of their rights let alone become able to exercise, and finally able to enforce their rights. The potential of the RTE depends a great deal on the advocacy and mobilisation campaigns initiated by Government, and the ability of parents and children to understand and exercise their new role relationships as far as elementary education is concerned.

The findings do not reflect the status of implementation of Right to Education Act all throughout the districts of Bastar and Dhamtari. However, the findings do focus on some important issues relating to the functional part of the Act. In future, further researches can be undertaken by enlarging sample size. Other districts from Chattisgarh can be selected as samples examine status of the implementation of the Act in the whole of the Chhattisgarh. Present study can help the future researchers in getting first hand information for further explorations as well as help state officials to seriously look into the implementation of the RTE Act towards providing quality elementary education to all children.

Bibliography

Aggarwal Y.P., 2000, *Quality Concerns in Primary Education in Primary: Where is the Problem?* National Institute of Educational Planning and Administration, New Delhi.

Aggarwal, D.D., 2002, *History and development of elementary education in India*, Sarup and Sons, New Delhi, Vol. 2.

Auguste, B., Kihn, P., Miller, M. 2010, *Closing the talent gap: Attracting and retaining top-third graduates to careers in teaching—An international and market research-based perspective*, McKinsey and Company.

Ball, S.J., 2006, *Education policy and social class: The selected works of Stephen J Ball.* London: Rutledge.

Barber, M. and Mourshed, M., 2007, *How the World's Best Performing School Systems Came Out on Top*, McKinsey and Company.

Census of India, 2001, Ministry of Home Affairs, Govt. of India, New Delhi.

Census of India, 2011, Ministry of Home Affairs, Govt. of India, New Delhi.

Ermisch, John; Francesconi, Marco, 2001, *Family Matters: Impacts of Family Background on Educational Attainments.* Economica, Vol. 68, pp. 137-156.

Evaluating Educational Inclusion, 2000, Guidance for Inspectors and Schools, of STED.

Fisher, R., 2002, *Creative Minds: Building Communities of Learning for the Creative Age*, paper presented at Teaching Qualities Initiative Conference, Hong Kong Baptist University, 2002.

Forlin, C., 2001, *Inclusion: Identifying potential stressors for regular class teachers. Educational Research*, 43 (3), 235-245.

Gardner, H., 1993, *Frames of mind: the theory of multiple intelligences* 2nd ed. New York: Basic Books.

Grubb, W.N. and Lazerson, M., 2004, *The education gospel: The economic power of schooling.* Cambridge, MA: Harvard University Press.

Heineck, Guido; Riphahn, Regina T., 2009, Intergenerational Transmission of Educational Attainment in Germany: The last five Decades. Jahrbucher fur Nationalokonomie and Statistik, Vol. 229, No. 1, pp. 36-60.

Kauffman, J.M., Landrum, T.J., Mock, D., Sayeski, B. and Sayeski, K.S., 2005, *Diverse knowledge and skills require a diversity of instructional groups: A position statement. Remedial and Special Education,* 26 (1), 2-6.

Lucas, B., 2001, *'Creative Teaching, Teaching Creativity and Creative Learning',* in Craft, A., Jeffrey, B., and Leibling, M. (Eds) (2001), *Creativity in Education.* London: Continuum.

McLaughlin, M. and Rouse, M., 2000, *Special education and school reform in the United States and Britain.* London: Routledge.

NCERT, 2002, Sixth all India Education Survey, New Delhi, Vol-1.

Russel, B., 1932, *Education and Social Order,* Unwin Paperbacks, London.

Sachchidananda, 1992, *Structural Constraints in the Education of Schedule Tribes and Scheduled Caste, Tribal Transformation in India,* Vol. IV (ed. By Chaudhuri, B), Inter India Publication, New Delhi.

Thakur, D., 1995, Tribal Education, Deep and Deep Publications, Delhi.

Torrance, E. Paul, 1967, Understanding the Fourth Grade Slump in Creative Thinking. Final Report. http://www.eric.ed.gov/ERICWebPortal/custom/portlets/record Details/detailmini.jsp?_nfpb= true&_& ERICExtSearch SearchValue_0= ED018273& ERICExtSearch_Search Type_0=no&accno=ED018273.

UNESCO, 2005, Children out of school: Measuring exclusion from primary education. Montreal: UNESCO Institute for Statistics.

Venkataiah, S., 2001, *Modern Tribal Education,* Anmol Publications Pvt. Ltd., New Delhi.

World Bank, 2003, *World Development Indicators* 2003, Washington, DC.

Index